EFFECTIVE TEACHING

ABOUT THE AUTHORS

Gilbert Harrison Hunt holds the Ph.D. and M.Ed. degrees from the University of North Carolina at Chapel Hill (1975, 1971) and the B.S. degree from Campbell University (1969). He is the Singleton Chaired Professor and Research Scholar in the Spadoni College of Education at Coastal Carolina University. Dr. Hunt has taught at the middle school level with the Harnett County, North Carolina, public school system. He is coauthor of *Effective Teaching: Preparation and Implementation* (3rd Edition); *Best Practice in Motivation and Management in the Classroom* (2nd Edition); *The Middle Level Teachers' Handbook: Becoming a Reflective Practitioner; The Modern Middle School: Addressing Standards and Student Needs;* and *Teaching at the University Level: Cross-Cultural Perspectives from the United States and Russia,* author of numerous articles in professional journals, and a member of Phi Delta Kappa, Kappa Delta Pi, National Middle School Association, and Association of Teacher Educators.

Dennis Gene Wiseman holds the Ph.D. and M.A. degrees from the University of Illinois at Urbana-Champaign (1974, 1970) and the B.A. degree from the University of Indianapolis (1969). He is Professor of Education in the Spadoni College of Education at Coastal Carolina University. He has taught with the Champaign, Illinois, and Indianapolis, Indiana, public school systems. He is coauthor of *Effective Teaching: Preparation and Implementation* (3rd Edition); *Best Practice in Motivation and Management in the Classroom* (2nd Edition); *The Middle Level Teachers' Handbook: Becoming a Reflective Practitioner; The Modern Middle School: Addressing Standards and Student Needs;* coeditor of *Teaching at the University Level: Cross-Cultural Perspectives from the United States and Russia;* and editor of *The American Family: Understanding its Changing Dynamics and Place in Society.* His teaching specialization areas are curriculum and instruction, social studies education, and educational psychology.

Timothy John Touzel holds the Ed.D. and B.S. degrees from the University of Tennessee-Knoxville (1975, 1969) and the M.Ed. from Memphis State University (1972). He is Distinguish Professor Emeritus at Coastal Carolina University. He has taught at the high school level for the Knoxville City and the Memphis City Schools and at the elementary level for the Oak Ridge Schools, all in Tennessee. He has also taught at the University of South Carolina, Winthrop University, and at Deakin University in Australia. Presently he is teaching K-college classes and conducting research in Qujing, China. He is coauthor of *Effective Teaching: Preparation and Implementation* (3rd Edition) and contributor to professional societies, books, and journals, mostly in the field of mathematics education. He is a member of Phi Delta Kappa, Kappa Delta Pi, the South Carolina and National Councils of Teachers of Mathematics.

Fourth Edition

EFFECTIVE TEACHING

Preparation and Implementation

By

GILBERT H. HUNT, Ph.D.

Coastal Carolina University
Conway, South Carolina

DENNIS G. WISEMAN, Ph.D.

Coastal Carolina University
Conway, South Carolina

TIMOTHY J. TOUZEL, Ed.D.

Distinguished Professor Emeritus
Coastal Carolina University
Conway, South Carolina

CHARLES C THOMAS • PUBLISHER, LTD.
Springfield • Illinois • U.S.A.

Published and Distributed Throughout the World by

CHARLES C THOMAS • PUBLISHER, LTD.
2600 South First Street
Springfield, Illinois 62704

© 2009 by CHARLES C THOMAS • PUBLISHER, LTD.

ISBN 978-0-398-07859-1 (hard)
ISBN 978-0-398-07860-7 (paper)

Library of Congress Catalog Card Number: 2008048227

With THOMAS BOOKS *careful attention is given to all details of manufacturing
and design. It is the Publisher's desire to present books that are satisfactory as to their
physical qualities and artistic possibilities and appropriate for their particular use.*
THOMAS BOOKS *will be true to those laws of quality that assure a good name
and good will.*

Printed in the United States of America
SM-R-3

Library of Congress Cataloging-in-Publication Data

Hunt, Gilbert.
  Effective teaching : preparation and implementation / Gilbert H. Hunt,
Dennis G. Wiseman, Timothy J. Touzel. -- 4th ed.
      p. cm.
  Includes bibliographical references and index.
  ISBN 978-0-398-07859-1 (hard) -- ISBN 978-0-398-07860-7 (pbk.)
  1. Effective teaching. 2. Teachers--Psychology. 3. Teacher-student relation-
ships. 4. Behavior modification. I. Wiseman, Dennis. II. Touzel, Timothy J.
III. Title.

  LB1025.3.H86 2009
  371.102--dc22

                                                              2008048227

PREFACE

Schools today have transcended from the chalkboard to the whiteboard and are populated by students who are not frightened to use the technology of this new digital age of learning. During this period of dynamic change, teachers must be ready to meet the challenges of preparing students for a global society characterized by diversity and ever-increasing expectations.

Effective teachers in the new millennium must prepare their students to function in a society that will be represented by several career changes before retirement. This societal complexity is due to the fact that knowledge is increasing, needs are changing, and opportunities sometimes seem endless for those individuals who leave school knowing how to learn on their own and solve problems in a dynamic environment.

It is little wonder that educators are held accountable for their students' learning more today than ever before in our history. Legislators, parents, and citizens in general are demanding that students be provided with a rigorous, standards-based curriculum that prepares them to function in the complex, challenging society of the twenty-first century. Because of this emphasis on high standards for student performance, which has resulted in more rigorous assessment of learning and higher accountability for teachers, one of the major issues facing teachers today is the need to provide high-level instruction in a learning environment that attends to expectations for academic rigor while remaining sensitive to all students' needs and providing each student an opportunity for success.

As professionals who have been school practitioners, who now are teacher educators, and who have evolved as students of teaching during a climate of change in public education and society, we prepared this textbook with the needs of both future and current teachers in mind. This study is organized around those teaching behaviors and instructional issues that are central to the dynamics of effective learning environments today.

We begin with a definition of effective teaching and best practice research that forms the basis for the development of the teacher as an effective practitioner. We proceed through discussions of planning for instruction, communicating as professionals, and research-based teaching behaviors and strategies. We complete the study with a discussion of managing student behavior and assessing student performance. Specifically, the textbook offers recommendations for planning, providing instruction, classroom management, and the evaluation and reporting of student progress.

Like teaching itself, learning to become an effective teacher must be approached on an individual though systematic basis. Successful preparation, characterized by formalized study, clinical experiences, and hours of reflection, along with an instructional philosophy which focuses on both student needs and content responsibilities, makes the possibility of becoming an effective teacher a reachable goal. We hope this textbook will guide as well as offer helpful insight in order that success in teaching becomes a reality.

Gilbert H. Hunt
Dennis G. Wiseman
Timothy J. Touzel

CONTENTS

EFFECTIVE TEACHING

Chapter 1

DEVELOPING A FRAMEWORK
FOR EFFECTIVE TEACHING

The desire to improve the quality of education for all students has become a driving force politically, socially, and even economically in the new millennium. In fulfilling this desire, teachers must focus on the development of educational practices and programs which will provide all students with the opportunity to develop the skills and knowledge necessary to contribute to a global economy and a diverse, ever-changing, world society. In reaching this end, teachers need to create environments in their classrooms that support and encourage success for all students, not just a few. Though a daunting challenge, teachers today are expected to maintain high and relevant standards for academic success while also maintaining student-centered, achievement-oriented classroom environments.

It is not possible to determine if certain teaching behaviors are effective without knowing whether or not students learn as an end result of these behaviors. This determination rests, in part, on the clarity of identified student learning outcomes, i.e., "What does the teacher desire for the students to learn?" A framework for effective teaching cannot stand alone in that it is relational to, and dependent upon, these outcomes. While educational research has identified many instructional strategies and behaviors which have come to be referred to as effective, it is not the case that each of these strategies and behaviors produces the same outcomes with all students and in all teaching situations. The challenge for the teacher is not only to identify and develop mastery of certain instructional strategies and behaviors accepted as effective practices, but the teacher is also challenged to develop the ability to effectively match these strategies and behaviors, at the appropriate time, to individual students and student groups, in specific teaching situations as these relate to the teacher's desired student learning outcomes.

This, however, still does not fully resolve the question of just what is desired as an end result of instruction. The answer to this question will depend on who is asking it and in what context the question is being posed. For example, "Does effective teaching result in student acquisition of a certain skill or body of subject matter knowledge?" "Does effective teaching result in students feeling good about themselves?" "Does it result in students liking, not disliking school?" "Does it result in students who obey the laws of society?" "Does it result in producing all of these possible outcomes?" While perhaps philosophical, this inquiry is important when deciding whether or not teachers are functioning in an effective manner, though it likely would be the more popular belief that effective teaching contributes in some way to each of these accomplishments.

Teachers today live and work in a world of cognitive and affective dissonance. Mixed messages abound. As an example, teachers often feel pressured to reach various desired outcomes popularly associated with effective teaching by the American public. Much of the critical attention now being given to American education has surfaced because America's teachers are expected to produce all of the desired outcomes previously mentioned, and more. Exploring the reasonableness of this expectation, however, goes well beyond the purview of this text. Though this is the case, the fact that American education and what goes on in America's schools and classrooms is of paramount interest to society should not, and cannot, be ignored.

In considering the many potential and desired outcomes associated with effective teaching, as discussed in this text, effective teaching has as its primary purpose the increased academic achievement of students which society expects of its schools and, consequently, its teachers. An effective teacher is one who is able to use certain strategies and exhibit certain behaviors which result in improved academic achievement, i.e., increased test scores, of students. Two additional points, however, are important. First, the most effective instruction associated with academic achievement also is instruction that produces positive affective ends. Second, no instructional strategy or behavior should be utilized for the purpose of achieving academic gain which results in affective loss.

A critical and difficult task facing today's teachers is the development of curricula and learning experiences that challenge students academically while remaining responsive to their individual needs. Much has been written about the importance of addressing individual learning styles, multiple intelligences, and numerous affective concerns. Each of these areas is important and needs to be considered as teachers develop their classroom learning environments. Teachers need to accept, however, that society sees the increase in academic achievement as the main purpose of schooling. Parents, school board members, legislatures, and concerned citizens hold schools and the teachers in them accountable for their students' academic achievement gains. Any education system that does not clearly strive toward, and reach, higher academic standards will face public disapproval. It is more critical now than ever before that teachers have the ability to develop and implement instructional programs that lead to greater academic success while also supporting the individual affective needs of their students. The balancing of these two concerns will no doubt be one of the greatest challenges for teachers in the future.

Ultimately, teachers determine the quality of schooling that students receive. In order to perform this important role effectively, an understanding of best practice research on effective teaching is needed so that a framework for effective teaching can be established and for effective teaching to take place. In studying this chapter, you will learn more about best practice research as you explore the following topics:

1. the characteristics of effective teaching,
2. the research on effective teaching, and
3. the process of analyzing best practice in the classroom.

CHARACTERISTICS OF EFFECTIVE TEACHING

Classroom teachers work at the core of a dynamic profession and hold the key position of responsibility for implementing high quality instruction for children. Effective teaching involves effective planning, communicating, managing, and evaluating, as well as the actual act or process of instructing. Each of these expectations is important in the successful pursuit of increased student learning.

Educational literature is replete with research on effective teaching. Some of this literature is empirically based while some is more conceptually grounded. Some is quite valuable and some, quite frankly, is much less so. The study of research on effective teaching must be approached and focused in such a way that it is based on the identification of those desired student learning outcomes previously mentioned. Once this has been accomplished, strategies and behaviors identified then can be studied and mastered with the understanding that, if they are exhibited properly, at the right time, at the right place, and with the right students, the desired learning outcomes will result. The enormous complexity of this undertaking is not only in identifying instructional strategies and behaviors that produce academic gains, but, as can be seen, also in using them properly at the right time and the right place and with the right students. This is where the need for a critical understanding of students, effective teaching practices, learning environments, teaching contexts, and rational decision making is essential.

Reflective Teaching

It is clear that not only does effective teaching include the successful use of certain instructional strategies and behaviors related to academic achievement, it also involves the ability to determine just when, where, and with whom these strategies and behaviors should be used. With these considerations in mind, effective teaching necessitates high levels of informed and reasoned decision making. A number of research studies and other publications support the significance of teacher reflection and the important role that reflection plays in student achievement (Glickman, Gordon, & Ross-Gordon, 2007; York-Barr, Sommers, Ghere, & Montie, 2005; Ross & Regan, 1993; Colton & Sparks-Langer, 1992; Tabachnick & Zeichner, 1991; Ellwein, Graue, & Comfort, 1990).

The need for teachers to be solidly grounded reflective professionals has emerged as a dominant theme in the field of education. As a result, there exist countless definitions of *reflective teaching* and ways to characterize the nature of reflective practice. *Reflective teachers* have and use the ability to critically examine what they do and the decisions that they make. Such an examination is referred to as reflection, and the process, in its totality, is referred to as reflective teaching (Cruickshank, 1987). Reflective teachers think deeply about what they are doing and are thoughtful, analytical, self-critical, and informed decision makers. They take the time to consider the impact of their work and the potential need to change or adjust their actions. Eggen and Kauchak (2007) refer to reflective practice as the process of conducting a critical self-examination of one's teaching. Reflective practice includes a deliberate pause taken by the teacher to examine beliefs, goals, and practices in order to gain new or deeper understanding that will lead to action to improve learning for students (York-Barr et al., 2005). Richert (1990) refers to the concept of reflective teaching as a period of time in the teaching process when teachers momentarily stop to reflect on their instruction in order to make sense of it. This allows teachers to grow as professionals by influencing how successful they are at learning from their own experiences. Reflective teachers think back over their teaching to analyze what they did and why and to consider how they might improve learning for their students in the future (Woolfolk, 2008).

John Dewey (1933) stressed the importance of reflective thinking as a foundation of the learning process. It is upon the ability of the reflective practitioner that the potential for high quality instruction rests. Reflective practitioners are professionals who are characterized by considering and weighing different points of view and perspective, explaining and defending decisions which have been made, and changing decisions once made when presented with new and relevant information. Reflective practitioners recognize and possess the skills, competencies, and knowledge essential to effective practice and recognize that they must continually seek to further develop their abilities in order to achieve and maintain high levels of effectiveness.

Because the classroom includes students of varied backgrounds, interests and motivations, ability levels and learning styles, reflective practitioners need an in-depth understanding of the principles of learning and growth and development so that they may make sound decisions regarding the selection of effective instructional strategies. Such teachers must be able to do their work with a high degree of efficiency. This often will require the use of different forms of technology and other instructional resources and aides. Teachers make virtually hundreds of learning-related decisions on a daily basis, not the least of these are those that involve the selection of effective practices for the students they have accepted the responsibility to educate.

Knowledge, Skills, and Dispositions

A clear though problematic characteristic of today's society is one that focuses on identifying quick solutions and "quick fixes" to problems. The American society has even been referred to as a "fast food" and "microwave" society. Unfortunately, some teachers take this same outlook into their classrooms with respect to finding quick solutions to the problems that they encounter there. There clearly are no quick solutions or fixes to difficult and complex problems of student learning.

Burden and Byrd (2007) suggest that, when examining effective teachers and building on the research reported, the most essential teacher characteristics may be placed into the three organizing categories of *knowledge, skills,* and *dispositions.*

Knowledge: To be effective, teachers must know the subjects that they teach. Although, this, in and of itself, is not sufficient to ensure effective teaching. Teachers must also have at least three other types of knowledge.

1. **Professional Knowledge:** Teachers must have knowledge about teaching in general; this includes knowledge about learning, diversity, technology, schooling and education, and the profession of teaching as a whole.
2. **Pedagogical Knowledge:** Teachers must have knowledge that includes the general concepts, theories, methods, and research about effective teaching, no matter the content area.
3. **Pedagogical Content Knowledge:** Teachers must have knowledge of teaching methods and approaches that are specific to the particular subject, or the application of certain strategies in a special way, that they teach. This includes an understanding of the content in

order to teach it in a variety of ways, drawing on the cultural backgrounds and prior knowledge and experiences of the students.

Skills: Teachers must have the necessary skills to use their knowledge effectively in making decisions about basic teaching functions such as planning for, implementing, and assessing instruction to ensure that all students are learning.

Dispositions: Teachers must have appropriate dispositions, i.e., values, commitments, and professional ethics, that influence their behaviors to promote learning for all students. Dispositions are guided by beliefs and attitudes related to values such as caring, fairness, honesty, responsibility, and social justice. While an affective concept, and in the minds of teachers, dispositions may be seen in teacher behaviors.

Many colleges, schools, and departments of teacher education are focusing on their faculty's definition of acceptable teacher dispositions. The National Council for Accreditation of Teacher Education (NCATE), one of the two national accreditation organizations for teacher education programs, has developed a disposition expectation for schools seeking NCATE accreditation. It is the position of NCATE that all candidates for teacher certification need to demonstrate behaviors consistent with the ideal of fairness and the belief that all students can learn (National Council for Accreditation of Teacher Education, 2008).

Much of what is known about best practice in teaching includes information related to *classroom planning and organization, goal setting and communication, teacher instructional strategies, time management, teacher-to-student interactions, relationships with students, and classroom management rules and procedures.* The following teacher behaviors represent a starting point to the investigation of effective teaching practices (Armstrong, Henson, & Savage, 1997). Effective teachers:

1. **play a central, dominant role in the classroom but involve students in planning and organization:** Effective teachers accept their important responsibility in classroom leadership, but also that students who are personally invested in their own learning will develop a greater sense of ownership for their learning and achieve at higher levels;
2. **set high goals and communicate these goals to their students:** It is important that teacher expectations be high though realistic; it is critical that teachers make their goals for their students clear, not only in terms of the learning experiences that they design, but also in terms of how students will be evaluated;
3. **work mostly with the entire class and less often with small groups, sometimes providing independent work for students:**

Teachers who are able to coordinate the learning of all students at the same time through large group instructional experiences develop a greater sense of community in the classroom and allow students to more clearly see their own progress, but also the work and activities of others at the same time;

4. **maintain a brisk lesson pace, requiring public and overt student participation:** Lessons that are seen by students as moving too slow, essentially only dragging along, allow for greater opportunities for students to drift away and become disengaged from the teacher; students who move forward with the lesson at a quicker pace, and who are overtly involved in the instruction, typically learn at higher levels and enjoy their learning more;

5. **use little criticism, shape student responses so that they are correct, hold students responsible for their work, and attend to students equitably:** Treating students fairly, providing uplifting rather than negative comments, and letting students know that they have responsibilities as learners, just as the teacher has responsibilities as a teacher, result in a more positive learning environment; students who feel safe in the learning environment, and who are meaningfully involved in it, are more successful in their work; and

6. **set and maintain clear rules for students' academic and social behavior:** Though perhaps not thought to be the case by some, students do desire and need clear boundaries in the classroom; students work better in environments that are well-defined in terms of the *do's* and *don'ts*, the *right's* and *wrong's*, than in settings where there is ambiguity and inconsistency as to what is acceptable and not acceptable behavior.

Five specific teacher characteristics related to teaching effectiveness have been described by Borich (2007) and organized into the broad categories of *lesson clarity, instructional variety, task orientation, engagement,* and *student success rate.*

Lesson Clarity

Lesson clarity refers to how well students understand the lessons of their teachers. It is not just important that teachers believe that they are clear, it is more important that their students truly understand them. Effective teachers make their points clear to their students, explain concepts in ways that help students follow along in a logical order, and have an oral delivery that is direct, audible to all students, and free from distracting mannerisms. Less effective teachers are vague, use vocabulary that students do not understand, are generally not well organized in their work, and typically are not considered as being clear in their teaching. Teachers who teach with a high degree of clarity spend less time going over material, i.e., the material is understood the first time it is presented. When students do not understand the various communications of their teachers, they will not be able to perform to their highest potentials. Students need to understand what their teachers are saying and expect of them in order to benefit the most from their learning experiences.

Instructional Variety

Instructional variety refers to the general teaching repertoire of the teacher. For example, "Does the teacher use a number of different teaching strategies or only a very few?", "Does the teacher utilize many different resources in his or her teaching or use the same resources over and over?" Having variety in instruction contributes to the perceived "energy" of the teacher and offers students different stimuli during lesson activities to which they may respond. Using different instructional approaches makes the teacher appear more interesting and exciting to students, piques students' natural curiosity to learn, and varies the stimuli in the classroom. Most students learn best through their experiences with a variety of different stimuli. The teacher with variability in the use of instructional techniques is able to offer students a greater number of connecting points as lessons are delivered. Consequently, the teacher who is skilled in using a number of different types of strategies is more effective than the teacher who is limited to only a few approaches.

Task Orientation

Time on task is a powerful concept when analyzing the teaching-learning process. When one considers that there are only a limited number of hours in the day in which students are in school, and that a portion of the typical school day is given over to non-instructional activities (e.g., moving from class to class, recess in the lower grades, lunch, and traveling to and from the restroom), the question of time available for learning becomes critical. Having a high level of meaningful and successful time on task communicates to students that the teacher is well prepared and "in charge." It also communicates where the teacher's instruction is headed and what students will be expected to know or be able to do at the end of the instructional period. Students who are on task are much less likely to present behavioral problems for their teachers. The more time that is allocated to a task or teaching a specific topic, the greater the opportunity students will have to learn it.

Engagement

Effective teachers use their time wisely. Wasted or idle time lead to problems in student management that should and can be avoided. Student engagement in the learning process, i.e., engaged learning time, is a key behavior that refers to the amount of time students devote to learning. Suggestions for increasing learning time and student engagement during learning include:

1. set rules that let students attend to their personal needs and work routines without obtaining permission each time;
2. move around the room to monitor students' seatwork and to communicate awareness of student progress;
3. ensure that independent assignments are interesting, worthwhile, and easy enough to be completed by each student without direction;
4. minimize time-consuming activities such as giving directions and organizing the class for instruction by writing the daily schedule on the board. This will ensure that students know where to go and what to do;
5. make ample use of resources and activities that are at, or slightly above, the student's current level of understanding; and
6. avoid timing errors. Act promptly to prevent misbehaviors from occurring or increasing in severity so they do not influence others in the class.

Time in schools and classrooms is often broken down into the following four dimensions:

1. **Allocated Time:** the amount of time a particular teacher or school designates to an identified course, topic, or activity;
2. **Instructional Time:** the portion of Allocated Time that is actually devoted to learning activities;
3. **Engaged Time:** sometimes referred to as time-on-task, Engaged Time is the portion of Instructional Time that students actually spend directly involved in learning activities; and
4. **Academic Learning Time:** Academic Learning Time takes all other forms of time into account and is characterized by students not only paying attention during instructional activities, but also interacting successfully with the content that is being taught; it is that portion of the classroom time where students are successfully engaged in meaningful learning experiences.

Teachers who have greater amounts of Academic Learning Time, i.e., time when students are actively and successfully involved in the lesson's activities, have students who learn at higher levels.

Given the multifaceted nature of any school, many events take place on a regular basis that compete for time which otherwise could be available for instruction. Instructional time is lost through different disruptions, interruptions, late starts, and less than smooth transitions. Out of a typical school year only 30 to 40 percent of the time is given over to quality Academic Learning Time (Weinstein & Mignano, 1993; Karweit, 1989). Research supports that, the greater the amount of Academic Learning Time in the classroom, the greater the level of student achievement. The best use of time in the classroom is determined, to a large extent, by the degree to which the teacher is fully planned for instruction. The better planned the teacher is for instruction that is relevant to the interests and needs of the students, and responsive to their learning styles and abilities, the greater the levels of achievement that will be reached.

Student Success Rate

Not only is wise use of time an important characteristic of effective teachers, effective teachers also have higher rates of student success in their teaching. Student success rate is defined as the rate at which students understand and correctly complete their work. Students should not be involved in just "doing things" in the classroom. What they do should be meaningful, learning-related as to what the teacher has planned for instruction, and result in successful achievement and productivity. Teachers need to know the abilities and interests of their students and plan their instruction accordingly based on this knowledge. Instruction where only a few students can be successful falls short of what is desired. This type of situation serves no one well. Success breeds success, and students who are successful one day will be better able to see themselves as being successful on another day. Likewise, students who experience little or no success have far greater difficulty in seeing themselves as being successful and, in the end, in being successful. If teachers desire for their students to be successful in their learning they must plan, teach, and evaluate in ways that ensure success for them.

Student engagement is closely related to student success rate. The average student in a typical classroom spends about half of the time working on tasks that provide the opportunity for high success. Researchers have found that students who spend more than the average time on high-success activities have higher achievement, better retention, and more positive attitudes toward school.

EDUCATIONAL RESEARCH AND
EFFECTIVE TEACHING PRACTICE

The Bush Administration's major education legislation, No Child Left Behind Act, has created much debate about the quality and worth of educational research since 2002. Central to the legislation is the position that federal money will not be awarded to any educational program that is not consistent with scientifically based research. Much debate has arisen over the definition of scientifically based research. As Woolfolk (2008) suggests, the Act's definition has five characteristics common to classical experimental research: (1) Researchers must use observations or experiments to gather valid, reliable data; (2) Data are analyzed using appropriate, rigorous procedures; (3) Researchers use experimental or quasi-experimental designs, hopefully with random assignment of subjects to conditions; (4) Research is replicable and easy to build upon by other researchers; and (5) The research has been blind refereed by a panel of independent experts.

In a classic article, David Berliner (2002) discusses his view on quality educational research. Berliner differs with the No Child Left Behind Act's position on the exclusive use of classical experimental or quasi-experimental design. Berliner stresses that the nature of education calls for the use of many types of data gathering and analyzing procedures; he feels there is great value in methods such as case studies, surveys and other descriptive, ethnographic research. It seems clear that educational researchers all agree about the importance of peer review and replicability, but many, including such respected researchers as Berliner, Woolfolk, and Olson (2004), to name a few, believe that education is a very different field of exploration than medicine. Because certain methods are exclusively used in medicine, it does not mean those methods should be exclusively used in education. There is little doubt that the Bush Administration took a position that education was a "weak science" and that the only way to improve the training of teachers was for educational scientists and training institutions in general to become more like the "stronger science" of medicine and the training of doctors. This debate is far from completed.

In spite of the tremendous amount of research ongoing in the field of education, Cruickshank (1990) identifies that almost all educational research suffers some shortcomings making much of it limited in its generalizability. A first limitation is the evident lack of agreement on the outcome variable used to determine effectiveness. Again, "What is the primary goal/role of the teacher?" "Is it to instruct, manage, bring about academic achievement, social change, affective change, or counsel?" These questions must be addressed when interpreting teacher effectiveness research and in determining a teacher's effectiveness. Additionally, any consideration of effective teaching research also must take into consideration the samples used, i.e., "Who are the students and teachers involved in the research, and what do they have in common with other students and teachers?", as one considers the usefulness of any results found. Finally, the research must be analyzed in terms of the methodology used, its focus and design, its attention to variables, and its statistical soundness. All of these considerations are relevant in drawing any interpretation or conclusion from research findings.

However, teachers and prospective teachers need to be able to read and understand research reports at a level that allows for application to classrooms (Eggen & Kauchak, 2007). Teachers should know the advantage of experimental research as discussed earlier is that it can be used to determine cause and effect when replication leads to consistent findings. On the other hand, teachers must be certain that the circumstances in the experimental study are similar to the circumstances in which they teach. For example, a study showing that high school students in inner city settings who do two hours of homework each night score higher on a standardized test than classmates who do thirty minutes of homework each night would tell nothing that is applicable to elementary school settings or even rural or suburban high school settings. Teachers must remember that, to the degree that variance exists (e.g., different students, different tests, different homework assignments, or different circumstances under which the test is given) between the research and the application setting, the ability to make inferences is radically decreased.

An important publication in this area by the Phi Delta Kappa Educational Foundation brought together a review of ten major studies from the 1970s and 1980s focusing on the characteristics of effective teachers as related to increasing academic achievement (Cruickshank, 1990). The results compiled were organized into seven cluster or trait areas (Figure 1-1).

---

1. Teacher Character Traits
2. What the Teacher Knows
3. What the Teacher Teaches
4. How the Teacher Teaches
5. What the Teacher Expects
6. How the Teacher Reacts to Students
7. How Teachers Manage

Figure 1-1. Cruickshank's clustering of effective teacher characteristics.

1. ***Teacher Character Traits:*** are enthusiastic, stimulating, encouraging, warm, task-oriented and businesslike, tolerant-polite-tactful, trusting,

flexible-adaptable, democratic, hold high expectations for students, do not seek personal recognition, care less about being liked, are able to overcome student stereotypes, feel responsible for student learning, are able to express feelings, and have good listening skills.

2. ***What the Teacher Knows:*** are knowledgeable in their subject fields and possess a great deal of factual information.

3. ***What the Teacher Teaches:*** ensure coverage of the criterion material for which students are accountable and go beyond it to provide maximal content coverage.

4. ***How the Teacher Teaches:*** demonstrate clarity, provide variety, establish and maintain momentum, make effective use of small groups, encourage more student participation, monitor and attend to students, structure teaching and learning, take advantage of unexpected events, monitor seatwork, use both open-ended and lower-order questions, involve students in peer teaching, use large-group instruction, avoid complexity by providing information in small amounts, use less busy work, use fewer traditional materials, show students the importance of what is to be learned, demonstrate the thinking processes necessary for learning, and anticipate and correct student misconceptions.

5. ***What the Teacher Expects:*** establish expectations for students, hold them accountable, and encourage parent participation in the student's academic life.

6. ***How the Teacher Reacts to Students:*** are accepting and supportive, deal with students in a consistent manner, make little but judicious use of student criticism, demonstrate withitness, make judicious use of praise, use incentives, adjust to student developmental levels, individualize instruction, insure equitable student participation, direct questions to non-volunteers, use appropriate wait-time when asking questions, use prompting, give immediate feedback to help students, and are aware of and sensitive to learning differences among socioeconomic status or cultural groups and adjust to these differences.

7. ***How Teachers Manage:*** demonstrate expertise in planning, have strong organization from the first day of class, are prompt in starting classes, make smooth transitions, are skilled in overlapping or handling two or more classroom activities at the same time, use group alerting especially to involve students who do not volunteer, are persistent and efficient in maintaining time-on-task, minimize disruptions, are accepting of some noise in the classroom, have a repertoire of control techniques, use mild forms of punishment, maintain a relaxed atmosphere, and hold students to work and success standards.

Berliner and Casanova (1996), in *Putting Research to Work in Your School*, provide another review of research on effective teaching offering a concise and application-oriented look at selected teaching practices, skills, and behaviors related to student achievement. The following ten teaching strategies are identified as being related to increased student achievement:

1. use of reciprocal teaching strategies,
2. placing personalized and informative comments on student homework papers,
3. specifically teaching metacognitive skills and skills for remembering,
4. use of peer tutoring,
5. use of cross-age tutoring,
6. use of reading aloud experiences,
7. use of participatory learning strategies,
8. use of project-based learning strategies,
9. establishing solid relationships with parents, and
10. involving parents in the learning experiences of their children.

Early Research on Effective Teaching Practice

One of the most thorough reviews of the research in the area of teacher effectiveness was conducted over thirty-five years ago (Rosenshine & Furst, 1971) and is still considered important reading in the field today. Although considerable research has been conducted more recently, this early research provides a sound foundation for the study of effective teaching behaviors related to student achievement.

Of particular importance to this work is the understanding given to the meaning of effective teaching. While teachers are expected to accomplish many things in their work, perhaps the most important accomplishment is guiding students to achieve academically. Defining effective teaching as teaching that results in higher levels of student achievement is not to discount the importance of students developing positive feelings about themselves and the world around them, and toward learning itself. It does recognize, though, that the primary purpose of the teacher is to guide and advance students in their learning. In their early research, Rosenshine and Furst (1971) report on eleven teacher behaviors or variables related to student achievement; they are presented here in the order of the degree to which they are so related.

1. Clarity
2. Variability
3. Enthusiasm
4. Task-Oriented and/or Business-Like Behavior

5. Student Opportunity to Learn Criterion Material
6. Use of Student Ideas and General Indirectness
7. Criticism
8. Use of Structuring Comments
9. Types of Questions
10. Probing Behaviors
11. Level of Difficulty of Instruction

Clarity

Teachers who have the ability to explain concepts clearly and who are able to answer student questions so that their students understand the answers given to them are characterized by clarity in their instruction. When teachers are clear in their communications, their students feel more secure in their learning and are better able to comprehend what is expected of them. As a result, they perform at higher academic levels.

Variability

Also referred to as instructional variety, variability is represented by the teacher's diversity of information-sending techniques or strategies used during the presentation of lessons. Teachers who have variability in their teaching utilize multiple strategies to get the main ideas of their lessons across to their students. Effective teachers have the ability to utilize expository lesson delivery as well as organize students for cooperative learning activities as appropriate to the purpose of the lesson. They are capable of exhibiting many different strategies in teaching and do so regularly. Through this variety, in particular when strategies are matched to student learning styles, students remain more interested in the lessons that their teachers have planned for them and learn more in the process.

Enthusiasm

Enthusiasm has been identified as the estimation of the amount of vigor and power displayed by the teacher. It also has been associated with the teacher's level of excitement, energy, involvement, and even interest regarding the subject matter, the students, and teaching. Although an abstract concept, students definitely have their own ideas about the enthusiasm of their teachers. Students feel they know when their teachers are enjoying their work and are excited about being in the classroom and when they are not. Students draw from the enthusiasm shown by their teachers, or at least from what they perceive as their teachers' enthusiasm, and respond accordingly. As a part of the teacher's overall attitude toward teaching, students, and student learning, teacher enthusiasm is related to the concept of teacher efficacy, i.e., the teacher's belief that he or she can be successful in bringing about increased student learning. Teachers who exhibit enthusiasm communicate that they are confident in what they are doing, not only in their own abilities, but also in the abilities of their students.

Task-Oriented and/or Business-Like Behavior

Task-oriented teachers project that they know what they expect concerning student performance and the lessons that they teach and how to attain the student performance that they desire. They are seen by their students as being in charge, knowing what they are doing, organized, and focused on what needs to be accomplished. Being task-oriented and business-like does not mean being impersonal, aloof, cold, or distant when working with students. Rather, it communicates that the teacher knows that something important needs to be done and that the teacher and students, together, will be successful in completing the task that is to be undertaken.

Student Opportunity to Learn Criterion Material

Teachers who are criterion-focused in their teaching communicate to students their expected instructional outcomes, i.e., desired student learning outcomes, prior to beginning their instruction and then teach specifically toward the students' successful attainment of these desired outcomes. What is desired is not kept secret; there is no mystery. Students know what is expected of them and how they will be evaluated (the criteria used) as to their level of success. This security of direction and understanding of the evaluation process is important to students as they engage in the teacher's planned learning activities. It also is important to the teacher in that it offers the teacher additional focus and direction with respect to teaching to stated learning objectives.

Use of Student Ideas and General Indirectness

The use of student ideas by teachers during instruction and, in so doing, communicating to students that their ideas and input are important enhances student achievement. The use of student ideas is a good way to personalize the instruction and is an important part of indirect teaching. Students have higher levels of meaningful participation and interest in their learning when their ideas are regularly incorporated into the learning process; they also have greater academic success as they believe their teachers value their ideas as well as them as individuals.

Criticism

A negative relationship exists between student achievement and the teacher's use of criticism. Teachers characterized by using criticism in their teaching, often seen by students as an attempt to justify their authority, typically have students who achieve less in most subject areas. Teachers who use frequent criticism are perceived by their students as being less prepared for their work and less sure of themselves. The use of criticism can create a threatening environment for some students, push students away, and detract from the learning process resulting in lower student achievement.

Use of Structuring Comments

The teacher's use of structuring comments in communicating with students, i.e., alerting students to the important instructional events which are to follow in the lesson, or important points to be made, is recommended. The use of structuring comments is appropriate at the start of lessons and at the start of different parts of lessons. Such comments help students focus on and attend to what will be taking place during the teacher's instruction. The use of structuring comments also projects to students that the teacher is well planned and clear as to where the learning activity is headed.

Types of Questions

Effective teachers are skilled at asking higher and lower level questions of cognition, and the use of both types is related to student achievement. This concept is vital to all levels and types of teaching. Some teachers consider the ability to ask good questions as the most significant teaching skill of all. This is particularly the case as question asking has the potential for great diagnostic value for the teacher as well the potential to advance intellectual thought for the student. The use of high and low level questions is discussed in detail in Chapter 4.

Probing Behaviors

Probing behaviors occur when the teacher requests students to go deeper into their thinking or to elaborate on comments made or positions taken.

Typically through the use of probing questions, the use of probing behaviors communicates to students that the teacher is interested in knowing more about their ideas. Probing behaviors cause students to review their ideas and explore them more deeply. They also help the teacher in creating a classroom atmosphere that includes student ideas and general indirectness that was described earlier. Since by its very purpose probing for student ideas does not involve looking at what students say as being either right or wrong, probing behaviors offer natural and excellent opportunities for teachers to praise students for their thinking. To be effective, such behaviors need to be carried out in a way that is seen by students as being nonthreatening and nonjudgmental.

Level of Difficulty of Instruction

Teachers who have created learning environments where students feel appropriately challenged, but not overchallenged, have established environments where students achieve at higher levels. Teachers should offer instruction that is neither too hard nor too easy for students. While much has been said about the importance of increasing academic rigor in schools and holding students to higher standards, this should not be done at the expense of students who are simply unable to reach the higher standards that may be established. If students perceive that the difficulty of instruction offered by the teacher is beyond their ability, they may either withdraw from the instruction or act out against it. In knowing the abilities and interests of their students, it is important for teachers to establish levels of instruction that are out of the immediate reach of their students (therefore not too easy), but which are reachable with effort and assistance (therefore appropriately challenging). In terms of fully knowing their students and utilizing this knowledge in planning and delivering instruction, it is helpful for teachers to understand how the concept of the *Zone of Proximal Development* relates to their teaching. The zone of proximal development is defined as a range of tasks that a student cannot yet do alone, but can accomplish when assisted by a more skilled partner (Eggen & Kauchak, 2007). To continually challenge students in appropriate ways, it is important for learning tasks to be presented at the outer reaches of this range or zone. Presenting tasks that are simply too complex and thought to be unreasonable by the students will cause student interest in the tasks to diminish as students will see the tasks as being too difficult for them to be successful. Working toward them will appear to be not worth their effort for this reason and whatever interest the students may have in the tasks will wane. Likewise, if the teacher too regularly presents tasks at the lower end of the zone and that represent no challenge, students also will lose interest because the tasks will be viewed as too simplistic and unimportant. Chapter 4 will present information on how proximal development can be used to improve instruction.

More Current Research on Best Teaching Practice

Considerable research on best teaching practice has been conducted since the research reported by Rosenshine and Furst in the early 1970s. Such factors as teacher knowledge, clarity and organization, and warmth and enthusiasm have been consistently reinforced over the years as characteristics of effective teachers (Woolfolk, 2008). Although more current research has expanded the knowledge base related to best practice in teaching, it has not contradicted earlier findings. Eggen and Kauchak (2007) report the following teaching characteristics or skills related to increased student achievement.

1. Attitudes
2. Organization
3. Communication
4. Focus
5. Feedback and Praise
6. Questioning
7. Review and Closure

Attitudes

The consideration of teacher *attitude* goes beyond seeing the teacher as merely having a "good" or "bad" attitude. Were it this simple, the influence of attitude on teaching and learning would have been more completely understood long before now. Teachers have studied attitude, researchers have reported on attitude, and students have responded to the attitudes of their teachers since the beginning of formal education. Teachers have a responsibility for the attitudes of their students, both positive and negative. Where students have negative attitudes toward themselves or their learning, teachers need to identify the causes of these negative attitudes so that they may help them become more positive in order for their learning to advance. An important aspect of this process relates to teachers and their own attitudes.

Teachers who hold the belief that they and their schools can have a positive effect on their students and their learning are said to have high efficacy (Hoy & Hoy, 2009; Orlich, Harder, Callahan, Trevisan, & Brown, 2007; Bruning, Schraw, & Ronning, 1995). Classrooms and schools with such teachers have increased student achievement. Teachers with high efficacy work well with low achieving students and use praise rather than criticism to motivate and reward them; they believe that all students can learn. Such teachers use their time effectively and are more accepting of the unique, individual qualities of their students. High efficacy teachers do not give up on students, but, more readily, change their strategies and adopt and adapt instructional materials as needed to meet their students' needs (Hoy & Hoy, 2009; Poole, Okeafor, & Sloan, 1989). Low efficacy teachers are more critical of their students and persevere less when seeking solutions to their learning problems. Such teachers do not hold strong beliefs that they really can make a difference in the lives of their students (Good & Brophy, 2003; Kagan, 1992). Teachers with low efficacy tend to stratify their classes more by student ability, or what they perceive to be student ability, while giving more effort, attention, and affection to their students felt to have higher ability (Ashton & Webb, 1986). Low efficacy teachers also perceive their students' behaviors, particularly those of their low-achieving students, in terms of potential threats to the orderliness of their classrooms. Teachers with high efficacy, on the other hand, are not as likely to feel threatened by the misbehavior or potential misbehavior of their students.

Organization

Being well organized does not mean being overly restrictive. Students can tell whether or not a teacher is organized. Teachers who are organized, or at least seen by their students as being organized, have higher achieving students than those who do not have or do not project this quality.

Organization involves management of the classroom in terms of its physical elements and rules and procedures as well as academic concerns with respect to the teaching process. *Management organization* in the classroom refers to the general organizational structure and procedures that the teacher has developed to keep the classroom running smoothly. Organized teachers have their teaching materials ready when it is time to begin their lessons, start on time, have established learning routines (e.g., certain ways of taking roll and collecting papers to minimize the time these activities take and making transitions from one activity to another quickly and smoothly), and engage their students throughout the entire instructional period. Established routines in the classroom enable teachers and their students to know what to anticipate as the teacher's instruction moves forward. Effective management organization allows for classroom time to be used more productively. Although the ability to be spontaneous as the situation dictates is important, and organized teachers certainly can be spontaneous, teachers who have well-established routines and procedures bring a positive predictability to their teaching, giving their students a greater sense of order, balance, and direction. This order and balance, i.e., equilibrium, in the environment, and the direction that results from it, contribute to higher levels of student achievement.

Where management organization deals with the organizational structure and procedures of operation in the classroom, the teacher's *academic organization* is reflected in the teacher's means of ordering and arranging information for instruction so that students will be able to understand the information communicated. Effective teachers have specific organization schemes to assist students in ordering and arranging information. Being well organized academically does not mean teachers lack excitement or the ability to teach to the moment. Rather, academic organization refers to the teacher being well prepared to carry out instruction in a way that assists students as they learn and remember what is being taught. The use of diagrams, outlines, hierarchies, schematics, and technology can be significant in not only helping teachers in presenting organized lessons but also in assisting students in making better organization of and use of the information being presented. The teacher's ability to be clear in communications with students is related to the teacher's ability to be academically organized. Good teacher organization is founded upon the routines and procedures the teacher has developed for instruction that effectively organize and use time wisely, thus enabling the classroom to run in an efficient and effective manner.

Communication

As previously noted, a strong, positive relationship exists between the clarity of the teacher and student achievement, reinforcing the importance of teachers being clear in the use of their verbal communication (Weiss & Pasley, 2004; Good & Brophy, 2003; Snyder, Bushur, Hoeksema, Olson, Clark, & Snyder, 1991; Cruickshank, 1985). Four aspects of language clarity have been identified related to effective teaching practice:

1. **Precise Terminology:** in using *precise terminology*, the teacher eliminates or restricts the use of vague and ambiguous words and phrases, e.g., perhaps, maybe, usually, might, and so on, from explanations and responses to students' questions, presentations, and interactions with students,

2. **Connected Discourse:** through *connected discourse* the teacher's presentation is thematically well connected and leads to a goal, going point by point; the absence of this type of discourse results in communication that may seem rambling to the student, being disjointed and not appropriately linked; if the lesson isn't clear, is presented in a poor order of events, or if incidental information is included without indicating how it relates to the topic, classroom discourse becomes disconnected,

3. **Transition Signals:** *transition signals* assist in smoothly blending one topic area with the next that follows; without such signals the teacher may be seen as abruptly moving or jumping from topic to topic or point to point; transition signals are verbal statements indicating that one idea is ending and another is beginning; since all students are not at the same place cognitively, a transition signal alerts the students that the lesson is making a conceptual shift, i.e., moving to a new topic, and allows them to prepare for it, and

4. **Emphasis:** *emphasis* denotes the teacher specifically identifying information that is to be remembered; phrases such as, "This is important," and "Be sure to remember this," are examples of the use of emphasis; if something is of special importance, the students should be told; emphasis consists of verbal cues that help students focus on important information in a lesson; repeating a point or asking a question about an important point previously considered can also be an effective form of emphasis.

Students will not display their best achievement when their teachers are not clear. Though a teacher may comment that a particular student does not pay attention and does not understand something, this may be more the teacher's problem than the student's. It is the teacher who must be expert in communicating and reaching students with the language used in the classroom.

Focus

Focus is an important aspect of the teacher's ability to communicate and attend to ideas in the classroom. Focus represents bringing student attention to the lesson at the very beginning of the instructional experience and then maintaining this attention throughout the remainder of the lesson. This focus also has been associated with establishing an anticipatory set (Burden & Byrd, 2007; Hunter, 1984). *Anticipatory set* is the mental or attitudinal foundation established by the teacher for the students at the beginning of the lesson that helps students understand what they may anticipate in the instruction to follow. When students are focused at the beginning of the lesson, they are better connected to the body of the lesson that is then presented. Teachers who have good introductory focus are able to gain and maintain student attention and more easily provide a stronger connection for the students with the material being taught as the lesson progresses. Focus serves to motivate students, increase their curiosity, and make the lesson more interesting. Teachers often can gain student attention successfully through the use of certain visual or auditory sensory techniques such as pictures, models, songs, concrete objects, riddles, the overhead projector, the white board or marker board, and the Internet and computer technology. The importance of using focus techniques, classically referred to as *advance organizers*, or the use of introductory statements or activities to frame new content as a part of the lesson focus, was developed in detail by Ausubel (1978). The use of such focus techniques brings students more into the overall mainstream of the lesson than into any specific part of it. This helps students avoid difficulties in understanding the main intent of the teacher's instruction but also assists them in attending to the important individual components that make it up.

Feedback and Praise

Few individuals function well in environments characterized by ambiguity and uncertainty. Students experience unnecessary stress and pressure when facing ambiguity. Teachers who regularly provide *feedback* to their students regarding the accuracy or appropriateness of their responses and their work have higher-achieving students. The most effective feedback provides instructive information, praise, and encouragement as appropriate and is immediate and specific. Individual feedback that is aimed at constructively correcting errors made during learning positively affects student performance and attitude (Elawar & Corno, 1985). Such feedback not only results in increased achievement, but also in increased motivation. It contributes to a greater sense of balance and self-regulation as students are able to monitor their own progress. It also helps students create associations that result in more meaningful learning and advancement toward stated goals. Simply put, feedback lessens student confusion which should be a major outcome of all instruction.

Feedback generally comes in one of two forms: written or oral. Providing written feedback poses a challenge for some teachers as it is more time consuming. Because of this, many teachers often provide only brief or sketchy written feedback for their students or information that is sometimes not terribly instructive in quality. Although it may take more time, written feedback that is specific to the nature of the students' performance is an important part of effective teaching and is positively related to student achievement. Specific written feedback helps students to focus on their weaknesses and make corrections through their own efforts. The time spent in giving more detailed feedback should eventually result in savings in instructional time. It should also result in improvements in student attitudes that will have a positive impact on classroom climate. It is suggested that teachers regularly ask themselves specific questions when they review their students' work, such as: (1) "What is the key error if there is one?" (2) "What is the probable reason for the error?" (3) "How can I guide the student to avoid the error in the future?"

and (4) "What did the student do well that could be noted?" Using questions such as these as guides in responding in written form to student work will result in benefits not only to student learning, but also to the learning environment as a whole (Elawar & Corno, 1985). In the future, as teachers use more and more electronic instruction, the ability to use written feedback will be especially important.

As compared to written feedback, oral feedback is more easily given as it can be used in ongoing discussions and question-and-answer periods. The instructive value of oral feedback also is important to enhancing student achievement. Quick, one word responses, or responses that merely inform the student that he or she is correct or not correct, are not as effective as more elaborate responses. More elaborate or extended responses let the student know that he or she was correct or incorrect, but also why this was the case.

Praise is one of the most common and adaptable forms of teacher feedback. Educational research has identified some interesting and not especially positive patterns in teacher use of praise (Brophy, 1981).

- Praise is not used nearly as often as most teachers believe, being used less than five times per class.
- Praise for good behavior is actually quite rare and occurs only once every two or more hours in the elementary grades and less than that as students get older.
- Praise is influenced by the type of student as much as on the quality of the responses that students give. High achieving, well-behaved and attentive students receive greater amounts of praise than do low achieving and inattentive students.
- Praise is often given by teachers based on the responses that they expect to receive as much as it is on the answers that the students actually give.

Alderman (2004, p. 254) provides a helpful analysis of the difference between the effective and ineffective use of praise (Figure 1-2).

Considering the positive impact of the use of praise in the classroom, in particular in the areas of student learning, motivation, and management, it is recommended that teachers should praise:

1. genuinely,
2. immediately,
3. accomplishments that students may not be aware of,
4. strategically with different types of students,
5. the effort as well as the answer,
6. specifically, and
7. judiciously.

Characteristics of Effective and Ineffective Use of Praise

Effective Praise	Ineffective Praise
Is delivered contingently	Is delivered randomly or unsystematically
Specifies the particulars of the accomplishment	Is restricted to global, positive reactions
Shows spontaneity, variety, and other signs of credibility; suggests clear attention to the student's accomplishment	Shows a bland uniformity, which suggests a conditioned response made with minimal attention
Rewards attainment of specified performance criteria (that can include effort criteria)	Rewards mere participation, without consideration of performance processes or outcomes
Provides information to students about their competence or the value of their accomplishments	Provides no information at all nor gives students information about their status
Orients students toward better appreciation of their own task-related behavior and thinking about problem solving	Orients students toward comparing themselves with others and thinking about competing
Uses students' own prior accomplishments as the context for describing present accomplishments	Uses the accomplishments of peers as the context for describing students' present accomplishments
Is given in recognition of noteworthy effort or success at difficult (for this student) tasks	Is given without regard to the effort expended or with meaning of the accomplishment (for this student)
Attributes success to effort and ability, implying that similar successes can be expected in the future	Attributes success to ability alone or to external factors such as luck or easy task
Fosters endogenous attributions (students believe that they expend effort on the task because they enjoy the task and/or want to develop task-relevant skills)	Fosters exogenous attributions (students believe that they expend effort on the task for external reasons — please the teacher, win a competition or reward, etc.)
Focuses students' attention on their own task-relevant behavior	Focuses students' attention on the teacher as an external authority figure who is manipulating them
Fosters appreciation of and desirable attributions about task-relevant behavior after the process is completed	Intrudes into the ongoing process, distracting attention from task-relevant behavior

Figure 1-2: From "Teacher praise: A functional analysis," by Brophy, 1981, *Review of Educational Research, 51*, 5–32.

Understanding the characteristics of the effective use of praise is important to the teaching process as they impact the student's motivation to stay and/or become involved in the teacher's lesson.

Additionally, teachers are advised to use variety as well as frequency in their approaches to praising their students. Some teachers fall into a routine pattern of using the same praise words over and over again, such as "good" or "well done." In that praise is a very special type of reinforcer, its potency is enhanced when it avoids being too routine. In an effort to add variety to their approaches used to praise, and keep themselves and their praise exciting and more interesting, it is recommended that teachers utilize as much variety as possible in their praising vocabulary. For example, words and phrases such as "terrific," "very good job," "outstanding," "stupendous," "excellent," and "wonderful," will make the teacher's praise efforts much more interesting and positively received by the students. In the end, the teacher's praise will be more motivational as it will be seen by the students as being more individual and dynamic.

Questioning

Research on teacher questioning strategies has increased considerably over the last twenty years. Questioning is considered by many to be the most important tool that teachers have for helping students build understanding. While it is important that teachers have well-developed questioning skills, such skills do not develop naturally. The development of good questioning skills comes only through specific question-asking applications that are consistently analyzed in terms of whether or not the questions, and the way they were asked and followed up upon, elicited the desired outcomes (Borich, 2007). Research continues to reinforce the relationship between the quality of a teacher's questioning skills and student achievement.

Though some might think that certain questions are preferred over others, such as low cognitive over high cognitive or vice versa, this is not the case. Different types of questions serve different learning and teaching purposes. The teacher should select questions as they relate to the learning outcomes desired. If the objective of the lesson is to focus on the development of certain basic skills or remembered information, low cognitive questions are of greater value. If the purpose is to place students in situations where they will be expected to analyze, evaluate, create information, or share their personal ideas, high cognitive questions should be used (Burden & Byrd, 2007; Good & Brophy, 2003; Anderson, Krathwohl, Airasian, Cruikshank, Mayer, Pintrich, Raths, & Wittrock, 2001; Bloom, Engelhart, Furst, Hill, & Krathwohl, 1956). Both high and low cognitive questions correlate positively with student achievement. *Frequency, equitable distribution, prompting,* and *wait-time* are considered to be characteristics of effective questioning strategies (Burden & Byrd, 2007; Eggen & Kauchak, 2007; Orlich et al., 2007; O'Flahavan, Hartman, & Pearson, 1988).

1. **Frequency:** generally, the more questions the better; greater numbers of questions allow for more students to be involved in the dynamics of a lesson and more opportunities for the teacher to monitor the students' and the lesson's progress; questioning increases the opportunity for student involvement and contributes to improved achievement;

2. **Equitable Distribution:** teachers should strive for a pattern of questioning in which all students are called on as equally as possible; more questioning with equal distribution across the class increases the opportunity for providing more feedback and helps students stay motivated and connected to the lesson; this reduces the likelihood that students will drift away from the instruction and become involved in misconduct behaviors;

3. **Prompting:** prompting is a technique to help students respond to questions by providing cues after an incorrect or incomplete answer or silence; an additional question or statement the teacher uses to elicit an appropriate student response after a student answers incorrectly is considered prompting; prompting is not appropriate if the question calls for remembering specific factual information, but is of value when studying conceptual, procedural knowledge and when using cognitive processes beyond remembering; and

4. **Wait-time:** wait-time is the period of silence before or after a student is asked a question and when the teacher speaks again; the use of wait-time increases student learning by giving students time to think; in most classrooms, regardless of grade or ability level, wait-times are very short, frequently less than one second (Rowe, 1986); research suggests that increasing wait-time to at least three seconds will positively impact student learning; wait-time should be implemented strategically; for example, if students are practicing basic skills such as multiplication facts, quick answers are desirable and wait-times should be short, but, if a question is asked to produce student ideas, where there are no right or wrong answers, wait-time should be longer.

Review and Closure

Clear review and closure consistently serve as aids to learning and enhancing achievement. *Review* is when the teacher summarizes important points from previous work in helping students to link what has been learned to what will be taught in the future. Review can occur at different points of the lesson, either close to the beginning, midpoint during the lesson, or at the end. When review is used effectively, teachers are able to guide students beyond a focus on only the specific information presented in the lesson into more substantive conceptual understandings (Dempster, 1991). *Closure* is a form of review that occurs at the end of the instructional period that enables the student to end the lesson with a better understanding of the topic and a place to build on in the future. Closure can be accomplished through a number of techniques such as the use of questions, short written assignments, or classroom discussion. The use of each technique should provide the teacher with valuable information related to identifying the most important place, or way, to begin the next lesson. An effective use of closure is to ask students to state, in their own words, important points of information covered in the lesson. While this enables students to end the lesson with a better understanding of the lesson's content, it also serves to inform the teacher. If teachers are uncertain as to what level of understanding their students have at the end of one lesson, they will not be well prepared to begin the next lesson that follows. They may know what they taught, but this does not mean that they know what their students understand.

Current Research Directions

Planning and Assessment

The need for teachers to be well planned and, therefore, well prepared is documented clearly in the literature. Many researchers support the connection between teacher effectiveness, planning of learning activities, and selection of appropriate materials (Hoy & Hoy, 2009; Morine-Dershimer, 2006; Emmer, Sanford, Clements & Martin, 1982; Evertson, Anderson, Anderson, & Brophy, 1980; Clark & Yinger, 1979). It also is clear that students learn more and rate their teachers higher when they can understand how facts, concepts, and principles are interrelated (Van Patten, Chao, & Reigeluth, 1986; Smith, 1985) and when instruction is logically sequenced and coherent in its design (Armento, 1997; Smith & Sanders, 1981). Research strongly supports the relationship between regularly and appropriately assessing student learning and enhancing achievement. Effective teachers approach the assessment of student progress specifically as this relates to stated learning goals (Hoy & Hoy, 2009; Reynolds, 1992; Porter & Brophy, 1987; Rosenshine, 1988; Brophy & Good, 1986). Such teachers are consistent in their assessment of student progress and in designing assessments that can be used to clearly provide for meaningful student feedback. Multiple assessments are used to more completely and accurately offer a total picture of student learning. The entirety of Chapter 2 is dedicated to this important topic.

Classroom Management

In the area of classroom environment, research supports the need for teachers to master the skills of classroom management before they can master the skills of effective instruction. Attention to routines, rules, and procedures, and the establishing of clear expectations for behavior are prerequisites to good instruction. The elements of the classroom environment are addressed while creating and maintaining an atmosphere of respect, caring, and commitment to important work. Good classroom management is a critical teacher skill and high student engagement in learning is both a cause and an effect of successful management systems.

Well-managed classrooms contribute positively to student engagement with and achievement on learning tasks. Where rules and procedures are concrete, explicit, and functional, they contribute to order and work accomplished (Good & Brophy, 2003; Doyle, 1986). Routines are standardized methods of handling particular situations which also are linked to student behavior (Burden & Byrd, 2007; Brophy, 1987). Teachers must maximize the time that students spend actively engaged in worthwhile academic activities and minimize the time that they spend waiting for activities to get started, making transitions between activities, sitting with nothing to do, or engaging in misconduct.

Finally, the connection between affective considerations such as climates of respect and the importance of self-concept also are supported in the research literature. The consistent projection of positive expectations and attributions are important in fostering positive self-concepts that contribute to prosocial behavior (Good & Brophy, 2003; Brophy, 1987). Students who are consistently treated as if they are well-intentioned individuals, who respect themselves and others and desire to act responsibly, are more likely to live up to these expectations and acquire these qualities than students who are treated as if they had the opposite characteristics. The entirety of Chapter 7 is dedicated to this important topic.

Instruction

In the area of instructional practice, educational research has brought attention to the importance of constructivist learning and has placed an important focus on conceptual learning and teaching for understanding.

Constructivist theories hold that learning develops as students try to under-stand their learning experiences. Students build mental models or schema and continue to revise them to make better sense of their experiences. Constructivists share similar goals for learning such as the emphasis that real learning is in its use of knowledge rather than in its storage. Learning goals include developing abilities to find and solve problems, critical thinking, inquiry, self-determination, etc. (Hoy & Hoy, 2009). The focus on construc-tivist learning builds on earlier work by Jean Piaget and John Dewey.

Effective practice research has shown that one approach or philosophy, however, is not necessarily superior to another as it relates to desired student results or outcomes. What is specific is the research base for questioning and discussion techniques. As previously noted, effective teachers use question-ing strategies that challenge students at several cognitive levels (Goodwin, Sharp, Cloutier, & Diamond, 1983). In teaching students to think, teachers should deliberately use structure, methods, and learning tasks that actively involve students in ample opportunities to develop concepts and skills in generating, structuring, transferring, and restructuring knowledge (Ellett, 1990). Clear and precise formulation of questions, waiting an appropriate interval for a student response, and follow-through using the student's response as a base are needed (Siegel, 1990). Problem-based and project-based learning, with students asking their own questions and conducting their own investigations with the teacher as facilitator or resource manager, also are supported in the research (Wilen, Hutchison, & Ishler, 2008; Gardner & Boix-Mansilla, 1994; Heckman, 1994; Perrone, 1994; Wiske, 1994; Brandt, 1992). Chapters 3, 4, 5, and 6 are dedicated to aspects of this important topic.

Professional Responsibilities

While teacher professionalism remains a relatively abstract construct and some lists of teacher professional responsibilities seem endless, expectations for teachers do go well beyond the walls of the classroom. Teacher reflection, discussed earlier, helps not only learning but continued professional growth and is important to teachers as they stay active throughout their careers (Steffy, Wolfe, Pasch, & Enz, 2000). Effective teachers are committed to the pursuit of their own life-long learning. As an example of reinforcing this belief, three of the five core propositions of the National Board for Professional Teaching Standards (NBPTS) (1991) reflect this observation. These are:

- teachers are committed to students and their learning,
- teachers think systematically about their practice and learn from expe-rience, and

- teachers are members of learning communities.

Effective teachers accept personal responsibility for student learning and behavior and engage in corrective, problem-solving approaches with failing students rather than punish them for their shortcomings (Porter & Brophy, 1987). The report *What Works* from the U.S. Department of Education (1987) identifies that students benefit academically when their teachers share ideas, cooperate in activities, and assist each other's professional growth. Collaboration is an important key to professionalism and effective teaching. Effective teachers interact with students, colleagues, and community members purposefully and effectively (Griffin, 1986). Such teachers see teaching as more than meeting with students but also collaborating with peers to identify and act on problems and issues related to their work. While more complicated to document, parent involvement and its relationship to student work is a well-established aspect of a teacher's professionalism. Parent involvement as related to academic achievement and to student behavior is not a debatable point, nor is the fact that there are a variety of ways for teachers to establish and enhance this involvement (Orlich et al., 2007; Powell, Casanova, & Berliner, 1991). The focus for the role of the effective teacher that goes beyond a presenter of lessons and having only a classroom-based orientation has strong support.

In a detailed study of teacher behaviors, Marzano (2003, pp. 82–83) identifies nine specific instructional strategies and related teacher behaviors that affect student achievement.

1. **Identifying similarities and differences:** assigning in-class and homework tasks that invoke comparison and classification; assigning in-class and homework tasks that invoke metaphors and analogies.
2. **Summarizing and note taking:** asking students to generate verbal summaries and/or written summaries; asking students to take notes; asking students to revise their notes, correcting errors and adding information.
3. **Reinforcing effort and providing recognition:** recognizing and celebrating progress toward learning goals throughout a unit; recognizing and reinforcing the importance of effort; recognizing and celebrating progress toward learning goals at the end of a unit.
4. **Homework and practice:** providing specific feedback on all assigned homework; assigning homework for the purpose of students practicing skills and procedures that have been the focus of instruction.
5. **Using nonlinguistic representations:** asking students to generate mental images representing content; asking students to draw pictures

graphic organizers representing content; asking students to act out content; asking students to make physical models of content.

6. **Cooperative learning:** organizing students in cooperative groups when appropriate; organizing students in ability groups when appropriate.

7. **Setting objectives and providing feedback:** setting specific learning goals at the beginning of a unit; asking students to set their own learning goals at the beginning of a unit; providing feedback on learning goals throughout the unit; asking students to keep track of their progress on learning goals; providing summative feedback at the end of a unit; asking students to assess themselves at the end of a unit.

8. **Generating and testing hypotheses:** engaging students in projects that involve generating and testing hypotheses through tasks such as problem-solving tasks, decision-making tasks, investigation tasks, experimental inquiry tasks, systems analysis tasks, and invention tasks.

9. **Using questions, cues, and advance organizers:** prior to presenting new content, asking questions that help students recall what they might already know about the content; prior to presenting new content, providing students with direct links with what they have studied previously; prior to presenting new content, providing ways for students to organize or think about the content.

Having skills and knowledge of instructional strategies, however, will produce only limited results if the teacher does not also know when to use these skills and apply this knowledge. Knowing and understanding skills may be identified as the science of teaching where knowing when to use certain skills, and with whom, may be considered the art. Marzano (2007) identifies a comprehensive model, i.e., framework, for ensuring quality teaching that balances the need for research-based information with the importance of understanding the strengths and weaknesses of individual students. The model is presented in the form of teaching and instructional design questions.

1. What will I do to establish and communicate learning goals, track student progress, and celebrate success?

2. What will I do to help students effectively interact with new knowledge?

3. What will I do to help students practice and deepen their understanding of new knowledge?

4. What will I do to help students generate and test hypotheses about new knowledge?

5. What will I do to engage students?
6. What will I do to establish or maintain classroom rules and procedures?
7. What will I do to recognize and acknowledge adherence and lack of adherence to classroom rules and procedures?
8. What will I do to establish and maintain effective relationships with students?
9. What will I do to communicate high expectations for all students?
10. What will I do to develop effective lessons organized into a cohesive unit?

The last ten to fifteen years has produced a special focus on teaching practices as related to student learning styles, brain research, and teaching and learning standards. The teaching practices identified by Tiletson (2000) can be important to teachers when paired with the best research linked to their implementation. The practices reinforce earlier research in the field as well as actual classroom experiences of teachers. Most teachers today are especially interested in guidance that is as real-world oriented and as practical as it can be. The following teaching practices are believed to meet these criteria.

1. Create an enriched and emotionally supportive environment.
2. Use a variety of teaching strategies that address different learning styles.
3. Use strategies that help students make connections from prior learning and experiences to new learning and across disciplines.
4. Teach for long-term memory as a primary goal.
5. Integrate higher-level thinking skills into learner activities.
6. Use collaborative learning as an integral part of the classroom.
7. Bridge the gap between all learners, regardless of race, socioeconomic status, sex, or creed.
8. Evaluate learning through a variety of authentic assessments.
9. Promote real-world applications of learning.
10. Provide a seamless integration of technology for high-quality instruction.

ANALYZING CLASSROOMS FOR BEST PRACTICE IN TEACHING

While it is critical that teachers have a solid knowledge base of information related to best practice in teaching, as discussed, having this knowledge base alone is not sufficient to ensure that instruction will be effective and that student learning will increase. Merely having or knowing information on best practice in teaching does not guarantee the appropriate application of this information to the teacher's behavior in the classroom.

The *System for the Analysis of Teaching Practices* (Wiseman & Hunt, 2008) has been developed to assist teachers as they systematically reflect on and review their teaching behaviors. The *System* is built on the knowledge base of effective teaching practices and can serve as a helpful tool for teachers for self-review, perhaps self-evaluation, and in making decisions to strengthen the instructional process.

System for the Analysis of Teaching Practices

Circle the appropriate number on the scale provided as you reflect on your teaching in each teacher characteristic area. Before making your selection, consider the accompanying statement(s) associated with each item as to how well the statement consistently describes your professional behavior.

Seldom   Always

1. **Clarity**   1 2 3 4 5

My students understand the words that I use in my teaching; I get my ideas across clearly without needing to repeat myself.

2. **Variability**   1 2 3 4 5

My teaching reflects the regular use of many different teaching strategies and resources rather than only a few.

3. **Enthusiasm**   1 2 3 4 5

I am energetic and my teaching reflects this energy; my enthusiasm shows in my teaching, my preparation, and the classroom environment that I establish.

4. **Task-oriented**   1 2 3 4 5

I conduct my classroom in a positive yet business-like manner. Students know where they are headed in their learning activities; my teaching is focused on the desired learning outcomes at all times.

5. **Students Learning Criterion Material**   1 2 3 4 5

My students know in advance of the learning activities what is important to be learned and how they will be evaluated. My assessments do not include "extras" that my students were not aware of.

6. **Use of Student Ideas**   1 2 3 4 5

My teaching is characterized by a heavy involvement of student ideas. Students know from the way I teach that their ideas are important.

7. **Structuring Comments**   1 2 3 4 5

I use structuring comments at the beginning of my lessons and as I move through my lessons to help my students stay focused on my objectives and know what is expected of them.

8. **Level of Difficulty**   1 2 3 4 5

My expectations are challenging but not beyond the reach of my students. Students are not "left behind" in my teaching; they know that they can be successful.

9. **Success Rates**   1 2 3 4 5

My students are consistently successful; no student considers himself or herself a failure as my approach to teaching ensures success for all.

10. **Attitude**   1 2 3 4 5

I know that if I plan my lessons thoroughly and select learning activities appropriately that all of my students can succeed. It may take extra effort, but I can make a positive difference with all of my students.

11. **Use of Time**   1 2 3 4 5

Students do not have idle time in my classroom, but stay actively and successfully engaged in meaningful experiences.

12. **Organization**   1 2 3 4 5

My classroom and teaching are organized, and my students recognize this. I am well prepared and my teaching transitions are smooth and controlled.

13. **Communication**   1 2 3 4 5

I communicate clearly to my students. This includes both verbal as well as nonverbal messages. I seldom need to repeat myself.

14. **Focus**   1 2 3 4 5

Students understand the purpose of my lessons, and my lessons stay focused. Spontaneous events do take place, but my students know where my lessons are headed and the outcomes that are desired.

15. **Feedback**   1 2 3 4 5

Students receive ample feedback related to their progress during my lessons and through my assessments. They regularly receive oral and written feedback that explains their progress to them.

16. **Questioning**   1 2 3 4 5

I routinely use both higher and lower order questioning. Students are asked many questions to develop their thinking and so I can know what they understand.

17. **Probing Behaviors**   1 2 3 4 5

My teaching includes probing students so that they may go deeper into and expand on their ideas, especially as their ideas relate to what I am teaching.

18. **Pacing**   1 2 3 4 5

My lesson pace is normally quicker as opposed to slower.

19. **Review and Closure**   1 2 3 4 5

I review at the beginning of my lessons what has just been previously taught. I review again through closure at the end of each lesson.

20. **Criticism**   1 2 3 4 5

My classroom environment is positive, open, and inviting. I seldom use criticism with my students.

Scoring Your Analysis

Twenty items make up the *System for the Analysis of Teaching Practices* with a maximum possible rating of 5 on each item. The instrument is not intended for evaluation purposes, but as a guide for reflection and determining instructional directions for the future. It offers a way to analyze individual teacher behaviors as well as a teacher's performance in its entirety by combining individual ratings together. Each behavior is treated as having the same level of importance.

The following rating scheme may be used when seeking a combined rating of all items.

Points	*Self-Rating*
93–100	Excellent
86–92	Above Average
79–85	Average
70–78	Below Average
Below 70	Unsatisfactory

A FRAMEWORK FOR EFFECTIVE TEACHING

As the discussion in Chapter 1 suggests, effective teaching can be defined in many different ways, and only where there is agreement with or understanding of the desired result or outcome of the teaching process will there be a realistic opportunity to truly explore effective teaching behaviors. Accordingly, this discussion has emphasized the importance of the need to establish a context for effective teaching. Effective teaching, through the application of research-based teaching strategies, results in improved academic achievement in students. The research base for effective teaching practices strongly supports the importance of the teacher being a highly trained, reflective professional. Such an individual will not only have a repertoire of strategies and skills related to improving academic achievement, but also will have the ability to know when, where, and with whom to use them.

The remaining chapters of this text expand on this first foundational chapter to provide an in-depth study of teacher behaviors considered to be effective in this context. A framework for effective teaching will be presented that builds on the research base that has sought to inform the profession. This five-part framework contains the following components: (1) *planning*, (2) *communicating*, (3) *instructing*, (4) *managing*, and (5) *evaluating*.

Through study of the components of this framework and research-based teaching behaviors, skills, and qualities associated with each component, practicing teachers as well as teachers-in-training will be able to develop the ability to be reflective teachers of high quality and to effect high achievement in students in a positive, supportive, and learner-focused environment.

Chapter 2

THE TEACHER AS A PLANNER
OF INSTRUCTION

The passage of The No Child Left Behind (NCLB) legislation of 2002 greatly impacted the way teachers plan for instruction. While we had seen a movement toward a strong emphasis on state standards and assessments which certainly affected the way teachers prepared instruction during the 1990s, NCLB raised the stakes to an even higher level. The concept of the highly qualified teacher that is promised to all citizens by NCLB entails not only a teacher who has quality, specialized training in his or her content area, but also someone who produces students that meet yearly growth expectations on standardized tests. This increase in performance expectations, due, at least in part, to student performance on high stakes, standardized tests has greatly influenced the curriculum and how it is taught. One of the obvious changes is the greater emphasis on time on task or, as it is sometimes called, engaged time. *Time on task*, as discussed in Chapter 1, is a term that refers to the amount of time students spend working on specific content. This typically is content that it is felt will be represented on high stakes tests that students will eventually take. As a result, instructional planning in many schools has focused on spending more time practicing skills and studying information that will be on high stakes tests while spending less time in the study of content that is not expected to be on such assessments. Nichols and Berliner (2007) argue that this heavy emphasis on preparing students for high stakes tests has caused *collateral damage* to the curriculum and the education process in general. They believe that, among other problems, students are being denied an adequate education because subject areas like art, music, drama, and health and physical education, not to mention science and social studies, are not given deserved time because students are too frequently completing worksheets day on end in preparation for high stakes tests where this content is not represented.

The very nature of instructional planning has changed because of the emphasis on testing. Teachers typically closely follow the state content standards of their individual states when planning lessons and units. State content standards are the documents to which the individual state tests are aligned. Many principals require teachers to write the exact standard and correlating desired learning outcome(s) on their daily plans (in this way the teacher can demonstrate that each learner outcome was taught and retaught on certain days prior to testing). Much of the importance of being able to choose and create good objectives, select appropriate instructional activities, and develop suitable assessment items that relate back to the objectives has been removed from the individual teacher because objectives, procedures, and assessments are often, in part or in whole, provided to teachers in state developed standards documents.

For better or worse, in the past, teachers had more freedom to select topics, write objectives, and design instruction than they do today. This observation, however, is not intended to imply that teachers have no responsibility in the instructional planning process. To the contrary, teachers may have an even more important and challenging task to perform. Given that learning outcomes and assessments are often, for the most part, provided by states and school districts, teachers must determine how best to teach students of various ability levels and backgrounds in a way that best ensures success for all students. If all students must address the same learning outcomes and take the same high stakes test, what is the best practice to use when teaching low ability versus high ability students? When students have English as a second or even third language, what is the best practice to use to ensure that no child is left behind? Of one thing we feel certain, the methods that work best for high ability students who have a history of performing well are not apt to be the best procedures to use with low ability students with a history of low performance. Planning for best practice is a very difficult process indeed. Since the standards, desired learning outcomes (objectives), and assessments are, to a great extent, predetermined, it is important that teachers understand the characteristics of their students and how to structure the teaching-learning environment to best help them meet their individual educational potentials.

Many points must be considered when preparing for high caliber instruction. Among the most important are questions concerning (1) *the needs of students*, (2) *objectives*, (3) *strategies*, (4) *resources*, and (5) *evaluative criteria*. Once these questions are addressed, the teacher's role in the classroom during the teaching process itself needs to be analyzed. Beyond these issues, the attitudes and the feelings of students, created by the teacher's behaviors, must be considered. Teacher behaviors and attitudes, as they impact student learning or other student behaviors, often prove to be the ultimate measure of success or failure. The development of prerequisite skills in planning for and delivering instruction does not come naturally but requires considerable determined and knowledgeable preparation.

In order to assist you in the development of successful planning skills, this chapter presents sections dealing with many important aspects of the planning process. After studying this chapter, you will learn more about the following topics:

1. characteristics of high and low ability students,
2. differences in learning styles, rates, and abilities,
3. classification of cognitive performances according to Bloom's taxonomy,
4. the planning process,
5. unit plans, and
6. daily lesson plans.

PLANNING FOR INDIVIDUAL DIFFERENCES

The most effective teachers think of their classes as being made up of individuals, not large group units. In order for success to be possible for all students, the classroom must be seen as a group of separate, individual students, not merely as one large, homogeneous group. At the very least, a classroom must be seen as a conglomerate of several small groups or a combination of small groups and distinct, individual students. A common misconception held by many teachers is that all of their students are equally able to gain information from classroom instruction. In a typical elementary, middle, or secondary classroom, however, a teacher, when making a presentation designed to be suitable for a large group, will most assuredly present material too difficult for some students while not challenging others.

This is not a great revelation to effective teachers as it is well known that some students have difficulty in school while others have to put forth little effort to do well. In spite of this knowledge, too many teachers are guilty of assuming that a teacher's obligation is fulfilled when correct information is presented in a sequential manner or when questions that students pose are answered. Regardless of the fact that this assumption has persisted for decades, it is obviously flawed. Not only do students vary in their ability to learn, students also vary in their rate of learning even when they are of similar ability. In other words, the excuse given by some teachers that their classes are homogeneously grouped and do not need further grouping is invalid. When students vary in their ability to learn, the variance in their rates in learning and the speed at which new material is mastered is likely to be even greater. Superimposed over the diversity created by differences in ability and rate of learning is the fact that many students do not learn equally well from all types of learning experiences. The reality is that students differ in what is termed *learning style preferences.*

One of the most difficult tasks that any teacher faces is adjusting instruction to the learning abilities, learning rates, and learning styles of all students. Successful adjustment will be challenging and will occupy considerable planning time. In fact, teachers will find that even the best planning efforts will sometimes fall short of meeting the learning needs of all students. No matter how complex the learning needs of a class may be, the teacher needs to begin planning for these needs by thinking of ways to best organize students for the most appropriate and effective learning tasks. Grouping students to enhance learning is a skill teachers at all grade levels must possess. Skilled teachers know how to arrange groups on a flexible basis in order for individuals within the class to learn as much as they can and at an optimum rate. They understand that students of different learning abilities cannot be taught effectively with the same instructional strategies because they learn in different ways and at different rates. Teachers cannot teach high ability students using the same strategies they use to teach low ability students if they wish to be effective with all students.

Students often differ markedly in a variety of ways because of a variety of factors. Two students of low aptitude may function at similar levels with the origin of their learning problems being quite different. Sarasin (1998), McCarthy (1990), and Reisman and Payne (1987) designate several factors which influence differences in learning. These researchers note that cognitive, social, psychomotor, physical, and sensory, as well as emotional factors combine to explain why some students do better than others in the classroom. Superimposed over all of this complexity is that more and more students are attending American schools each year where English is not their first language. It is highly probable that any given teacher will have one or more students in the classroom who have little or no facility in English. Too, it is not uncommon that a classroom may house multiple Spanish-speaking students who have difficulty communicating with each other because Spanish is spoken differently in various parts of the Spanish-speaking world. Even with these challenges, teachers must design instruction and assessments to ensure that all students acquire the knowledge, skills, and dispositions being taught.

Working with the High-Ability Student

There has been considerable debate over the best ways to meet the needs of students and to adapt instruction to individual learning differences. Snow (1988) notes that three main academic factors are vital when examining student aptitude as it affects learning in school: academic intelligence, academic motivation, and specific prior knowledge. Teachers must be aware of their students' abilities to perform academic tasks and the conditions under which they learn best (their learning style preferences). This is critical information to have when planning instructional adaptations to match student learning needs. As a group, students with high aptitudes need less direct instruction and time to complete learning tasks than those whose aptitudes are lower. Snow suggests that students of differing abilities often use different strategies when learning to solve problems, even the same problem. For example, it may be that students low in spatial and verbal ability are helped most by visual training while high-ability students learn best through a practice/feedback condition (Kyllonen, Lohman, & Snow, 1981). Before reading the following portion of this section, carefully study Figure 2-1 which provides an outline of some of the more definitive characteristics of high ability students.

High–Ability Students

High–ability students:

- are able to complete their work faster than many of their classmates,
- have an extensive background of competencies,
- are able to tie new information to their relatively large accumulation of experiences,
- have a history of academic success,
- are confident,
- are eager to become involved in new learning experiences,
- work well on their own,
- often are class leaders,
- are frequently outgoing,
- are willing to take on problems,
- often interact in groups,
- ask searching questions,
- deal with some ambiguity,
- accept responsibility,
- tend to complete tasks, and
- often have positive self-concepts.

Figure 2-1. Characteristics of high-ability students as adapted from Blair (1988).

It is important that teachers be able to challenge and motivate the students of high ability in their classrooms. High-ability students are usually, in the traditional academic sense, more talented, learn faster, and retain more content more easily than their lower ability peers. The typical scope and sequence of a conventional school curriculum, however, may leave these students unmotivated or even alienated. Regrettably, such students can annoy teachers and peers to the point of being labeled troublemakers (Wiles & Bondi, 1989) when the basic problem is that their teachers have not responded effectively to their learning needs.

In order to challenge the more advanced and faster working students, teachers must design strategies which allow them to complete their assignments in a more realistic timeframe and, at the same time, provide them with opportunities to explore an enriched curriculum. An elementary teacher, for example, may choose to use a learning center designed for advanced students while a secondary teacher may provide the necessary materials and resources for students to pursue an individual project. In each case, students who finish their basic assignments have the opportunity to pursue additional areas in which they have a special interest and which serve as enrichment. Work on such enrichment activities frequently takes place while other students in the class are completing their required, basic assignments. High-ability students, when working through a given curriculum area, should be encouraged if not expected to work independently at their own rates of speed. They should more frequently be working in a curriculum that is individualized and self-paced. An individualized, self-paced curriculum is one where students are accorded the opportunity to experience instruction geared to their individual ability levels and learning styles which allows them to complete the instruction at their own personal rates. Working with high-ability students in this way will:

- allow students to extend themselves by completing more work in a shorter time span and going into greater depth on given topics,
- diminish the amount of disengaged instructional time during the school year,
- allow teachers to spend more direct instructional time with lower ability students, and
- make it possible for advanced students to progress through the curriculum fast enough to allow them extra time which can be used for other activities such as peer-tutoring sessions with classmates or self-directed study.

Teachers often spend too much time giving direct instruction to students who need it the least while less motivated, lower ability students suffer from the absence of needed direct teacher guidance. Although the use of an individualized strategy is strongly advised for high-ability pupils, it is important to realize that such an independent approach to learning may not work as well with low-ability students. Only the more skilled students with a background of successful learning experiences are likely to have the competencies, personal organization, and motivation needed to work effectively on their own for extended periods of time.

Working with the Low-Ability Student

Figure 2-2 provides the more typical characteristics of low-ability students. As with high-ability students, low-ability students need to move through the curriculum at a pace that is commensurate with their personal needs while allowing for a greater amount of attention from the teacher. Low-ability students generally benefit less from large group or independent instruction than high-ability students and often make better progress in a dyadic situation with the teacher or a tutor. Immediate reinforcement and feedback are of the essence. The teacher should look for those things that the low-ability student does well and provide reinforcement for the accomplishment. The teacher also must identify curriculum materials that are of high interest to each student and written on an appropriate level to engender success. When instructing a low-ability student, it is important to remember that it is much worse to place the student in material which is too difficult than in material which is too easy. The low-ability student is one who typically has had a history of failure and frustration. If such students are to realize success, it is important that they be given the opportunity to view themselves as capable individuals.

The most realistic, nonthreatening environment for low-ability students is a situation in which they work closely with a supportive teacher in a curriculum area where they do not have to worry about adjusting their rate or

---

Low-Ability Students

Low-ability students:

- require more time to learn a concept or skill,
- have a minimal level of readiness for new instruction,
- have generally had fewer past experiences with which to link new information,
- have a history of failure,
- are unsure of themselves,
- are hesitant to become involved in new learning situations,
- tend not to work well in groups,
- may be difficult to motivate,
- are often more successful with concrete as opposed to abstract work,
- frequently require visual, active presentations,
- tend not to work well independent of close supervision,
- are often over-dependent on teachers,
- rarely ask searching questions,
- easily give up on problems,
- often depend on others for answers, and
- frequently have poor self-concepts.

Figure 2-2. Characteristics of low-ability students as adapted from Blair (1988).

style of learning to other students in the class. Additionally, the teacher must not approach the low-ability student with a corrective attitude but should concentrate on what the student does well. The importance of reinforcing the low-ability student in a highly supportive environment cannot be overstated (Van Houten, 1980; Purkey, 1976). If low-ability students are constantly corrected and reminded of their weaknesses, their most common reaction is anxiousness and withdrawal from the instructional situation.

By definition, the low ability student is a student who does not have the skills and knowledge that are required to function in the typical curriculum for average learners at the assigned grade or level. Such students need to be accepted for who they are and not judged by standards more appropriate for others. It sometimes may be an unrealistic goal to expect such students to move to the norm in the span of one school year. A more appropriate goal would be to work toward steady, although perhaps slow, progress from the point at which they are presently functioning. The teacher should be concerned more with what any student learns rather than what the student does not already know. One might think of low ability students as if they are glasses that need filling. In the past, much water has been spilled instead of going into the glass. Now is the time to ensure that water goes into the glass and not worry about what has been previously spilled outside.

ADJUSTING INSTRUCTION
TO LEARNING STYLE PREFERENCES

In addition to the fact that students learn at different rates and have various levels of learning ability, all students do not achieve at their optimal levels through the same instructional methods. While some students achieve well through some methods, other students will find it difficult to learn when these same methods of instruction are used. Individual preference for a particular method of instruction is known as learning style preference (Woolfolk, 2008). In their classic work, Dunn, Dunn, and Price (1989) suggest that there are four elements that make up all of the possible learning styles and that these elements can be categorized into one of the following areas: (1) environmental elements, (2) emotional elements, (3) sociological elements, and (4) physical elements. Sarasin (1998) also recommends the need to investigate areas of sense perception in conjunction with learning styles in order to create the optimal learning environment (Figure 2-3). In analyzing the learning style preferences of students, a teacher has a great many stimuli to be aware of in planning the best learning experiences for all students.

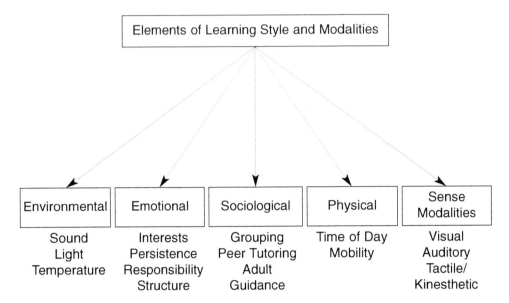

Figure 2-3. Basic elements of learning style and modalities affecting the learning environment.

Environmental Elements

Many factors associated with the classroom environment can be rather easily controlled by the teacher (e.g., light, room temperature, and furniture). Some students seem to learn best in a quiet setting as noise disrupts their learning process while others are quite able to learn in a busy, active environment which might seem noisy and bothersome to others. The amount of light also has an effect on the learning of some students. While light variations do not affect as many students as sound variations, some students should not sit near windows or bright lights if they are to do their best work. Room temperature has also been found to have an effect on learning. Some students learn best when the temperature is warm while others simply cannot function unless they feel the temperature is cooler. If possible, the classroom should be arranged so that there are variations in room temperature. At the very least, the teacher needs to be aware of how close or how far away from heaters and air conditioners certain students should sit to do their best work. A final consideration about the environment is its degree of casualness or formality. Some students simply do not learn well in a restrictive environment that requires them to sit quietly without moving. One can only speculate about how many students have become behavior problems because they could not adjust to the restrictive environment of the classical teaching-learning setting. It also should be noted, however, that there are many other students who cannot learn at their best unless they are in an environment that provides a quiet, peaceful, disciplined, and controlled setting.

Emotional Elements

Motivation is an important emotional element in determining how well a student will learn a given body of information. Great variance typically exists among students in terms of how much motivation they exhibit as a response to different learning activities. Some students show little interest or, at the most, very short attention spans when many classroom activities are undertaken and often need special instructional strategies to help them stay engaged and learn. Such students may need to be given greater choices in order to vary the way they work. Teachers are encouraged to provide students opportunities to work in groups and practice self-evaluation as a part of this variability.

Persistence is also a very important aspect of a learner's style. Some students can only stay on task for about ten to twenty minutes, others less time, while others can work an hour or more at the same assignment. Because of this variance in student persistence, it is suggested that students who have shorter attention spans be given assignments that have specific time limits and end points that are more realistic for them. It is important that time limits be set so that students can legitimately be required to come to closure.

A final important emotional element is that of *responsibility*. Many students are unable to work on any task unless they are closely supervised finding it difficult to work independently in a self-paced situation. Such students need less demanding work while they build their confidence. Closely related to the other elements of emotional stimuli is the concept of *structure*. Many students have a need for ongoing supervision to complete a task. Students who have special learning styles based on their emotional needs are those who probably need the closest attention of all from the teacher. Students who do not have these needs are more likely to be able to work independently.

Sociological Elements

The third set of elements is referred to as the sociological elements of learning style preferences. Students often vary greatly in terms of the type of learning group in which they work best. This variety ranges from learning alone to learning in small groups and large groups. Some students prefer learning with a teacher or other adult present while others prefer almost total independence. Teachers need to know in what type of setting students work best and adjust their organizational structures accordingly.

Physical Elements

The fourth set of learning style preferences is referred to as physical elements. Though some students actually seem to learn best when they are eating or drinking, few teachers would be able to accommodate such student preferences in the classroom. As difficult as some teachers may find it to adjust to a student's need for the intake of food or drink, it does seem reasonable to suggest that students' schedules could be adjusted to coincide with the times at which they learn best. If it is known that a student learns best during the latter part of the morning, for example, this is the time to provide the more demanding tasks. Finally, some students tend to function best in a more informal learning environment because of their need to move, stretch, and even walk around before they can successfully adjust to the teacher's classroom expectations.

In spite of these personal needs, it is unrealistic to suggest that a teacher develop a completely different learning environment for each and every student in the classroom. Nevertheless, it is reasonable for a teacher to be conscious of the fact that some of the students' learning may be affected by group size, room temperature, time of day, room design, noise, and other variables.

How many students are greatly affected in the public schools by the fact that their learning style needs often go unsatisfied is difficult to determine. As Fischer and Fischer (1979) point out, many students are eclectic learners and can adjust their learning to virtually any instructional style. The best of these students cope very well in school and teachers have a tendency to give them high evaluations. Since it is the better students who adjust to any teaching style, teachers often conclude that all students should be able to make these adjustments. Dunn, Dunn, and Price (1981) suggest that all students simply cannot adjust their learning to all teaching styles. And, many students are unable to meet their full learning potential because they cannot learn in the environment that the teacher has established for the total class. These students suffer more with a teacher who feels that all students should be taught in the same way. One solution may be to give such students greater freedom to take more responsibility for their own learning and, in effect, have a greater role in creating their own best learning environment (Glasser, 1993).

Sense Modalities

High-ability students, by definition, adapt well to the varied instructional styles of their teachers. It is the successful adaptation of the low-ability student that is in need of much more careful analysis. Barbe and Milone (1981) observe that the greatest analysis should be done in the area of sense perception. These channels of perception are usually referred to as sense modalities. Some students, for example, can learn best visually while others learn best through the senses of hearing and touch. The matching of instructional styles with learning styles embraces the understanding that many students are unable to learn well through certain sense modalities or in certain learning environments. It is important that students not be expected to learn in situations that only lead to anxiety and failure. Teachers need to vary their approaches to instruction with students who are having difficulty until a best approach is identified. The goal of the teacher is not to use all approaches for each student but to find the optimal approaches and then use them. The result will be a variety of approaches within the same classroom, not within the instructional program of a given student.

Multiple Intelligences

Related to the research on learning style preference is the work of Howard Gardner and others in what is referred to as multiple intelligences or MI (Armstrong, 1994; Gardner, 1993, 1983). Gardner posits that individuals develop more than one type of intelligence and that each person possesses varying degrees of each type. Eight intelligences have been identified with the resulting affect that some students are more likely to learn and retain information based upon the way that information is presented. Traditional classroom and school settings have focused most on linguistic and logical-mathematical intelligences and this has been a detriment to the learning of many students who do not have these intelligences as their primary strengths. Table 2-1 displays each intelligence, along with examples and characteristics of each (Hunt, Wiseman, & Bowden, 2003). Students with high linguistic intelligence, for example, may best learn from reading and being told about information whereas the student with high interpersonal intelligence may learn better from a teaching method that emphasizes group work. The most effective teachers address all of the intelligences in their classrooms in order to reach all of their students and not just a few.

BEGINNING THE PLANNING PROCESS

Terry Crawford, a student teacher, and Carolyn Williams, an experienced teacher, were talking one day in the teachers' lounge about planning. Both believed that planning was extremely important to the effective presentation of content. Their agreement, however, ended with the need to plan. They disagreed strongly about what was needed in a plan.

Table 2-1
GARDNER'S EIGHT TYPES OF INTELLIGENCE

Intelligence	Example	Characteristics
1. Linguistic	Author-Ernest Hemingway Orator-Jessie Jackson	Great ability to understand the meaning and functions of oral and written language.
2. Logical-mathematical	Mathematician-Isaac Newton Scientist-Albert Einstein	Great ability to handle in-depth reasoning and to understand numerical patterns.
3. Spatial	Artist-Michelangelo Architect-Frank Lloyd Wright	Very accurate visual perception of spatial reality and the ability to transform those perceptions.
4. Bodily-kinesthetic	Athlete-Michael Jordan Dancer-Martha Graham	Great ability to create high levels of physical movements and skills.
5. Musical	Musician-Ray Charles Composer-Leonard Bernstein	Great ability to create and appreciate rhythmic, musical expressions.
6. Interpersonal	Political leader-Bill Clinton Religious leader-Billy Graham	Strong capacity to understand and properly respond to the moods and needs of other people.
7. Intrapersonal	Analyst-Sigmund Freud Reformers-Jesus, Buddha	Keen sense of self-actualization with great insight into self.
8. Naturalist	Frontiersman-Daniel Boone Scientist-Charles Darwin	Great ability to discriminate among living things as well as sensitivity to the natural world.

"My professor at the college wants me to include all my actions as a teacher because he says he wants me to be thoroughly prepared. Without complete plans, he says, I am liable to forget a critical procedure, question, or explanation."

"Well Terry," Carolyn responds, "After six years of teaching seventh grade science, I know what I am doing. My principal realizes that there is no reason to put down everything that I'm going to do. As a professional I know that rigid plans sometimes can impede the development of learning—especially spontaneous learning. Since I am familiar with the content, and past achievement test scores of my students reflect my ability to teach it skillfully, I just write the outline of the tasks I want students to do."

"I understand what you're saying, but my professor says that complete plans allow an evaluator to assess both the teacher's and the student's achievement; plus, a substitute can come in and teach from the plan. A true professional should have professional looking plans!"

"Terry, I am sure your professor is giving you good advice, but if you're inferring that I ought to have longer plans or that I'm unprofessional, I think you need to reflect a little more on the intent of your professor's advice. His suggestion is to be prepared, to understand totally your objectives and the learning strategies you will use to accomplish them. I have much of that in my notes, but I don't specifically teach from them anymore. Perhaps I should occasionally look over some of them. Since you're helping me this semester, I'll have time to review the lesson on atoms – it is a difficult one. As a matter of fact, we could put our heads together; with your recent work at the college and my experience, we could come up with some better methods of achieving the designated objectives. Let's give it a try!"

Discussions such as this one reinforce not only the importance of planning but also how different teachers have unique needs, perspectives, and purposes in planning, especially when compared to student teachers. Research analyzing how professionals at different skill levels think about their craft reveals that planning is approached differently by novices and experts (Borko & Niles, 1987). Using a metaphor to describe teaching as following a map may help identify distinctions between novices and experts. Whereas novices need to follow a map closely, more experienced travelers who are familiar with the terrain, the troubles along the way, and the destination do not rely on the map in the same way. Expert travelers who have been down the road many times simply do not need the detailed road maps required by novices. Specifically in the field of education, it has been found that experts require or at least spend less time planning and focus more of their efforts on the flow of activities for extended periods of time than novices. This is contrary to the identified needs of novices who require more time to plan while placing less focus on the weekly flow of activities and more focus on the individual lessons themselves.

Planning Needs

The tremendous complexity of classroom life has increased the challenge of analyzing student-to-student and student-to-teacher interactions, as well as analyzing the instruction and learning that occurs (Jackson, 1990). Because the environment of the classroom is at times difficult to control, and so potentially overwhelming to teachers, especially beginning teachers, there is a greater need now than ever before to develop plans in order to organize and anticipate the flow of interactions and potential problems.

How a teacher plans will be determined by the level of skill the teacher possesses. The more experience and knowledge a teacher possesses about (1) what is to be taught, (2) what materials are to be used, and (3) the students who are to be instructed, the easier will be the planning for that lesson. Though the planning process may be easier for experts, their decision making in the classroom and their understanding of planning have been found to be more sophisticated than novices (Borko & Niles, 1982). Experts simply have more established mental images and constructs for organizing subject matter and managing classroom behavior. They also are more likely, when presented with a prepared plan, to add to it and transform what has been prescribed to fit the needs of the particular learning situation (Yinger & Clark, 1983). Additionally, experts' mental images of classroom life permit them an understanding of group dynamics that novices do not yet have, thereby making spontaneous as well as written planning for learning activities easier. Planning is most beneficial to teachers who (1) are aware of their students' backgrounds, (2) understand the complexity of instruction, and (3) have insight into the nature of instructional tasks.

In discussing planning, it is helpful to designate times when it occurs and purposes for the plans themselves. Though it may be surprising to some, planning can occur long before, directly before, during, or even after the lesson is taught. For example, before a student teacher prepares a history lesson on the French Revolution, some planning likely happened when the student studied World History. That initial learning may have had a significant impact on subsequent use of that material. Then, as the lesson is taught, the student teacher may make mental notes about how it should be taught the next time. Finally, after a lesson is taught, a thorough analysis of the lesson will lead to more insights and even more refined plans for future use. When this description of the planning process is coupled with the fact that it is completed in diverse ways by both novices and experts, it is evident that planning is truly a complex mental activity. Teachers actually begin in college to form mental images or structures for planning and then elaborate on them later as the need arises and as their experiences expand.

An effective teacher will remember that instructional planning involves deciding *what* you are going to teach, *how* you are going to teach, and *how well* you expect your students to know the material when you have finished. If the teacher does not have these planning points well in mind, inconsistent instruction and classroom confusion may be expected. Not only may students become confused, but the teacher may also lose direction. Good planning, of course, will not ensure good teaching, but it is a very important prerequisite to quality classroom instruction. In fact, good planning is a first step to good classroom management which will be discussed later in Chapter 7.

The planning process in today's accountability environment begins with each teacher examining the appropriate state standards documents. It is essential that teachers be familiar with all standards related to their specific grade levels and/or content areas. In some areas, school districts also have developed standards that may supplement or go beyond the state documented standards and teachers need to be familiar with any such standards as well.

Standards documents typically identify indicators or skills that students need to learn in order to demonstrate mastery of the specific standards by the end of the school year (actually, by the time the state standards examination is given when such a test is used). These indicators are extremely important to the planning process because, as representing observable student outcomes, they will become the objectives of both long-term and daily instructional plans.

Mapping Indicators (Student Performances)

Curriculum mapping is a concept that has become a central part of the planning process in many schools (Jacobs, 2004). The curriculum mapping process is a somewhat simple activity that allows teachers to make connection between content and assessments while, at the same time, ensuring that each aspect of the lessons being taught align with each other and any mandated set of standards. Succinctly, curriculum mapping is a process that outlines the content, skills, and assessments taught within a classroom, department, school, or district. The intent of curriculum mapping is to organize this information into an easily accessible visual that provides a timeline of instruction. Mapping is a process that allows teachers to see a graphic visual of the scope and sequence of what is to be taught at each level and to see the interrelationship of all segments of the curriculum.

For those educators who are interested in developing sophisticated curriculum structures such as *integrated curriculum* (Beane, 2001, 1993), mapping is a valuable process indeed. Curriculum mapping allows teachers to integrate instruction in multiple content areas around several standards in the same instructional unit. Figure 2-4 shows a planning web (i.e., one teacher's adaptation of the curriculum map to be used in an individual classroom) for a specific section of an integrated unit.

WRITING INSTRUCTIONAL OBJECTIVES

Good teaching will facilitate learning on behalf of all students in the classroom. But, how is one to know if learning has been facilitated? If the teacher is not certain of what it is that is being facilitated, it will be impossible to determine when it has been accomplished. It is for this reason that instructional objectives, as a formal planning aid, become necessary. Through the use of well-planned objectives tailored to the student or student group, the teacher has a much clearer indication of how learning may be directed and enhanced.

There are many types and styles of instructional objectives that a teacher might adopt and use. The classic three-part objective described by Mager (1962) is used here as an example to demonstrate the objective writing

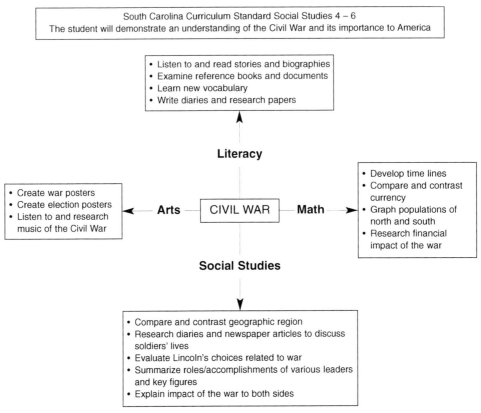

Figure 2-4. A fourth grade planning web.

process. Mager stated that objectives should consist of (1) a **performance statement** identifying the desired terminal behavior of the student, (2) a **conditions of performance** statement, and (3) a **criterion statement** to indicate the quality of performance expected by the teacher. We feel that this model can successfully guide the novice teacher's thinking, in particular, through the planning process. Regardless of which type of objectives teachers may be asked to write at their given schools, the ability to write a three-part objective such as this will prepare them to write quality objectives that can lead to student success.

Performance Statements and Domains of Learning

Performance statements describe the behavior that students will be able to perform or exhibit following instruction in order to demonstrate that learning has taken place. Performance statements typically consist of a verb followed by the object of that verb. Bloom and his associates classified all learning into three basic categories or domains: *cognitive, affective,* and *psychomotor.* In order to better teach the whole student, performance statements should be developed for each domain (Harrow, 1972; Krathwohl, Bloom, & Masia, 1964; Bloom, Englehart, Furst, Hill, & Krathwohl, 1956). Anderson, Krathwohl, Airasian, Cruikshank, Mayer, Pintrich, Raths, and Wittrock (2001) revised the original categorization of these domains; the revised categories in each domain can be seen in Figure 2-5.

Domain	Categories	Description
Cognitive	1. Remembering	involves recall of information
	2. Understanding	refers to comprehending something
	3. Applying	the use of prior knowledge in particular situations
	4. Analyzing	the dissection of something into components revealing the relationship between the parts of the whole
	5. Evaluating	the judgment about a person, place, or thing
	6. Creating	the putting together of ideas or things in a unique fashion
Affective	1. Receiving	an awareness of the existence of certain ideas so as to become willing to receive or listen to them
	2. Responding	a response which goes beyond attending; it implies some commitment to be involved
	3. Valuing	a profession that something has worth
	4. Organization	the elementary internalization of values into a system
	5. Generalization	the more refined internalization of values which are consistent and interrelated with other values
Psychomotor	1. Reflex Movements	involuntary movements; precursor to voluntary, fundamental movements
	2. Basic Fundamental Movements	simple, learned movements, (e.g., crawling, walking, grabbing) which are inherent and form the basis for complex movements
	3. Perceptual Abilities	all perceptual modalities that are carried to the brain for interpretation
	4. Physical Abilities	general body vigor such as endurance and flexibility demonstrated by efficiency in performing complex movement tasks
	5. Nondiscursive Communications	behaviors related to expressive or interpretive movement which communicate a message to the viewer

Figure 2-5. Major categories of the taxonomies in the cognitive, affective, and psychomotor domains.

Thinking of learning as involving one of three discrete categories or domains has proven useful in planning and organizing instruction. *Cognitive domain* behaviors or performances are intellectual. They involve such mental skills as *knowing, understanding,* and *thinking.* Behaviors in this domain are those which traditionally receive greater emphasis in formal education as they are those that are most reflected in the standardized tests that students take. Any curriculum contains a certain, rather large, body of information that educators feel is important for students to learn. Along with this body of information, teachers strive through their instruction to develop rational thinking abilities in their students in using this information.

Learning in the *affective domain* consists of *attitudes, interests,* and *appreciations.* Behaviors or performances in this domain are products of feelings, emotions, and values. The emphasis in formal education in this domain involves attempting to generate learner enthusiasm for the subject matter the teacher is presenting. The emphasis also includes the development of a positive disposition toward learning regardless of the subject matter.

The *psychomotor domain* involves *motor* or *neuromuscular* skills such as handwriting, typing, assembling or using apparatus, and performing athletic/movement skills. See Figure 2-6 for a brief summary of the three domains and examples of performance statements in each. As can be seen, overlap exists among the domains reinforcing the interrelatedness that they possess.

It should be noted that within each domain performance statements will reflect varying degrees or levels/depths of learning. The performance statement *conduct an out of school project,* for example, indicates a more positive attitude toward the subject than the statement, *actively participate in class discussions.* Similarly, *recite the first multiplication table* indicates less intellectual activity than *write a paragraph about your pet.* The cognitive domain is especially useful in instructional planning to differentiate between levels of performance expected of students. While it is also useful to differentiate between levels of the psychomotor and affective domains, due to the content emphasis of public school curricula, levels of the cognitive domain will be stressed here. Knowledge gained studying subject matter in the cognitive domain is readily transferable to work in the other two domains should the teacher wish to develop planning around the specific levels of each domain. Regardless of whether or not the domains are divided into discrete categories, they provide a useful guide for the teacher in planning for instruction.

Cognitive Levels

Although educators have agreed that there are many levels of thinking or cognition, no attempt at delineating the levels of thinking gained general

Domain	Sample Performance Statements
Cognitive: Intellectual Activities	Define energy in your own words.
	Identify the rhyming words.
	Formulate a generalization to explain recent weather trends.
	Write a paragraph about your summer vacation.
	Discriminate between a triangle and a square.
	Solve problems using the given formula.
Affective: Attitudes, Interests, Appreciations	Volunteer to care for the aquarium after school.
	Take care of the school garden.
	Conduct an after school research project.
	Rewrite a book report voluntarily.
	Bring current news stories to class.
	Voluntarily pick up trash in the lunchroom.
Psychomotor: Motor Skills	Roll a kickball.
	Color a picture.
	Assemble a model airplane.
	Copy a graph from the chalkboard.
	Measure the classroom.
	Focus a telescope on a given point.

Figure 2-6. Sample performance statements for the three domains of learning.

acceptance until a committee of the American Psychological Association addressed the problem in the 1950s (Bloom, Englehart, Furst, Hill, & Krathwohl, 1956). This taxonomy (popularly called Bloom's Taxonomy) or classification system for educational objectives in the cognitive domain was revised more recently (2001) under the leadership of Lorin Anderson (see Figure 2-5). The resultant taxonomy is composed of the following six levels: *remembering, understanding, applying, analyzing, evaluating,* and *creating.* The original categories developed by Bloom and others were *knowledge, comprehension, application, analysis, synthesis,* and *evaluation.*

The classification levels listed in the cognitive domain comprise a hierarchy; that is, they are ranked with *remembering* being the lowest and *creating* being the highest. As a hierarchy, to function effectively at the more complex levels (*analyzing, evaluating,* and *creating*), the student must first master the lower and simpler mental processes (*remembering, understanding,* and *applying*). For example, if a student solves a problem at the analyzing level, it is assumed that the student has the ability to deal with the same subject matter at the preceding, less complex levels.

For consistency in classifying student performances, the teacher should categorize behaviors in the highest (most complex) category that is appropriate. If a student is required to use remembering, understanding, and applying, the performance statement developed for the desired behavior would be classified under the applying category.

Remembering, the lowest level of the cognitive domain, includes situations and conditions in which the student is expected to remember, memorize, or recall information previously learned. Remembering level functions are those that develop almost directly from one's experiences, particularly those experiences at the concrete level. At this level the student is expected to store certain facts derived from experience and then, at some later time, recall the information with minimum assistance. Remembering level performances typically refer to the recall of facts, concepts, or principles. Examples of remembering level performance statements are:

- Name three types of sentences.
- Match the meaning of selected road signs with the correct picture.
- Recall the date of Darwin's voyage.

Understanding, the level most emphasized in schools today, requires the ability to know the meaning of material or ideas and make some use of it. Understanding builds on remembering in that the student has achieved a higher level of comprehending of the information which has been memorized and recalled. Performance statements in this category indicate that the student understands a particular fact, concept, or idea. Examples of understanding level performance statements include:

- Explain the kind of information found on a particular chart.
- In your own words, define subtraction.
- Paraphrase written statements, retaining the original meaning.

Applying is essentially the act of using some understanding in a new or unique situation without being directed to do so. The distinction between the levels of understanding and applying is that, in applying, the student is able to use information in an appropriate situation without being told to do so by the teacher. It is useful to think of the student comprehending a principle or rule at the understanding level and then knowing when and how to use that principle or rule in a practical situation at the applying level. Applying, then, requires the student to remember, comprehend, and also apply knowledge or skill at the right time and place. There is a great deal of difference in knowing how to multiply and knowing when to multiply. Examples of applying level performance statements are:

- Calculate how much paint will be needed to paint our classroom.
- Select and use the appropriate verb wherever it has been left out of a list of sentences.

- Demonstrate what our class should do if we were to see a tornado coming.

At the *analyzing* level, students should be able to break an idea into its constituent elements or internal organizational principles and identify relationships among those elements or principles. Analyzing, in its fundamental form, is recognizing similarities among and differences between things. Although higher on the taxonomic scale, analysis may be easier to understand than some of the previous levels because analysis basically involves breaking down material into its component parts and finding relationships among them. Performance at this level requires the student to *get into* something to see clearly what is there. Examples of analyzing level performance statements are:

- Identify, from a written passage, which statements are statements of fact and which are opinions.
- Identify the bias of a writer in an article.
- Distinguish between two classroom speakers as to their point of view on the topic presented.

Evaluating includes making judgments about the worth of something according to specific criteria. Performances at this level also involve a justification of the judgment which is made by reference to facts, examples, or specific criteria of another sort. Evaluating is considerably more than simply saying that one thing is better than another. The judgment must have some basis, or criterion, for being made in the first place. Care must be taken in writing evaluation level performance statements to exclude those dealing with the affective domain or personal values. Evaluating requires the identification of standards and ascertaining the degree to which whatever is being evaluated meets the standards. Whenever students are required to assess, appraise, rate, or judge some event, message, object, or situation on the basis of distinct criteria, the intellectual skill of evaluating is being developed. Examples of evaluating level performance statements are:

- Rate information in the *Weekly Reader* on the basis of accuracy, completeness, and relevance of the included data.
- Compare the worth of the scientific contributions of Einstein and Newton.
- Appraise the quality of a given recipe according to your analysis of the product.

While *analyzing* involves reducing wholes to identify their component parts, *creating* is the ability to put known parts together to make a unique entity or whole which is new to the student. Using a musical analogy, when they attempt to develop a new composition, composers may begin with basic chords and, using music theory principles, develop these logically into a melody. It should be remembered that students must have mastered material in the area at the preceding levels before they can be successful at the creating level. Even then, developing something that is unique is often not an easy task. Performance statements dealing with creating require students to synthesize something that is distinctly their own. The product to be created may be a communication (e.g., poem, essay, editorial), a plan of operation (e.g., diagram, outline, model), or a set of abstract relations (e.g., unique interpretation). The distinctive quality of creating is the freedom it allows students in deciding what is to be produced. A performance statement dealing with creating, in other words, never has only one correct response and, consequently, often poses assessment challenges for the teacher. Examples of creating level performance statements are:

- Prepare a bulletin board depicting your view of the 1920s.
- Write a poem about winter.
- Design a model bridge.

Any cognitive performance statement can be categorized into one of these six levels. Because certain mental processes can overlap several categories, the exact classification of a performance statement is sometimes difficult. This does not necessarily decrease the instructional quality or value of that performance statement since a wide range of intellectual activities for students will be provided as a result of this type of planning.

Each of the different intellectual skills just identified can be adapted to any subject area and grade level. Less able students and able students alike can perform at each level of thinking with some measure of sophistication. Students of lesser ability, however, may experience more difficulty in analyzing, evaluating, and creating though they can engage in these higher mental processes if the subject matter is familiar to them. It is characteristic of lower ability students not to function as well at higher levels when using abstract ideas.

In practice, the cognitive domain can be appropriately used in the development of curricula and instructional objectives which address both lower as well as higher level thinking skills. Through the categorization of performance statements as they relate to the cognitive domain, the teacher can readily see what mental challenges the student will experience. Figure 2-7 presents a brief summary of the typical behaviors and the definitions of the six levels of the *Taxonomy for Learning, Teaching, and Assessing*. Becoming familiar with this taxonomy is an important step in using this very valuable aid in planning and sequencing instruction.

Level	Typical Action Verbs	Definition
Creating	design, devise, formulate, hypothesize, plan	Creating involves organizing elements into a new structure, putting parts into a whole, creating new forms or ideas, or developing plans.
Evaluating	appraise, compare, criticize, judge, justify, rate	Evaluating is to make a judgment based on specific criteria; more than choice is involved. One must also provide a rationale for whatever evaluation is made.
Analyzing	detect, infer, relate, distinguish, differentiate	Analyzing is the breaking down of something to reveal its parts or structure and making clear what they are and how they relate to one another.
Applying	calculate, solve, determine, compute	Applying involves the use of facts, ideas, principles, or formulas in *new* situations. The appropriate fact, idea, or formula must first be selected and then used in the given situation.
Understanding	convert, estimate, explain, paraphrase, summarize, translate	Understanding emphasizes gaining the meaning or intent of something. The student must do more than recall memorized knowledge.
Remembering	define, identify, list, name, state	Remembering involves recalling specific facts, definitions, terms, names, or formulas.

Figure 2-7. A summary of the *Taxonomy for Learning, Teaching and Assessing* as adapted from Anderson et al. (2001).

The most basic part of a quality objective, the performance statement, may be more clearly defined through the use of this category system. With the students' expected performance better delineated, the teacher has a clearer indication of the answer to the question: "What do I expect my students to do?"

Criterion Statement

A second important component of an instructional objective, the criterion statement, serves to further clarify expected student performance by identifying how well the student is expected to complete the specified activity.

While it is very important to know *what* students are expected to be able to do, it is also important to know *how well* they are expected to perform. This latter point becomes helpful for four reasons: (1) it serves to clarify the initial performance statement of what is expected, (2) it becomes a valuable aid in helping identify individual students who may need remedial instruction, (3) it provides information for the teacher to use in revising instruction, and (4) it informs the student as to what level of performance is expected.

The criterion statement is an expression of the level of learner proficiency expected as a result of mastering a stated objective. The teacher may express this in a variety of ways. For example, if the performance statement involves solving addition problems with two digit numbers, the criterion statement may be stated in terms of the number correct out of the total number possible, such as nine out of ten. A criterion could also be stated in terms of a percentage of correct responses, e.g., 90 percent. If the criterion statement is absent from an objective, 100 percent proficiency by the student is implied. The criterion, along with the conditions statement, adds greater specificity and a higher dimension of quality to a performance statement. The performance statement, however, remains the heart of the instructional objective.

Conditions Statement

The conditions statement communicates what the students will be given or have at their disposal at the time they are to demonstrate accomplishment of the learning involved in the performance statement. It may be useful to think of a conditions statement as a description of the setting in which the students will function before or during their evaluative performance. The student, for example, may be provided with pictures to match with names for performance statements such as: *Match the name of the animal with its habitat.* Or, the student may simply use paper and pencil to demonstrate the performance as in: *Write a brief summary of a story.* In this instance, the conditions statement may be implied; it is not necessary to state *given paper and pencil.* Previous instruction may also be referred to in the conditions statement. The conditions statement, *Given class discussion and a filmstrip*, describes information that the student will need to complete a performance statement such as: *Give examples of the use of the question mark.*

Assembling Objectives

After performance statements, criterion statements, and conditions statements have been developed, all that remains to arrive at a well-stated objective is to combine the three components. The following is considered as a complete objective:

- *After observing plant growth, name three of four life requirements of plants.*

The performance statement is *name life requirements of plants.* The expression, *after observing plant growth* is a statement of the necessary conditions for mastery of the performance. The criterion statement is three of four requirements. Another example is as follows:

- *Given ten straight line segments, measure the length of each line segment to the nearest centimeter.*

In this example, the performance statement is *measure the length of each line segment.* The expression, *given straight line segments* describes the conditions inherent in the testing of the students' ability to perform the measurement. The criterion statement is embodied in the phrase *to the nearest centimeter.* This indicates the level at which the student must perform. Consider the following final example.

- *Given the names of twenty common animals, identify the habitat of at least eighteen.*

This objective represents the use of a quantitative criterion (i.e., eighteen of twenty must be correct). The conditions statement indicates that the learner will receive a list of animal names and be expected to write an answer beside each name.

WRITING INSTRUCTIONAL PLANS

Examination of the curriculum map discussed earlier will allow the teacher to see the major topics to be learned and the order in which they should be presented. Having this knowledge, the teacher can begin the long-range planning process. Long-range plans are typically developed around units of instruction which can last from several days to several months depending on the age level and interest of the students and the content being presented. Units can be organized around a topic within a single content area or a theme that cuts across and unites several content areas (often referred to as thematic units). After the long-range plan has been developed, daily plans are taken from the unit to meet specific learning objectives.

Unit Planning

Notice that at the top of the suggested daily planning format in Figure 2-9 the teacher is asked to provide the name of the unit in addition to the title of the lesson. A unit refers to a designated segment of study and may be defined in many different ways. To some teachers a unit consists of one to two weeks of instruction; to others it may constitute six weeks or more of teaching. Regardless of its length, a unit represents a series of learning experiences or the study of a body of information related to a general topic. To be complete, a unit should include all necessary materials such as tests, manipulatives, library resources, and audiovisual aids.

Unit planning typically has been thought of as a method of structuring the curriculum in order to organize several kinds of activities, or even subject areas, so that they focus upon one general topic. This type of planning can be utilized to ensure that the learning rates, abilities, and styles of the students, as well as their experiential backgrounds, are taken into consideration during ongoing daily lessons. For example:

> Mr. Jorge is a third grade teacher who utilizes unit planning and is currently teaching a unit on fractions. He plans to have five groups working on a variety of projects which will culminate in five separate activities to be shared by the entire class. Mr. Jorge began his planning by generating five major goals; in this particular case, there is one goal statement for each group. After the goals were generated, Mr. Jorge created several specific instructional objectives based on each goal. In this unit, one goal deals with problem solving.

> A specific objective was written as follows: Given ten problems from *Riddles for the Superintelligent*, the student will explain in writing the steps needed to solve six problems. Each group is given five to ten such specific objectives. Mr. Jorge then meets with each group to suggest ways to accomplish the objectives. He is always ready to take student suggestions and often modifies certain objectives to coincide with student interests.

> During their group meetings, Mr. Jorge makes certain that all students understand exactly how committee and individual work is to be evaluated. In Mr. Jorge's class, several activities go on at once. The students are involved in some talk because Mr. Jorge understands the importance of sharing ideas in a socially stimulating environment. However, he never allows some students to disturb other students. Mr. Jorge has definite plans for the culmination of the unit after three weeks. The culminating activities will include role playing, the exhibition of art work, the reading of individual poems and essays, and the exhibiting of projects.

Most daily lesson plans should be thought of as small parts of a larger, more encompassing plan called a *unit*. It is not suggested that all instruction must be planned within a unit format as many important and interesting lessons will stand alone in any instructional program (Shepherd & Ragan, 1982). Nonetheless, several advantages of a unit planning system may be identified (Figure 2-8).

Advantages of the Unit Format in Planning

1. It unifies several subject matter fields around a general topic.
2. It lends itself to students learning *how* to learn on their own.
3. The students' rates, abilities, and styles of learning can be taken into account.
4. The experiential background of the students and the resources of the community can easily shape planning.
5. Unit planning helps the teacher get away from an over-reliance upon a single textbook.
6. A format is provided to allow the teacher to be flexible and creative.
7. Unit utilization aids in the development of quality long-range plans.

Figure 2-8. Advantages of unit planning.

As noted in Figure 2-8, developing units may result in developing quality *long-range* plans. Since long-range plans often consist of some unit plans, the achievement of long-range goals generally is made easier when unit planning is used. The long-range, decision-making process includes: (1) identification of goals, (2) selection of topics, (3) specification of the approximate time requirement for each topic, and (4) determination of an appropriate sequence for the units or topics. Once these steps are completed, the outlining of long-range plans is finished. It now remains for the teacher to prepare individual units as needed.

Once teachers have their unit plans, the scheduling of daily and weekly plans becomes easier because the scope and sequence of the total content to be taught is much more visible. Lessons now may be readily sequenced in weekly and, finally, daily order. Weekly and daily planning tasks are primarily ones of continuity, reviewing, and taking care of last-minute details. Weekly plans are necessary to ensure a smooth fit with each week's objectives and to find all needed materials and have them ready to use. Daily plans accomplish the same purpose but on a daily basis.

Daily Lesson Plans

Because novice teachers have certain unique planning needs, a basic three part lesson plan is often suggested that includes: (1) what to teach (objectives), (2) how to teach (strategies), and (3) how to evaluate (assessment). When such planning is done, the format in Figure 2-9, which incorporates these three main parts, is suggested.

Teacher _____

Lesson Title _____

Unit _____

Goal(s):

Objective(s):

Materials:

Procedures:

    Motivation
    Introduction
    Presentation of Lesson
    Exploration/Practice

Assessment:

Figure 2-9. A basic lesson planning format.

Goals and Objectives

Goals and objectives along with a lesson title comprise the first part of a lesson plan, procedures and materials the second, and evaluation the third. Since the writing of objectives was discussed in the previous section, only goals and standards for evaluation will be addressed here. Essentially, goals are broader and more long-range statements of intent than objectives. *Develop good health habits* or *develop good citizenship behaviors* are examples of goal statements. The purpose of using goals is to clearly identify the *big picture* of a unit of study where the **learning indicators** found in state and district standards documents function as the **performance part** of an objective. Because of their specificity, learning indicators generally are not a part of goal statements.

Procedures

The procedures section of the lesson plan describes how the teacher and students will interact during the lesson. The lesson typically will begin with a segment designed to stimulate student interest. There are many ways in which teachers can begin their lessons. Depending upon the purpose of the instruction that is to follow, Gage and Berliner (1988) note that the teacher might begin the lesson with (1) a motivational attention-getting beginning, (2) a simple interaction that establishes rapport between teacher and students, or (3) a way of relating past experiences to the class presentation. The function of the review at the beginning of the lesson is to build upon the readiness levels determined by the cognitive, affective, and psychomotor entry behaviors of students. For example, if the topic to be studied is reducing fractions, a necessary step before teaching fractions may be to review the skills of division. By specifying and summarizing the attributes and processes of division, the teacher is more assured that the student has the major prerequisite knowledge that is necessary to learn the new objective(s) of the lesson. The review should be a short part of the overall lesson lasting from perhaps one to five minutes.

The second phase of the procedure is designed to introduce the content that is to be learned. An outline of the topics and information to be discussed as to how they are related to real world applications is appropriate. Simply giving directions regarding how to do an activity is an insufficient orientation. Elaboration, description, and insight are the focal points in developing a successful introduction to the content. The introduction portion typically is less than five minutes in duration. At the beginning of a lesson on physical geography, for example, the teacher could write on the board: *Landforms are land surfaces that have characteristic shapes and compositions.* Drawings of plateaus, hills, and mountains may be included with this beginning. This preparatory statement would facilitate learning about landforms in the lesson to follow. Ausubel (1968), in his classical study of advance organizers, found that students are better able to associate past learning with present learning when given some preparatory understanding of what they are about to study.

The major portion of any lesson will be some type of presentation structured by the teacher. Where the review and overview are typically composed of only one activity, the presentation should be composed of several activities. These primarily will be a combination of showing, telling, or doing activities. In reference to the previous example with landforms, the teacher could include a variety of activities that influence students to (1) observe the drawing on the chalkboard or whiteboard, (2) listen to the teacher explain the different kinds of landforms, (3) compare their maps with the standard on the board, (4) get feedback from the teacher about their answers, (5) see additional examples of landforms in pictures and/or slides, and (6) respond to questions about landforms and participate in other showing, telling, and doing activities. An important key in using such showing, telling, and doing methods is to vary their implementation for the purpose of maintaining the students' interests and improving retention (Woolfolk, 2008; Eggen & Kauchak, 2007; Gage & Berliner, 1988; Cooper, 1986). The change of pace from one perceptual sense to another, from one task to another, and from previously learned material to novel material enhances learning. Teachers who vary their activities have faster paced lessons that are usually characterized as being more motivating and interesting. The presentation is generally the major portion of a lesson and may take as much as three-quarters of the class time and usually no less than one-quarter.

The fourth portion of the lesson is designed to allow students time to explore and practice new learning. When a physical education student practices the correct form in shooting free throws, when a fourth grade student practices the multiplication tables, and when a student in English practices sentence combining, all are exploring newly introduced skills. They are, in effect, applying what they have learned by shooting, reciting, or writing. This is practice of new learning, but it also has the added benefit of providing feedback for the teacher and the student. Without watching the ball go into the hoop, without checking the multiplication tables, without examining the different sentences formed, the student or teacher would have no real knowledge, no feedback, of how well the material is being mastered. Knowledge of feedback is effective because it increases the students' likelihood of being more responsive and productive. If the practice that the teacher requires the students to do is to achieve its greatest benefit, the teacher must be sure to provide ample amounts of feedback. The practice or exercise that students are asked to complete is often written but can include oral drill, recitation, or physical manipulation and demonstration. It should be a type of performance that has been taught in the lesson but also could include some material from content previously mastered. The purpose of practice and exploration is to allow students the opportunity to actively apply what has been presented. The length of this component is variable. In a second grade spelling lesson or a high school geography lesson, practice and exploration could be as short as five minutes. When conducting a values clarification or a science laboratory activity, however, the process could include one-half of the lesson and perhaps even more.

The final phase of the lesson should involve some type of summary or conclusion. Unfortunately, the conclusion of a lesson is often neglected by some teachers because they tend to concentrate their attention on the body of the lesson, not because the ending of a lesson is considered unimportant. Since the presentation component may be lengthy, usually between one-quarter and three-quarters of a class session, the use of a summary at the end of a lesson helps ensure that the main points of the lesson are reinforced. Summaries can be structured by the teacher in many ways. Some teachers prefer to have students answer questions as a summary activity at the end of the lesson. Student answers can be accepted orally, in writing by individuals, or by the whole class. Such variation tends to improve the classroom climate by keeping the lesson routine novel, not monotonous. Other variations also are possible. Many teachers, for example, choose to present a summary themselves either orally or through the use of the white board or PowerPoint.

The use of test-like questions is an excellent way to conclude the class. Using test-like questions has been shown (McKenzie 1980, 1979) to be important in raising achievement because such questions stimulate thought and students' construction and elaboration of knowledge (Eggen & Kauchak, 2007).

Summaries also may involve the use of prepared posters or transparencies to save time in the presentation. Such approaches provide students with materials to examine or copy after the lesson. It is important to note that summaries may also have diagnostic benefits that help teachers in the planning of future lessons. The goal of the procedure section of the lesson plan allows the teacher to develop activities that are consistent with sound psychological principles of learning and deliver logically organized instruction from beginning to end.

Assessment

The final portion of any good lesson is the assessment of the students' performance on each stated objective. Assessment is an integral, ongoing part of the teacher's responsibility and is discussed in detail in Chapter 8. It is a tool in providing the teacher with feedback information for meeting future student needs. Teachers are advised to prepare assessment activities or instruments to comprehensively assess student learning efforts and achievement. Each objective in the daily lesson plan is to be fully assessed. The Mager three-part model requires that the teacher think specifically in terms of assessing each objective.

Assessment usually occurs daily but can occur weekly, monthly, or, in the case of standardized tests, yearly. Generally speaking, the more frequently students are evaluated and receive feedback, the better their achievement. Daily assessment can be achieved in many ways. Assessment might simply consist of the teacher asking questions orally during the lesson with subsequent feedback to students about the accuracy of their answers, or a written response might be required. Short quizzes could be given daily. Recitation, drill, and question-answering serve to provide students with feedback about their degree of proficiency. Such approaches as these communicate to students and teachers whether the material is being learned correctly and whether this results in increased achievement (Bloom, 1980).

In planning lessons, it is advisable not only to (1) have one or more definite objectives identified; (2) plan appropriate, stimulating instruction; (3) prepare a culminating assessment exercise; but also, (4) develop test-like situations that function as learning aides during instruction which can be used later in preparing for student assessment. These four steps in planning for instruction are beneficial teacher routines and are sound preparation for effective instruction.

Planning Overview

Figure 2-10 is an example of a completed lesson plan for a kindergarten mathematics lesson. Study the plan and compare it to the criteria identified in the lesson plan checklist (Figure 2-11). All checklist items for this lesson plan could be checked *yes*. Differences in ability levels and rates of learning are accommodated by providing guiding questions to those needing help or more challenge and an enrichment learning center for those who finish early. Differences in learning style preference are also accommodated by the variation in showing, telling, and doing activities. Study Figures 2-10 and 2-11 and see if you agree.

Figure 2-10

Kindergarten Mathematics Lesson

Teacher: Joan Smith

Lesson Title: Sorting by one attribute

Unit: Classification

Goal:

To develop classification skills.

Objective:

Given objects of varying size and color, sort the objects using one attribute.

Materials: 4 boxes, 24 total objects — for each of the 4 basic shapes you need a big and a little of 3 different colors (i.e., 1 big red square and 1 little red square, etc.), chart paper and marker. You will also need a Ziploc bag with 24 small shapes (same as above) for each child.

Procedures:

A. Motivation
   Teacher will begin lesson by dumping the box of 4 shapes of 3 different colors and 2 sizes on the floor.
B. Introduction
   Ask students to describe what they see. Teacher writes responses on a chart eliciting shape, size, and color as the three characteristics addressed today.
C. Presentation of Lesson
   I have four boxes that I want to put these materials in. Ask one child to choose one object and put it in a box. The teacher picks up a square (nonexample) and places it in the box with the circle. The teacher asks children "did I put this in the correct box?" Repeat another nonexample sometime during the process. Ask another child to choose a **different** object to go in a **different** box. Continue until you have a different shape in each box. When all the shapes have been distributed into the appropriate box, ask children to discuss the attributes of the objects in each box. For example, the squares have four sides that are all the same. "What label could we put on this box so anyone would know what belongs in it?" Continue until all the shapes in each box have been described and boxes are labeled correctly. Recap what has been

Continued on next page

Figure 2-10 – *Continued*

learned by asking students to explain how they sorted the objects.

D. Exploration/Practice

Provide each child with a Ziploc bag of materials similar to those used in the lesson presentation and 3 paper plates. Ask children to find a way to sort their materials. Teacher moves among the tables providing assistance to those struggling and asking those at a higher level to sort using 2 attributes. Those who finish early are to work at the enrichment <u>learning center</u>.

E. Summary

Ask children to define shapes and provide nonexamples of shapes. Ask children to explain how they can sort objects into smaller groups. Conclude lesson by asking how sorting can help them in their daily lives.

Assessment: Children correctly sort the 24 objects based on one attribute.

Figure 2-11

Lesson Plan Checklist

	Yes	No
Goal(s):		
Does the goal statement represent a long-range purpose for study?	_____	_____
Objective(s):		
Does the objective(s) include conditions, performance, and criteria for assessment?	_____	_____
Is each consistent with the stated goal?	_____	_____
Materials:		
Did I identify all necessary materials?	_____	_____
Procedure:		
Did I address each component? Motivation	_____	_____
Introduction	_____	_____
Lesson Presentation	_____	_____
Exploration/Practice	_____	_____
Summary	_____	_____
Did I plan for differences in: Rate of Learning	_____	_____
Learning Preferences	_____	_____
Ability Levels	_____	_____
Assessment:		
Did I plan appropriate assessment for each objective?	_____	_____
Did I plan for the communication of feedback to all students?	_____	_____

PLANNING WITH THE INTERNET

Teachers can find an almost unlimited number of ideas and plans on the Internet. However, care should be taken that all aspects of any plan that may be found reflect accurate information and are appropriate for the age and developmental levels of the students being taught. Teachers must remember that any plan retrieved from any source will have to be modified to accommodate for individual differences in abilities and learning preferences of the students. Moreover, as previously discussed, it is important that the objectives of the lesson align with stated state and district standards. Before teachers can use any of the information accessible to them, they must be confident that the content is accurate and the presentation is objective. The following questions are suggested as a way to determine the quality of plans located through the Internet: *Is there a creation or revision date? Are there links to outside sites? Are links in working order? Does the information show evidence of political or ideological bias? How accurate is the information? Does the information represent fact or opinion?* After these questions are answered sufficiently to ensure the accuracy of the information and objectivity of the presentation, any resulting creations of the teacher's instructional activities can at least be considered reasonable and supportable. If such information is used, the teacher should be sure to copy the document's URL and the date the information was found. This will allow for credit to be given to the original author and help the teacher to retrieve or share it in the future.

The intellectual demands on teachers in recent years clearly have increased to higher and more intense levels. Though demands on teachers to achieve specified standards are at an all-time high, the assistance that is readily available has increased as well, and this helps somewhat to ease this pressure. Teachers today must be able to efficiently locate information, reflect on and determine its worth, make changes where necessary to meet the needs of students, and implement effective instructional plans. Simply downloading plans from the Internet, even though they may represent viable instructional suggestions, will not produce better learning or higher achievement. Teachers must carefully reflect on the intent of each plan that they develop and weave it into the greater curriculum while ensuring that it is sensitive to the students' learning styles, abilities, and rates of learning.

Chapter 3

THE TEACHER AS A COMMUNICATOR

Communication takes place throughout the educational environment even before the teacher enters the classroom. Messages are sent and received, some clearly understood and some not. Teachers communicate, students communicate, building administrators communicate, and so on and so on. As the focus here is on the classroom teacher, Chapter 3 addresses specifically the role of the teacher as a communicator. Consider the following examples of teacher communications which commonly take place within the classroom; the fact that teaching is communication and, in many ways, communication is teaching is illustrated through just this brief listing. The classroom teacher:

- discusses classroom assignments,
- explains a new concept,
- writes information on the whiteboard,
- reads instructions for an activity,
- corrects students' homework,
- talks with teacher aides,
- reviews student papers,
- asks questions about student understanding,
- presents overviews of main ideas,
- announces forthcoming activities, and
- communicates with families.

The above list is not intended to be exhaustive of all of the types of teacher communications in any given classroom on any given day, but only to illustrate the many and varied communications in which teachers are involved. It also should be noted that the list only illustrates examples of what may be termed verbal communication. Nonverbal communication and verbal communication make up the two forms of communication exhibited by teachers on a regular basis.

Because teachers are expected to communicate often and well, this chapter is dedicated to the study of several aspects of the role of the teacher as a communicator. Since much of what a teacher wishes to transmit to students is subject matter knowledge or skills to be learned, various types of knowledge to be communicated are also discussed. The chapter concludes with a special example of teacher communication: communicating for conceptual understanding. Since concepts comprise a significant part of the curriculum, the study of concept communication is given special attention. In this final section, specific aspects of planning concept lessons and the application of planning skills are addressed. In this chapter you will learn more about the importance of communication for teachers through the study of the following topics:

1. communication as a three-part process,
2. verbal and nonverbal communication,
3. seven types of nonverbal language symbols,
4. facts, generalizations, values, and concepts,
5. abstract concepts and concrete concepts, and
6. teaching concept lessons.

TEACHING AS COMMUNICATION

Because the classroom teacher must be expert in communication in order to achieve an optimum level of effectiveness, it is essential that the teacher be knowledgeable of the many facets of communication utilized in the classroom. With this in mind, a basic definition of communication with relevant examples is provided.

Defining Communication

Communication is a systemic process in which people interact with and through symbols to create and interpret meanings (Wood, 2008). Communication is an evolving process, not a set of isolated events. As such, it involves a number of key elements necessary to make it effective. In the classic model of the communication process (Figure 3-1), three key elements are identified: *source, message,* and *destination.* Communication must have a beginning point of origin, a message to be sent, and an ending or receiving point. The *message,* in the traditional sense represented by subject matter to be taught, is sent to its *destination,* the students in the classroom, by the *source,* the teacher. The medium by which the message is sent is referred to as language or symbols.

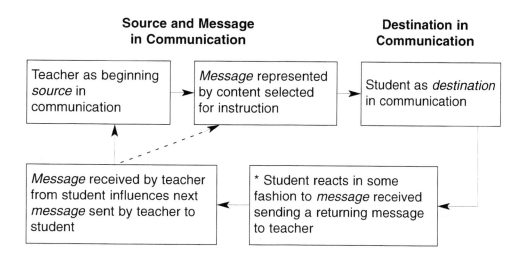

**Source and Message
in Communication**   **Destination in
Communication**

| Teacher as beginning *source* in communication | → | *Message* represented by content selected for instruction | → | Student as *destination* in communication |

| *Message* received by teacher from student influences next *message* sent by teacher to student | | * Student reacts in some fashion to *message* received sending a returning message to teacher |

* In this return communication process
the student becomes the *source* of the
message and the teacher becomes the
destination

Figure 3-1. Source, message, destination model of communication as applied to a teaching situation (influenced by Schramm, 1945).

In the communication process, an idea or message exists with the source or message-sender (e.g., the teacher) who develops symbols or language so that the receiver or message-recipient (e.g., the students) may understand the communication. In the teaching process, the teacher identifies what is to be communicated and develops procedures so that students will understand what is being transmitted. Communication may be thought of as a transaction in which changes or exchanges occur (Sereno & Bodaken, 1975). Once the communication transaction has taken place, a meaning has been communicated from the teacher to the student. If the communication transaction has been successful, the student has changed in some way because something is now known that was not known previously. The teacher also has changed, as the teacher now recognizes the student as having new information, i.e., in a new light. The meaning attached to each message sent is the most central feature of effective communication; this meaning must be communicated clearly and effectively for optimum learning to take place.

In its most basic form, communication involves (1) a *sender*, (2) a *receiver*, (3) a meaningful *message*, and (4) a *language* with which to send the message. The language possibilities which exist in this process are represented in two broad categories: verbal language and nonverbal language (Figure 3-2).

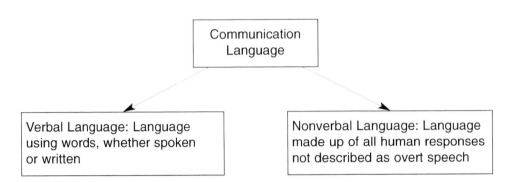

Figure 3-2. Communication as verbal and nonverbal language.

Whether the teacher uses primarily verbal or nonverbal language messages, the language which is chosen always will involve the use of some type of language symbols to constitute the basis of the message transmission.

Verbal Communication

Verbal communication, or language, consists of symbols in the form of spoken or written words (Wood, 2008). Whether spoken or written, words are verbal symbols. These symbols relate to ideas about things. Linguists have identified four basic verbal language vocabularies: *reading, listening, writing,* and *speaking.* Communication problems, which may arise through the use of any of the four vocabularies, develop primarily because senders (teachers) and receivers (students) do not share the same meaning for the symbols (words) used. This is because they put the symbols together in different patterns, or because there is some interference that creates a misunderstanding between the sender and receiver. Communication breakdowns can occur quickly when word symbols are abstract as opposed to concrete. For example, words such as *fair, just, helpful,* and *love* are more easily misinterpreted because of their abstractness than such words as *chair, house, car,* and *cow* which are concrete. Abstract word symbols also are much more difficult to understand in the absence of common background experiences. Because of this, it is important that teachers, especially those in multicultural and more heterogeneous settings, further their understanding of the cultural and linguistic backgrounds of the students in their classes so that they may establish a basis for clear communication. In so doing, teachers can better serve the needs of each individual student and more effectively facilitate the communication process.

Particularly in the teaching environment, various thoughts occur at different levels of sophistication and abstraction. The clearest communication occurs when language, thus thought, is made as concrete as possible. In spite of this, it is a major part of the teacher's responsibility to make sure that students also understand abstract ideas which are communicated and taught on a daily basis. This can be accomplished best when the teacher provides experiences for students with the language being used in order to develop familiarity and concreteness. Although the communication of an abstract message is often more difficult for students to understand, it is a necessary and important part of what is learned in school. It is often the understanding of abstractions that provides the greatest long-term benefit for students.

More than any other aspect of communication, the skill of listening is the least studied and the most taken for granted. No matter how much teachers would like for listening skills to develop naturally, the development of skills in listening is not predictable nor guaranteed even though the spoken language surrounds students daily. Competency in the listening process requires awareness, concentration, and practice. It is important for teachers to realize that the ability to be an effective listener is not necessarily first dependent on one's intelligence or reading skill. In fact, many linguists have suggested that one's ability to read as well as one's measured intelligence are dependent, at least in part, on an individual's ability to listen.

Various techniques can be utilized to enhance all types of verbal communication in the classroom. Consider the following suggestions.

1. Reading communication should be integrated into all subject matter areas in an interdisciplinary approach and on a school-wide basis. To relegate such communication development to the reading or language arts specialist at the elementary level, or the remedial or English teacher at the secondary level, represents stereotypical thinking. All teachers have responsibilities in this area. Whether the question is textbook reading, whiteboard reading, or perhaps the study of teacher-given notes, there exists a sender, a message, and an intended receiver. Unless the student has an appropriate level of mastery of the reading process, clear communication of the message may not take place.

2. Students should be encouraged to feel that they have something important to say. Like teachers, students need encouragement, praise, and a forum to express their ideas. Written messages such as *interesting idea* and *good point* serve as positive reinforcers to students. Such reinforcers are important even if the student's work is not of the highest caliber possible. To assist the student in maintaining a positive approach to the task, it is important that the teacher be able to incorporate a sound blend of positive reinforcement with necessary constructive criticism.

3. For students to understand what is being said, they must understand the verbal symbols being used. There is a direct relationship between words and thoughts. When the teacher uses certain words, the student has certain thoughts. In successful communication, the intent is to develop better control over what thoughts the student has when certain words are used. Teachers need to be alert to word misunderstandings and ask frequent questions designed to determine student comprehension of the verbal presentation.

4. Teachers must be good listeners and pay close attention to student responses in all language vocabularies: reading, listening, speaking, and writing. The role of the teacher as a model of effective communication can have a significant impact on students in the development of their own communication skills.

5. Teachers must regularly provide opportunities for students to practice their verbal communication skills in all four language vocabularies. For example, teachers at each grade level should occasionally read aloud to help students develop listening skills as well as provide extensive opportunities for students to write in order to improve their writing skills.

6. Teachers should design the classroom physical environment in a way that encourages and enhances the enjoyment of communication. Care should be taken in making seating and grouping arrangements to ensure that all students can easily see, hear, and participate.

A characteristic of teaching in the twenty-first century is that most teachers will teach in classrooms populated with some children who are English Speakers of Other Languages (ESOL). ESOL students often have difficulty communicating with both their teachers and fellow students. Such students may have much difficulty following the thoughts of others in the classroom and communicating their thoughts to classmates and teachers. This is such an important issue in the education of today's youth that teachers should focus some portion of their professional development in the area of best practice in instructing ESOL students. There is a multitude of quality materials available for teachers seeking more information on the education of ESOL students. *Take Action* (de Ramirez, 2009) and *Fifty Strategies for Teaching English Language Learners* (Herrell, 2000) are recommended.

Nonverbal Communication

Imagine the teacher as a picture sending out messages or symbols without actually using verbal communication. Even though this may sound unusual, as it is often said, a picture is a worth a thousand words. Nonverbal language communication involves transactions through nonverbal symbols rather than verbalizations (Crable, 1979). Nonverbal communication includes all aspects of communication other than spoken or written words (Wood, 2008; Knapp, 1972). In addition to gestures and body language, nonverbal communication includes how words are uttered (inflection, volume), features of the environment that affect meaning (temperature, lighting), and objects that affect personal images and interaction patterns (dress, jewelry, furniture) (Wood, 2008). O'Hair, Friedrich, Wiemann, and Wiemann (1997) note that nonverbal communication involves behavior rather than the content of spoken words, i.e., not involving the content of traditional speech, and that in the communication process meaning is attributed to this behavior.

Nonverbal communication accounts for 65 to 93 percent of the total meaning of communication (Mehrabian, 1981; Birdwhistell, 1970). It is unusual for verbal and nonverbal symbols to occur in isolation from one another. It has been estimated that, in simultaneous verbal and nonverbal communication, approximately 65 percent of the meaning of the communication is created by nonverbal messages. Research also suggests that, when verbal and nonverbal messages seem to conflict, the nonverbal symbols are the ones to be believed (Galloway, 1982). It is important to remember that nonverbal symbols do not really have meaning by themselves; their ultimate meanings are given by the receiver. A yawn, for example, may mean *boredom* to one or *fatigue* to another. Someone's hand waving could mean *good-bye* or a call for *help*. As with verbal communication, to a great extent, interpretation depends on the context of the message and the background of the receiver.

Of particular interest to the classroom teacher are the following types of nonverbal symbols (Figure 3-3): (1) *kinesics*, (2) *proxemics*, (3) *haptics*, (4) *oculesics*, (5) *paralanguage*, (6) *chronemics*, and (7) *environmental factors* (O'Hair, Friedrich, Wiemann, & Wiemann, 1997; Smith, 1995; McCroskey, 1972).

Kinesics

Kinesics refers to the way gestures and body movements, e.g., postures and head movements, body positions, body motions, and facial expressions, send messages (Wood, 2008; O'Hair et al., 1997). Related to teaching behaviors, posture which includes leaning toward someone is generally seen as expressing interest or positive feelings; leaning away expresses more negative or cold feelings (Smith, 1995; Mehrabian, 1969). Similar conclusions are drawn concerning head movements. Head nodding typically is seen as acceptance and active listening while shaking the head suggests a lack of acceptance and lack of attention or interest. Some moderate level of gestural activity often is associated with the abstract concept of enthusiasm, and

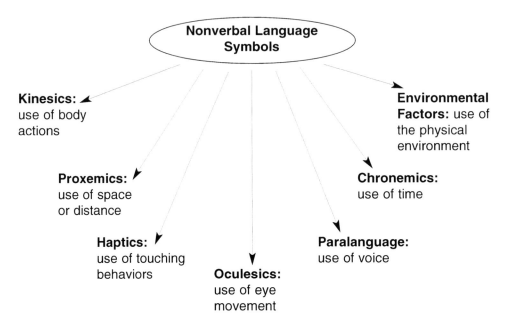

Figure 3-3. Nonverbal language symbols relevant to classroom communication.

educational research has linked enthusiasm to teaching effectiveness. Interpretations of physical or bodily gestures are far from absolute and point only to general impressions or feelings. Interpretations of *kinesic* messages, consequently, are only open to some general conclusions. It is observed, however, that teachers who have better control of their classes and who are accessible to their students tend to manifest a relaxed and open bearing toward them (Smith, 1995). Such teachers demonstrate fewer signs of defensiveness and anxiety (e.g., hands on hips and tightly crossed arms). Teachers whose nonverbal behaviors indicate they have the energy or vigor to take care of themselves and who move quickly are less likely to be challenged in their classroom leadership roles than teachers whose posture communicates otherwise and who move with less vitality (Gunns, Johnston, & Hudson, 2002). Additionally, teachers who smile and project a pleasant demeanor toward their students signal that they like others and are happy being around them (Gueguen & De Gail, 2003; Walker & Trimboli, 1989). This can produce a comparable response in return from students.

Proxemics

The use of space or distance in the communication process is referred to as proxemics and applies to the use of one's social and personal space in situations that typically involve other people (Smith, 1995). People tend to define their own territory, claiming territoriality, and then protect it. Concern for privacy, intimacy, dominance, and status all influence how individuals position themselves during interactions (Goss & O'Hair, 1988). Some teachers, for example, have desks that face their classroom or office doors and a chair beside the desk to promote open communication with people who come in. Others turn their desks away from the door and place chairs opposite their desks, which configures the space hierarchically (Wood, 2008). Some teachers are notorious for defining their territory as that space around their desks or in front of the classroom. This kind of proxemic message tells students that there is an area best suited for them, and one best suited for the teacher. Students should not go into the teacher's space unless invited. Many teachers also are not comfortable going into what they have allowed to be defined as the students' space. Such a territorial arrangement in a classroom environment generally proves to be counterproductive. Individuals become protective and defensive, and this type of setting often results in a breakdown of positive communication. When teachers and students are in whole-class situations, the closer teachers are to students the greater the amount of student participation and focus may be found in class activities.

When seatwork is assigned, a greater percentage of students complete their work when the teacher circulates about the room during work time. This type of nonverbal communication, an application of the understanding of the concept of proxemics, communicates to students that the teacher is interested in their performance and comfortable being near them. Although a somewhat simple criterion for success, the academic payoff is clear. When students perceive the teacher as truly being interested in their work, and attend to the task at hand, their achievement improves.

Haptics

Nonverbal language communication through touching behaviors is known as haptics (Wood, 2008). O'Hair et al. (1997) identified that, while people have different perceptions of touch and some are more accepting of it than others, touch is a primary means of communication. Touching is a common method of communicating among early childhood and elementary school teachers and their students and far less so between teachers and students in the middle and high school grades. Many educators point to the warmth shown by a hand on the shoulder but also recognize how this may be misinterpreted by some students. Research suggests that there are gender differences in touching behavior. Compared to men, women are more likely to engage in touch to show caring and warmth (Anderson, 1999), whereas men are more likely than women to use touch to assert control (Jhally &

Katz, 2001). While touching is a common means of nonverbal communication, the potential for misinterpretation in touching can make its use awkward. It is important for the teacher to accept that interpretations of touch are varied and are influenced by cultural backgrounds. For example, Ishii (1987) identified that in the Japanese culture little touching is used after childhood. Teachers are advised to not be afraid to touch but, also, to be alert to the various interpretations that touching may invoke. There are people who are touchers and those who are nontouchers. A non-touching student may label a touching teacher as being overly forward or aggressive. Other students, often younger students, however, may perceive a nontouching teacher as unfriendly or cold-natured. Touching in the classroom should emerge as a natural part of the classroom situation and be used only by teachers who feel comfortable in using it (Smith, 1995).

Oculesics

The study of how the eyes and eye movements can communicate is termed oculesics. Eye contact with another person can command involvement (O'Hair et al., 1997). If teachers desire that their students be involved in the learning process, attention to oculesics is important as the eyes influence the quality of communication. Four major factors influence or determine how much eye contact will exist in a communication transaction (Argyle & Dean, 1965). First is the role of the communicator; the person receiving the message usually demonstrates more eye contact than the person who is initiating the message being sent. Second is the nature of the topic to be communicated; making and maintaining eye contact is easier with impersonal topics. If the topic is personal, eye contact generally decreases. Gender is the third factor; women tend to engage in more eye contact than men. The fourth factor is relationship. If the people communicating are friends or otherwise are individuals who have a positive relationship, greater eye contact will be established. In the role of classroom leader, the teacher can improve communication channels by establishing good eye contact with students. When students are speaking, eye contact from the teacher should be evident. This tells students that the teacher is interested in what they are saying. No eye contact communicates disinterest.

Eye messages can serve the teacher in many ways; perhaps the two most important are in promoting positive relationships in the classroom and in communicating some form of teacher dissatisfaction to students in order to influence behavior change. Looking at students promotes their attentiveness, involvement, and positive regard for the teacher (Smith, 1995). Not looking at them can promote the opposite. Strong eye contact tends to heighten the credibility of the speaker (Wood, 2008). However, this illustration is another example of the importance of teachers having an understanding of and respect for the cultures of all students. For example, some children come from cultures where it might be a sign of disrespect to look an adult in the eye when speaking or being spoken to. An understanding of cultural differences is needed if teachers are going to effectively communicate with all students in a positive fashion.

Paralanguage

Paralanguage is communication that is vocal but not actual words (Wood, 2008). It refers to nonverbal characteristics of speech such as voice pitch, volume, tempo and intensity, intruding sounds, murmurs and gasps, and pauses (Smith, 1995). While judgments about people are continually made based on vocal quality, research shows that these judgments are accurate only about 50 percent of the time (Knapp, 1972). Nevertheless, as decisions about individuals will be made, whether right or wrong, they are all too often assumed accurate and acted on accordingly. Because of this, it is important that the teacher have a good working knowledge of just what can be done and communicated with the voice. Students generally prefer listening to voices that change in inflection. They do not prefer a voice with a lack of pitch variety as seen in a monotonic presentation. On the other hand, voices which have patterns of a singsong nature are received as annoying as a monotone. Changes in pitch, volume, and rate of speech create interesting, more stimulating communication transactions resulting in more favorable student reactions (Crable, 1979). People who speak at slow to moderate rates are perceived as having greater control over the interaction than those who speak more rapidly (Tusing & Dillard, 2000). The selected use of vocal cues by the teacher can influence persuasion and aid in comprehension (Knapp & Hall, 1992). In general, teachers who use lower voice volume and pitch are perceived to be more in charge of their classes than teachers who speak constantly at a higher voice pitch (Smith, 1995).

Many teachers, the novice as well as the experienced, include in their verbal repertoire the distracting overuse of repeated words or phrases. Vocalizations such as *um, er, ok,* and *ah* are often used to fill a pause in the speech pattern. The use of these utterances, however, typically communicates that the teacher is nervous, excited, or unsure (Goldman-Eisler, 1961). The pattern of *filling* speech pauses in this manner also can communicate that the individual is attempting to keep control of the conversation or situation (Maclay & Osgood, 1959). The pause also is an important form of nonverbal communication. When pauses are few and not obvious, the teacher is seen as being extroverted and outgoing, perhaps even confident. When this is not the case with the teacher using many and longer pauses, the opposite interpretation of the teacher is made. The intended use of the pause in teaching, sometimes called *wait time* when following a question, can be used to the teacher's advantage in provoking student thought and investigation (Rowe, 1972). Used appropriately, *wait time* can be an extremely important teacher strategy to encourage higher order thinking and reflection. It is the overuse or unplanned use of the pause that is of concern. In its extreme usage, this speech pattern displays a lack of confidence and evidences insecurity on the part of the teacher.

Chronemics

Chronemics refers to how individuals perceive and structure time (Wood, 2008; O'Hair et al., 1997). Teachers have no control over the beginning time of the school day or when the school day ends. Many have little control, in particular in the middle and high school grades, over beginning and ending times of their own classes. Within their immediate instructional time, however, their control of time is critical. Skilled teachers have developed a sense of rhythm or pacing which allows sufficient time to conclude needed tasks and for smooth transitions from one activity to another (Smith, 1995). Teachers not skilled in the use of time, as seen by erratic rhythms in their teaching and uneven transitions between activities, often have more student misbehavior and lack of student attentiveness. A quicker pace in the class as opposed to a more methodical, slow pace has been related to higher levels of student learning. Time management, in terms of beginning lessons promptly on time and ending them on time, is considered an important aspect of teacher effectiveness.

Environmental Factors

Environmental factors are elements of settings that affect how people feel, think, and act (Wood, 2008). In nonverbal communication, they refer to the effects of the physical attributes of settings on behavior (Smith, 1995). Restaurants use environmental factors, for example, to control how long people spend eating. Low lights, comfortable chairs or booths, and soft music often are part of the environment in upscale restaurants. Fast food restaurants have hard plastic booths and bright lights which encourage diners to eat and move on (Wood, 2008). The appearance of the teacher's classroom is important in this regard. Even the type and arrangement of furniture can promote or hinder various activities. Cold, stale, undecorated rooms, in general, push students away while warm, colorful, decorated surroundings tend to draw them in. The work of Kovalik (1994) reinforces the importance of the classroom environment. It is important for the teacher to remember, for example, that the display of student work can be a significant part of an inviting atmosphere. Students whose work or contributions have a place in the environment become a greater part of the classroom themselves. Constructive use of bulletin board and wall space, desk arrangement, and even personal preferences such as plants and the playing of soft music say a great deal about the teacher's concern for the learning environment and testify to the professionalism produced. Various studies have identified that an abundance of soft color, flexible lighting, comfortable seats, and the incorporation of student ideas and materials can substantially influence pupil attitudes and behavior, even when academic performance is not affected (Smith, 1995). The work place reflects both personality and professional effort. The need to create a comfortable place in which to work is no different for teachers than for those in other professions. The warm, inviting environment is preferred and more productive than the cold.

TYPES OF KNOWLEDGE IN CLASSROOM COMMUNICATION

Look at the pages of any textbook at any grade level and at least four kinds of information being communicated can be noted:

- factual statements,
- value statements,
- concepts, and
- generalizations.

Factual statements, perhaps the most commonly represented type of knowledge taught in the classroom, represent something verifiable or thought to be verifiable. Factual statements represent something considered to be true or known. *Value statements* typically function either as justification for a course of action or as a basis of rating objects, events, persons, or situations. Value and factual statements, however, actually have less importance in the thinking process except as they are given some kind of order in the construction of concepts or generalizations. *Concepts*, as opposed to factual or value statements, define or categorize objects, events, or situations. They are expressions, usually consisting of one or two words, or ideas having common characteristics (Orlich, Harder, Callahan, Trevisan, & Brown, 2007). Concepts are often thought of as representing a mental image or abstraction of something and are popularly referred to as the building blocks of knowledge. Teachers say that students need to understand the proper facts with which to think, when, sound thinking is impossible without sound conceptual understanding (Hunt & Metcalf, 1968). Concepts are the basis of all thinking and knowing. Extending beyond concepts, *generalizations* are statements of fact, but are probabilistic in nature. Generalizations are inferential statements that express relationships between two or more concepts (Orlich et al., 2007) and offer guidance and predictability. Good instruction involves the teaching of facts so that this factual knowledge can help the student have an understanding of important concepts. Effective teachers guide students in their conceptual development so that they will be able to form sound and accurate generalizations. Because of the significance of facts, concepts, and generalizations to understanding the thinking process and to the logic of teaching, communication, and learning, they will be discussed at some length.

Facts, Generalizations, and Values

The easiest mistake a teacher can make with concepts is to confuse them with facts. In one study, an attempt was made to rate, according to their relative importance, 938 *concepts* in United States history (Hunt & Metcalf, 1968). Nearly every alleged concept on the list was actually a factual statement such as *Christopher Columbus, attempting to reach Asia by sailing west across the Atlantic, discovered America in 1492.* This statement is not a concept; it is a fact. A convenient way to describe a fact is to consider it as a well-grounded, clearly established unit of information. It is a fact, for example, that George Washington was the first president of the United States.

There is an important difference between teaching facts and teaching concepts. Effective teachers use facts while teaching or communicating concepts, but it is possible to communicate many facts without teaching a single concept. Facts should not be taught as learning end-points. Facts should be taught to enable students to better understand concepts and, in turn, understand broader, more life-applicable generalizations. Factual knowledge (remembering) represents the lowest level of the cognitive domain.

Another confusion can arise when concepts are defined as generalizations. The basic difference is that concepts are definitions and axioms. By comparison, generalizations possess a synthetic content. Their truth or believability rests upon their proof through the investigation of evidence. Such expressions as *people migrate when they are hungry,* or, *generals are babes in politics,* are often erroneously labeled as concepts. Actually, they are generalizations. Generalizations are law-like statements which express a relationship among concepts. Part of the special nature of generalizations is their predictive power. As noted earlier, generalizations are probabilistic in nature and represent what is at the heart of teaching for transfer of learning. Generalizations have the following qualities (Martorella, 1986).

- They are true or have been verified by the best tests of evidence available (i.e., facts).

- They predict things in the sense of allowing one to make *if . . . then* statements.
- They apply to all relevant cases without exceptions.
- They express significant relationships among concepts.

The generalization, *people who have common interests are attracted to one another*, is a law-like statement expressing a relationship between the concepts *people, common interests,* and *attraction.* The teaching of concepts such as these should not be ends in themselves. Their greater purpose is to enable students to develop the ability to create sound generalizations for the purpose of transferring their learning to situations and environments away from the classroom and school. In considering the acquisition of information for its future use, it is the generalization which has far greater usefulness.

It could be argued that most decisions, whether thought of as intellectual or not, are motivated by one's values. An individual's values serve as the reasons for completing or not completing actions and as the basis for rating the worth of something. Such statements as *the rose is a beautiful flower, Doctor Seuss is the best author of children's books,* and *communist sympathizers cannot be trusted* all reflect value-based decisions which, in a given situation, could be the reason for an action taken or a position held. As compared to other areas of knowledge such as facts, generalizations, and concepts, values are much more tentative though they are ever-present. They are grounded in belief systems and personal interpretations, sometimes based on small and, at other times, large amounts of information. For some people, their values are embraced as facts, when, in actuality, they generally lack the proof and verifiability factors needed for them to be facts.

Values held are formed through understanding of or interpretation given to information at any particular point in time. Considering their relationship to classroom instruction, values or value statements are frequently felt to hold greater potential for controversy and less common agreement. Their universal acceptance is something which cannot be expected. With this said, it is recommended that values, or at least the analysis of value statements, be explored as a formal part of instruction when they can serve to provide clarity in the understanding of concepts and generalizations and in how they are different from facts. Taught as ends in themselves, values may lead to a narrow, less-than-objective investigation of knowledge and its use.

The following are examples of factual statements, value statements, and generalizations:

Factual Statements

1. There are 12 inches in a foot.
2. Red is a primary color.
3. George Washington was the first president of the United States.

4. A circle has 360 degrees.
5. Each state is allowed two senators in Congress.

Value Statements

1. Harvard has the best university library.
2. Bill Cosby is the funniest comedian.
3. Jefferson Square is the richest section of town.
4. Philadelphia is the most historic city in the country.
5. The movie *Titanic* is well worth seeing.

Generalizations

1. Changes in climate affect the way people live.
2. Friends generally help one another.
3. New challenges are sometimes confusing.
4. Clubs are made up of common interest areas that tie people together.
5. Domestic animals often have difficulty when put in the wild.

Facts, concepts, and generalizations are important logical tools of language and thought and are the primary basis of communication in the learning process. Nevertheless, it would be an error to assume that all that is taught in schools can neatly be classified as facts, concepts, and generalizations. Many subject matter areas have a skill or performance orientation as well. Understanding and instruction in skill areas, however, are enhanced and many times dependent on an accompanying understanding of related concepts associated with the skill performance.

One of the major reasons for learning concepts is to use them in solving problems. These could be quantitative problems where correct answers are to be anticipated or higher order problems where the logical use of problem solving skills is what is desired, not an accepted, correct answer to the problem. Knowledge of logical problem solving is a skill performance in and of itself. In some subject matter areas, using problem-solving skills is a natural extension of concept development where an important process takes place within the student (Gagne, 1985). The use of problem-solving skills, through concept development, causes the student to become engaged in higher level cognitive skill performances. Skills in the areas of mathematics, reading, and map and graph interpretation, for example, involve the development of an approach to seeking solutions dependent on an understanding of related concepts. While the argument may be made that activities of this type are skill oriented, and indeed they are, their successful attainment is based on a sound understanding of relevant concepts.

Concepts

The distinction to be made in reference to the study of a concept is that a concept *defines*. The verbal expression of a concept is thought of as its *definition* or its *concept rule*. A dictionary might be looked upon as a book of concepts. Bruner, Goodnow, and Austin (1956) offer a helpful interpretation of the term *concept* when they define a concept simply as a *category*. In this view, a concept may be thought of as a basket into which one may place those objects that belong together because of their common attributes (i.e., characteristics). These categories typically include a range of discriminately different items which are treated as if they are the same. For example, many discriminately different wars are placed together to form a category called *civil war*. This is done in accordance with certain relevant criteria. Bruner, Goodnow, and Austin call these relevant criteria the *defining or critical attributes of the category* as they represent the various characteristics of the concept. A particular war can be classified as a *civil war* only by first defining *civil war* according to its attributes and then showing that any war in question has those unique characteristics. Merrill and Tennyson (1977) describe a concept as being a set of specific objects, symbols, or events which are grouped together on the basis of shared characteristics and are referred to by the same name. Students will only have learned a concept at that point in time when they can name the concept and identify its class membership with its defining characteristics.

A concept also is helpfully thought of as a mental construct or representation of a category that allows one to identify examples and nonexamples of the category (Schunk, 2004) or as a mental image held by an individual accounting for a level of familiarity with, or understanding of, objects, events, or the relationships among objects and/or events. Following the mental image idea, one might think of the phrase *in your mind's eye* when considering what is pictured when a concept is brought to mind. For example, when someone says the word "lightening," all who have heard the word or seen lightening have an image form in their minds. Other examples could be "Paris," "urban area," "desert," or "border guard." The examples are endless as the world of concepts is endless. Concepts also may be considered as *hooks* upon which to hang new experiences. When a student is confronted with a novel situation for which there are no existing *hooks*, the student must either force the new information on a present hook which is related in some aspect (assimilate the information) or create a new one (accommodate the information). Concepts, then, serve to help an individual organize knowledge and keep it from becoming unwieldy and dysfunctional. If students do not have the appropriate mental *hooks*, the concept cannot be appropriately communicated and understood. When they do not have the appropriate hook, the teacher needs to help them acquire or develop the hook.

Concepts and Schema Theory

Bartlett (1932, 1958), a British psychologist, is identified as first proposing the concept of schema suggesting that memory takes the form of schema which provides a mental framework for understanding and remembering information. Understanding the concept *schema* will help one better understand how concepts are learned, stored, and used. A schema (pl. schemas or schemata) is an individual's collection of prior knowledge that provides a context for meaningful interpretation of new information (Anderson, 1984). Schemas have been defined as abstract knowledge structures that organize vast amounts of information (Gagne, Yekovich, & Yekovich, 1993) and as cognitive constructs that organize information into meaningful systems (Anderson, 2005; Schunk, 2004). Bruning et al. (2004) identifies schemas as scripts or representations for events that provide plans for action in particular situations, such as a student having a script to prepare for a test. Scripts contain procedural knowledge and often have information about physical features, people, and typical occurrences. As individuals encounter new information, they add this information to their schemas, which are organized into different interrelated categories (Cooper, 2006). It can be seen that, in this way, the words *concept* and *schema* can be used interchangeably.

Schemas are personal and individually organized, e.g., two individuals can have two different schemas for the same information. If new information can be related to existing schemas, using these schemas can help students develop expectations about the nature of the new information, attend to its most important elements, and fill in gaps where information is implied rather than stated explicitly. For this to work optimally, an individual's schema, or concept, for something must be well-organized, allow for information retrieval, and based on accurate information. When it is not, i.e., not well-organized and inaccurate, the new information will itself be poorly received, organized, and perhaps used in an inaccurate way.

Long-term memory has been usefully compared to a library of books or set of file folders. The way students retrieve information is said to be similar to the process they use to locate and check out a book or find a folder. The process of retrieving information from long term memory, however, is not always precise. When a student searches through his or her long-term memory storehouse of information, the student does not always find the book or folder desired, or might find the desired book or folder but discover that some pages are not intact. This is often based on the completeness of the information and/or how the information was filed or stored in the first place.

Anderson (1978, 1977), an educational psychologist, played an important role in introducing schema theory to the field of education. Schema theory is based on the belief that every act of comprehension involves one's knowledge of the world developed up to that point. Schemas provide a form of representation for complex knowledge. This construct, for the first time, offered a principled account of how old knowledge might influence the acquisition of new knowledge. Schema theory lays out a picture of how people organize the truly enormous amount of background knowledge which they accumulate about the world. Such knowledge is organized into mental units, i.e., *schemas*. When people learn, when they build knowledge, they are either creating new schemas, or linking together preexisting schemas in new ways. Schema theory states that, when students reconstruct information, they fit it into information that already exists in their minds. As they attempt to retrieve information from their long-term memory, the searches sometimes are not very exact and they do not always locate precisely what they want. When asked to retrieve information, students often fill in the gaps between their fragmented memories, sometimes not well organized and/or with incorrect information, with a variety of accuracies and inaccuracies. In the end, communication can go forward well or be misdirected, based on what a student has not organized or learned well previously.

Concepts, Schemas, and Learning

What application does memory and schema theory have for communication in the classroom? The answer is quite simple, while in practice, quite complex. Teachers need to teach their students how to store information for efficient and accurate retrieval; they must guide their students in the development of accurate schemas and teach them so that they logically build upon knowledge already gained.

Information that does not accurately fit into a student's existing schema may not be understood correctly. In schema theory, students actively build schemas and revise them in light of new information. Each schema depends on the student's prior experiences and cognitive processes. Most schema theorists hold that there is not just one body of knowledge available to students at any given stage of development, but, a network of situation-specific bodies of knowledge that students apply to specific situations. Situation-specific schemas help to explain the difference between expert and novice interpretation of knowledge. Having more complex and developed schemas in a particular subject area, experts can function better in any given domain than novices with no schema or inadequate schemas to help them interpret new information.

How students acquire knowledge through schema theory is similar to Piaget's model of the process of cognitive development. In this model, (1) through *accretion*, students take in new information and assimilate it into their existing schema without making any changes to the overall schema; (2)

through *tuning*, students realize that their existing schema is inadequate for the new information and modify the existing schema; or, (3) through *restructuring*, students create a new schema to deal with inconsistencies between the old schema and newly acquired information (Driscoll, 1994). Piaget's theory emphasizes the ways that schemas change as children develop and assimilate or accommodate new information. Bartlett's research (1958, 1932) suggests that, not only does information change children's schemas, their schemas may also affect the information that they learn. Students' prior knowledge and expectations may cause them to remember information in a distorted way as it fits into their existing cognitive frameworks (Sternberg & Williams, 2002).

Schemas and Teaching

The most important implication of schema theory in teaching is the role of prior knowledge in processing. When people learn, they are either creating new schemas or linking together preexisting schemas in new ways. For students to effectively process information, their existing schemas related to the new information need to be activated. This can be done by using outlines, organized activities, advance organizers, and meaningful materials such as handouts, guides, specific questions, etc. This activation stimulates prior knowledge and, in turn, students are better able to process the new information and link to it. In reading, for example, Miller (2002, pp. 71–72) notes that readers:

- activate their prior knowledge before, during, and after reading;
- use schema to make connections between the text and their lives, between one text and another, and between the text and the world;
- distinguish between connections that are meaningful and relevant and those that are not;
- build, change, and revise their schema when they encounter new information in the text, engage in conversations with others, and gain personal experience; and
- use their schema to enhance understanding.

Teachers are encouraged to use analogies and comparisons in their teaching in order to draw attention to students' existing schemas and to help them make connections between existing schemas and new information (Armbruster, 1996). Teaching should focus on schema-building strategies, in particular strategies for building functional problem-solving schema, as a foundation for further developing the student's problem solving ability (Price & Driscoll, 1997). Teachers are advised to use familiar examples in their teaching rather than more conventional, abstract information. Instruction can facilitate schema-building by providing students feedback in the form of numerous, fully worked out and explained examples that explicitly guide them in building their own schemas. To assist students in their learning and to capitalize on connecting to a student's prior knowledge, the teacher's materials should be organized according to conventional structures with which students may already be familiar. Teachers also must acknowledge the cultural differences in their students, in particular as these differences impact their students' familiarity with their teaching materials, the examples that they give, and the contexts for learning that they establish in their teaching.

The strength of understanding a concept, or schema, depends upon the number of established relationships the students can see between it and other concepts or schemas. Of great importance for the student is the fact that concepts are really the student's own, somewhat private, mental images generated by thinking about personal experiences. In the communication process, teachers can only utilize available language to attempt to make interpretations of a concept understandable to their students. Whether or not a student exposed to these communication techniques and this language is able to produce an appropriate concept or image is dependent upon many factors. The potential for error or misunderstanding is significant. In some instances the communication of verbal language may be the weakest technique a teacher can use to communicate concepts to some students because what may be effective for one student may not be effective for another (Lewis & Greene, 1982). Most individuals benefit from visual presentations, illustrations, or even demonstrations. Wherever possible, the use of pictures, actual objects representing concepts under study, or hands-on experiences is highly recommended.

Types of Concepts

Concepts have been placed in different categories, typically based upon their comprehension difficulty. As a classroom teacher approaches the decision of which concepts to teach and how, the complexity of the concepts selected will have bearing on how easily students will be able to form the desired understandings.

A popular distinction made in the classification of concepts is the degree to which they are perceived as *concrete* or *abstract*. Concrete concepts are those which may be perceived directly through one of the five senses: taste, smell, sound, touch, and sight. Abstract concepts cannot be perceived through the senses. Concrete concepts are much easier for the teacher to communicate than those which are abstract. For example, it is easier to communicate an image of *apple*, something which can be touched, smelled, tasted, and seen, than it is to provide such an image of *honesty*, which is very

abstract in nature. Consider Figure 3-4 for additional examples of concepts
in the concrete and abstract categories.

Concrete Concepts	Abstract Concepts
1. wagon	1. hope
2. test tube	2. beauty
3. computer monitor	3. sharing
4. kitten	4. peace
5. automobile	5. time

Figure 3-4. Concepts as classified as either concrete or abstract.

Many years ago, Bruner et al. (1956) suggested that, classified according
to their nature, there are three kinds of concepts: the *conjunctive*, the *disjunctive*, and the *relational*. Since various teaching strategies are affected by the
kind of concept being taught, it is helpful for teachers to be able to distinguish among these concept types.

- **Conjunctive** – the simultaneous presence of several critical attributes.
- **Disjunctive** – various sets of alternate attributes.
- **Relational** – shows a connection among defining attributes.

A *conjunctive concept* is a concept that is defined by the simultaneous presence of several critical attributes which are required for the concept to be
complete. Most of the research on the teaching of concepts has dealt with
concepts of this type. A good example of a conjunctive concept is *social class*
when it is defined according to several attributes: a person's occupation,
source of income, neighborhood, and type of housing. Note that a conjunctive concept connects its attributes with the coordinating conjunction *and*.
Conjunctive concepts typically are learned by looking for elements that are
common to several examples. *Mammal, orchestra instrument*, and *cathedral* are
other examples of conjunctive concepts.

A *disjunctive concept*, on the other hand, is a concept defined by various sets
of alternate attributes. A disjunctive concept separates these attributes with
the coordinating conjunction *or*. An example of a disjunctive concept is *citizen*. A citizen may be defined as a person who was born in this country, or
one whose parents were born in this country, or an individual who has
passed certain examinations. Another example of a disjunctive concept
would be a *strike* in baseball. A strike in baseball could be a pitch within a
certain zone, or a pitch that the batter misses, or a pitch that the batter hits
outside the foul line when the count is less than two strikes. Any of these
alternate definitions is acceptable.

The concept *triangle*, which is conjunctive, can be taught by presenting the student with an array of triangles, each one very different from the others, and asking the student to determine what the triangles have in common. It would be a mistake to try to teach a disjunctive concept in this manner. Imagine a baseball coach trying to teach someone foreign to the game an understanding of the activities on a baseball field. The coach might start with an attempt to communicate the concept *strike*. After each strike, the coach could say "that was a strike." If the individual then tried to invent a concept of strike based upon an attribute or set of attributes common to all strikes, failure would likely occur resulting in the feeling that baseball simply was too complicated a game to understand. This kind of frustration also will be created in a student when a teacher attempts to teach disjunctive concepts as if they were conjunctive. The teacher would be better advised to begin by providing the student with a basic definition of the concept or concept rule. This definition would include all of the different instances of the concept which are possible. From this knowledge base, the teacher then could proceed to offer examples of each instance to reinforce the learned definition.

Finally, a *relational concept* is a concept that shows a connection among attributes. A numerical law of physics is one example of a relational concept; for example, *density* is defined as *mass per unit volume*. If one knows the values for two of the attributes, the other may then be computed. Another example of a relational concept is *area of a rectangle*, defined as a relationship between *length of rectangle* and *width of rectangle*. For an understanding of this concept, the student must understand what is meant by the related concepts of *length* and *width*. If either of these concepts is not understood, the relational concept *area of a rectangle* will not be clearly understood either.

COMMUNICATING FOR CONCEPTUAL UNDERSTANDING

Teachers are communicators and their effectiveness rests on how well and what they communicate. Because so much of the teacher's effort in communication involves the teaching of concepts that lead to an understanding of generalizations, special consideration has been given in this section to teaching for conceptual understanding. Additional strategies for the application of these skills will be presented later in the text.

Concept Acquisition

Concepts are largely derived through *inductive reasoning. Induction* is a form of reasoning used to draw a conclusion or make a generalization from specific instances (Borich, 2007). It is the process whereby the student collects an assortment of separate pieces of information and puts them together in a manner which makes them meaningful. When this occurs, the student actually creates a mental image of the concept which synthesizes these pieces of information. The mental image created is what is termed the student's concept of whatever is being investigated. Any new information encountered by the student can result in a revision or expansion of the concept, as was discussed earlier related to developing schema, to make it even more meaningful, and, therefore, better understood (Wiseman, 1975). This revision or expansion is arrived at through a combination of inductive and deductive processes. *Deduction* is reasoning that proceeds from principles or generalizations to their application in specific instances (Borich, 2007). Working definitions of inductive and deductive reasoning have been long accepted as:

- **inductive reasoning** – reasoning from a set of particular points to a general principle
- **deductive reasoning** – reasoning from a general principle to a set of particular points

What actually occurs in most school settings related to concept learning is a process which combines, in some way, both deductive and inductive features of thinking (Carroll, 1970). By providing descriptions and definitions of the concept in question, the teacher uses deductive aspects of thinking. The component parts of a selected definition identify the critical attributes or critical aspects (i.e., characteristics) of the concept necessary for its understanding. By citing numerous positive and negative instances of the concept, in contrast, the teacher uses inductive aspects of thinking. Teachers should be mindful that concept learning is facilitated more by the use of positive rather than negative instances, although both are helpful and can be necessary to develop the concept completely for instruction and student understanding. In classroom practice, the student is frequently provided a verbal presentation of the concept. This often involves the stating of a concept rule or definition – a deductive process. The student then is assisted in understanding the concept by learning to make correct identifications of positive and negative instances of it – an inductive process. The ultimate value of formal inductive procedures in concept acquisition is in providing students with the opportunity to test their understanding of the concept, its definition, and description in new situations and applications.

Borich (2007, p. 282) identifies the following comparison of steps in inductive and deductive teaching.

Teaching Inductively	**Teaching Deductively**
1. Teacher presents specific data from which a generalization is to be drawn.	1. Teacher introduces the generalization to be learned.
2. Each student is allowed uninterrupted time to observe or study the data that illustrates the generalization.	2. Teacher reviews the task-relevant prior facts, rules, and action sequences needed to form the generalization.
3. Students are shown additional examples and then nonexamples containing the generalization.	3. Students raise a question, pose an hypothesis, or make a prediction thought to be contained in the generalization.
4. Student attention is guided first to the critical (relevant) aspects of the data containing the generalization and then to its noncritical (irrelevant) aspects.	4. Data, events, materials, or objects are gathered and observed to test prediction.
5. A generalization is made that can distinguish the examples from nonexamples.	5. Results of the test are analyzed and a conclusion is made as to whether the prediction is supported by the data, events, materials, or objects that were observed.
	6. The starting generalization is refined or revised in accordance with the observations.

A Systematic Approach to Concept Instruction

Assume that the teacher plans to teach a middle school social studies unit on the topic *war*. The teacher already has decided that one of the broad goals of the instruction will be to: *develop an understanding of the different types of wars and their effects.* The teacher also has tentatively planned to teach a lesson on *civil war* with the following objectives. The student will be able to:

1. after studying several examples, define *civil war* using at least two characteristics of the concept.
2. given a short history of the Vietnam conflict, explain in writing why this was or was not a civil war citing two reasons for the decision made.

Though these objectives include many concepts beyond the concept *civil war*, *civil war* is the significant concept that the teacher wishes to teach. How should the teacher proceed in order to teach the concept *civil war*? As with any lesson, the communication of this concept should be approached formally and systematically. Confusion should not arise out of the selection of awkward or inappropriate teaching procedures. Procedures for instruction should be chosen with the difficulty of the concept and intellectual sophistication and background of the students in mind. During the instructional planning and development stage of the lesson it is recommended that the teacher proceed as outlined in Figure 3-5.

Instructional Planning and Development Stage

1. Analyze and clearly define the concept.

2. Plan the lesson procedures and materials portion to include:

   • set induction,
   • presentation of examples and nonexamples,
   • use of cues, questions, and further directions, and
   • assessment of minimal level concept mastery.

3. Plan the evaluation portion of the lesson to include:

   • assessment of advanced levels of concept mastery.

Figure 3-5. A systematic approach to concept instruction (adapted from Martorella, 1986).

As further preparation for instruction, a working knowledge of the following concept-related terminology will be helpful.

- **Concept Rule:** the basic, verbalized definition of the concept.
- **Critical Attribute:** an essential, defining characteristic of the concept.
- **Noncritical Attribute:** a defining characteristic often associated with the concept but not really necessary to its understanding.
- **Example:** positive instance of the concept.
- **Nonexample:** negative or non-instance of the concept.
- **Cues:** suggestions, directed thoughts, or hints for the student to consider as the concept is being communicated.

Analyzing and Defining the Concept

The teacher will carry out a number of important tasks when preparing for instruction. As a beginning point, the teacher must decide (1) whether or not the concept is important enough to even be taught; (2) if the concept is best learned through formal, instructional means; and (3) if there is sufficient agreement on the critical attributes of the concept to make its communication clear. In this initial phase, the teacher should analyze the appropriateness of the concept and its level of complexity for the students. Besides assessing the appropriateness or relevance of the concept for instruction, the teacher also should analyze the concept in order to help organize the basic elements of the lesson. In this activity, certain questions need to be asked and answered. For example:

- What is the concept rule or definition to be communicated?
- What are the important critical and noncritical attributes of the concept?
- What examples and nonexamples of the concept will be included to enhance communication?
- What are some basic questions or cues which may be used in the lesson to facilitate concept understanding?
- What will the student need to be able to know or do to demonstrate an acceptable understanding of the concept?

Figure 3-6 presents the results of an analysis of the concept civil war against these questions. This figure helps to illustrate how helpful a concept analysis can be in lesson planning.

	Concept: Civil War
Concept Rule or Definition:	A civil war is a war between different sections or factions of the same country.
Critical Attributes:	1. Occurs within a country 2. Participants are citizens of the same country 3. Begins with an uprising against some form of government
Non-Critical Attributes:	1. Length 2. Nation involved 3. Point in history 4. Cost 5. Historical significance 6. Numbers involved
Examples:	1. U.S. Civil War 2. French Revolution 3. Bolshevik Revolution 4. War of the Roses
Nonexample:	1. World War I 2. World War II 3. Spanish-American War 4. War of 1812

Continued on next page

Questions and Cues: 1. What might cause one group of citizens
                              to conflict with another?
                           2. Was the Korean conflict a civil war?
                           3. What does the word *civil* mean?
                           4. How can civil wars be resolved?
                           5. Think about inter-country and intra-country
                              conflict.
                           6. Describe how citizens might feel fighting one
                              another.

Figure 3-6. Analysis of the concept: *Civil war.*

Teaching the Concept

As with any type of instruction, the teaching of a concept should have an eye-catching, motivational beginning. The introduction (1) should present the concept, (2) include its rule or definition, and (3) set the stage for the lesson to follow. The beginning of the instructional sequence might include a short story or a description of a concept-related experience. It also could contain a series of questions to stimulate thinking on the part of the students directed toward an investigation of the concept. This part of the lesson is sometimes referred to as the lesson's *set induction* or *anticipatory set.* The set induction occurs early in the lesson wherein a special *set* is established on which the remainder of the lesson will build. The set induction establishes the foundation for the lesson and pulls together a common student outlook for the concept being studied. For the concept *civil war*, the following introductory questions could be helpful as a part of the lesson's set induction.

- Have any of you ever studied wars in other classes?
- What do you think of when you hear the term civil war?
- Did any of your ancestors or relatives fight in a civil war? Which war?
- Why do you think they fought in this war?

One common element in concept instruction is the presence of examples and nonexamples of the concept. Such examples and nonexamples also are referred to as positive and negative instances of the concept. Illustrations in the lesson which portray the concept are called positive instances; those which do not are called negative instances. Where possible, it is recommended that all examples and nonexamples, positive or negative instances, be presented simultaneously. In this way, where such experiences are presented in close succession or proximity to one another, the student can quickly compare or discriminate between/among all of the cases. If the concept is understood, the student should be able to point to examples in new and novel situations. The student also should be able to identify instances which do not represent the concept.

Returning to the concept *civil war*, the teacher might present the examples and nonexamples listed in Figure 3-6 in close succession and in as short a time period as possible. As these instances are presented, the student will develop the ability to discriminate between that which is defined as *civil war* and that which is not.

Throughout the lesson, the teacher should draw close attention to the finer differences or distinctions among the examples used. An understanding only of gross differences is not sufficient. In making reference to such differences, the teacher should have the students focus on the critical as well as the non-critical attributes of the concept. The teacher can do this by asking questions to determine the degree to which the students are advancing and, at the same time, encourage them to ask questions.

In assessing for in-depth levels of concept formation, the teacher might seek answers to the following questions. This approach recognizes an increasingly complex understanding of concept acquisition. Are the students able to:

- state the meaning of the concept in their own words?
- identify both critical and noncritical attributes of the concept?
- separate positive instances of the concept from negative instances?
- relate the newly acquired concept to other concepts?
- use the concept in a novel way?

If the answers to these questions are *yes*, the teacher may conclude that the concept has been taught successfully. Explaining the meaning of something in one's own words, identifying examples and nonexamples, critical and noncritical attributes, relating the concept to other concepts, and actually using the concept in a novel way point to a high level of learning. Chapter 2 provides a discussion of the development of teaching objectives, planning of instructional procedures, and the application of assessment procedures to determine student progress toward stated learning outcomes.

Chapter 4

THE TEACHER AS
AN EFFECTIVE PERFORMER

This chapter is dedicated to an examination of the teaching process. Factors will be discussed that are pertinent to all instruction regardless of grade level or content. It is important to think of the effective teacher as someone who functions as a decision maker in a learning environment that is responsive to the interests, needs, and abilities of all students. Effective teachers constantly assess both instructional behaviors and learning behaviors to determine what changes, if any, need to be made to maximize student learning. Effective teaching is an interaction of (1) student developmental levels, interests, and abilities to learn and (2) the teacher's ability to manage the classroom environment.

Determining those behaviors which lead to effective classroom instruction is difficult and has occupied a significant amount of educational research for some time. This chapter focuses on teacher performance in the complex instructional environment and examines those teacher behaviors which should be considered in effectively addressing the intricate social system of the classroom. Such a review of the instructional environment will help put the need for appropriate teacher skills and performances in their proper perspective across subject matter areas and grade levels. After studying this chapter, you will learn more about the following topics:

1. positive learning environments,
2. seven generic characteristics of effective instruction,
3. a classification of questions according to four cognitive levels, and
4. guidelines for better classroom questioning practices.

CREATING POSITIVE LEARNING ENVIRONMENTS

Any teacher entering the classroom for the first time will be confronted with decisions to make concerning just what type of teaching-leadership role is most effective. How should teachers lead students to accomplish stated objectives? Which teaching style is best? What is the preferred relationship of the teacher to the students? In the end, of course, these decisions will need to be made on an individual basis. What suits one teacher, student, or group of students may not suit another. Nevertheless, there is information available that relates to these questions that you should consider in determining your classroom teaching and leadership behavior. This information also lends assistance in dealing with the overall issue of student involvement in the learning process. To facilitate the development of a productive teaching-learning environment, teachers must know their students very, very well.

Knowing the Students

In order to motivate and instruct students effectively, teachers will first need to know their students as individuals. Classrooms today tend to be very diverse in terms of the backgrounds and characteristics of students. Students in a single class may come from a variety of ethnic and racial backgrounds, may have differing learning preferences, may have special learning needs that require accommodations, and may represent a variety of socioeconomic groups.

One major educational issue that has arisen over the last twenty years in the American educational system is the question of how best to educate students who use English as a second language (ESOL learners). In the 1950s, Noam Chomsky's (1957) landmark research demonstrated to us that there exists an important link between language and the human mind. In the late 1970s, linguistic research began focusing more on the social and pragmatic issues associated with literacy education in a multicultural/bilingual society (Minami & Ovando, 2004). Although America has always been diverse, the increase in immigration over the last several decades has resulted in many students coming to our schools who are ESOL learners. Gumperz (1996) and others believe that many teachers are unprepared to work with ESOL learners and urges all teachers to learn more about the cultural backgrounds of their students. Gilzow (2001) feels that progress is being made in addressing the needs of ESOL students as demonstrated in the increase of such educational initiatives as foreign language instruction in elementary schools. However, the fact remains that middle class teachers and students are speaking and writing with a language system very different from the one used in homes of many Latino, African American, and Native American students coming from lower socioeconomic status segments of our society. This mismatch between the language used in homes and schools has put many students at an educational disadvantage in terms of success in the school system as well as, later on, in the job market.

Teachers today will teach in classrooms with a vast diversity of students: students of many races, ethnic groups, and levels of social status. In our schools, certain groups of students tend to do less well than others on academic endeavors and standardized tests. Students of poverty, African American males, ESOL students, and students needing special learning accommodations are a few such students who frequently have difficulty realizing success. In order to help all students achieve their full potentials, teachers need to understand their students' cultural and socioeconomic backgrounds in order to better guide their educational experiences.

Leadership Styles

There is little doubt that the image that teachers project as instructional leaders influences what types of success may be expected. Different behaviors and attitudes send different messages to students which, in turn, help to determine outcomes following the teaching process. These teacher behaviors create an image that is often referred to as *teaching style*. Since the teacher is the leader of the learning group, one may conclude that a teaching style, in reality, also represents the teacher's leadership style. Because of the impact that a teacher's leadership style has on student accomplishments, knowledge of style as it relates to outcomes is essential. Glasser (1993) states that teachers must make the difficult adjustment from bossing to leading in order to promote optimal student learning. The skill in leading people develops over time as a result of the decisions we make about classroom events and about ourselves in relationship to them. William James observed that teachers gain confidence as soon as they believe that a particular method has theory as well as practice behind it (Heck & Williams, 1984).

A popular comparison of leadership styles is the three-category system which includes the *authoritarian, laissez-faire,* and *authoritative* styles. In order to reach a logical conclusion concerning (1) one's most preferred style, (2) the question of student involvement in learning, and (3) student response to various leadership styles, it is helpful to investigate what the different styles mean in relation to student development, both personal and intellectual.

The authoritarian style of leadership is noted for its firmness of control. Authoritarian teachers demonstrate leadership not only by doing the planning and issuing class directives but by making all significant decisions in the classroom; they might well be considered as analogous to the captain of the ship. In the authoritarian classroom, the teacher acts primarily as the active point of instruction and sees students as passive receivers of information. Consider the following example:

Mrs. Peabody, a second grade teacher, always follows a definite routine for beginning class. At the moment the bell rings, she positions herself behind the desk and stares at the students until they become quiet and ready for instruction. She expects that students will have a pencil and paper ready as she begins the morning's lesson. She typically writes an outline of the day's activities on the chalkboard. Students know what they are to read, what worksheets to complete, and where finished assignments go. Mrs. Peabody believes that students need structure. Moreover, students know that any deviation from this plan results in punishments. She has taught them well that she is the teacher and they are the students; her job is to know the subject and theirs' is to learn it as she prescribes. She is conscious of her position as leader in the classroom and strives to be visible to all students at all times. The front of the room is her territory, and she does not expect students to approach her desk. On the other hand, she frequently stands behind it. Should a student need help, the student is expected to raise his or her hand. It is rare that she sits at a student desk or kneels beside a child.

Mrs. Peabody's classroom in many ways is a traditional classroom. She is well mannered and expects her students to be also. In short, she likes the regularity of a highly structured curriculum. She has relatively few discipline problems since students know exactly what is expected of them. However, it is also true that she does not encourage genuine inquiry, self-motivation, and love of learning. Students may behave but the love of learning is missing. Indeed, in Mrs. Peabody's classroom students are often bored because of the rigid nature of her class routine and the fact that they do not have an opportunity to actively participate and feel genuinely appreciated.

Mrs. Peabody is a good example of the distinction between efficient and effective. She is efficient in maintaining class order and in presenting the material she selects, but she is not effective in developing important, positive attitudes toward learning and a sense of autonomy and self-worth in her students. Difficulties with Mrs. Peabody's type of leadership have been recognized for quite some time. An early study by White and Lippitt (1960) concerning this style of instruction found that students in authoritarian groups tended to be apathetic, dependent, and unable to show serious initiative for self-directed work. When the teacher left the room very little was accomplished. Students being instructed under this leadership style tended, on occasion, to display hostile behaviors toward fellow class members. While aggressive behaviors were evidenced in this manner toward classmates, little open resentment was shown toward the authoritarian leader. More recent studies of group leadership have produced similar results (Woolfolk, 2008).

The laissez-faire teacher is found at the opposite end of the continuum from the authoritarian. Teachers operating with this style of instruction are really not committed to getting involved. Students are frequently left on their own to make their own decisions. The laissez-faire teacher tends to avoid giving directions, thoroughly planning lessons, and, for all practical purposes, does not lead at all. Consider the case of Mr. Pinkerton.

> Working in a high school, Mr. Pinkerton teaches ninth and tenth grade English. Mr. Pinkerton, unlike Mrs. Peabody, is often not even in the room when it is time to begin class. Upon arrival, he usually spends considerable time chatting with two or three students near the front of the room while other students talk among themselves. When his class finally does begin, he usually has to ask the students to identify which page of the textbook the class is to study next. His opening remark is often the question: "What do we do today, group?" Mr. Pinkerton's philosophy is that students must be given freedom to express their inborn leadership skills and not be dominated by the teacher. He follows the text almost exclusively because he feels that since someone smarter than he went to so much trouble to write it, he does not need to plan his lessons but, instead, merely follow the book. His class often ends in the middle of a topic and, as they are leaving, the students yell out questions concerning the intent of the next assignment. He often replies with, "Oh, just keep reading ahead."

Students under Mr. Pinkerton's laissez-faire leadership style seem to get along better than those enduring Mrs. Peabody's authoritarian style. Left on their own, Mr. Pinkerton's students will even complete some instructional tasks. As far as personal development, they tend to be insecure, continually seeking assistance from Mr. Pinkerton or some other leader figure. And, their learning is haphazard and far from optimal.

In authoritative leadership situations, the teacher becomes a group leader rather than the *ship's captain*, as was noted in the authoritarian style of teaching. The primary purpose of teaching as seen by those teachers employing this style of leadership is to guide students in the pursuit of investigations in specified content areas. While the teacher is still the expert in relation to knowledge of the subject matter in question, student ideas, recommendations, and input play a greater role as well. The classroom is arranged so that students may become active participants rather than passive recipients in the learning process. The students, as well as the teacher, play a major role in what takes place in the classroom. Students come to believe that they have some control over their successes, that they can deal with future challenges, and possess the motivation to deal with difficulties when they arise. For an example of how this may be done, consider Mrs. Nakato's class:

> Mrs. Nakato's kindergarten class routines vary considerably from day to day. She definitely believes in structuring class activities, but her entire

approach is characterized by flexibility and concern for helping the students learn. She strongly believes that her job is to teach students – not subject matter; however, she expects her students to achieve high levels of content mastery. On many topics students have a choice of ways in which they may actively participate because Mrs. Nakato uses a variety of activities and strategies to accomplish the objectives. Her students even have some input into the selection of topics to be considered through the use of individual projects. Difficult topics are dealt with by careful planning which helps her to prepare for students' frustrations and mistakes. Use of group work and individualized instruction addresses students' problems. Students in Mrs. Nakato's class experience instruction in a variety of organizational patterns, individual, small group, and large group, and feel free to communicate within and among groups as necessary. There are ample opportunities for discussion and solution of personal dilemmas.

Unlike Mrs. Peabody, Mrs. Nakato does not fear loss of classroom control during group work because she realizes that there are several kinds of classroom noise (e.g., productive noise and disruptive noise). Through her enthusiasm, genuine interest in their progress, and keen understanding of performance tasks, she has taught the students well that learning can be interesting and even fun. Mrs. Nakato's students feel free to discuss issues or problems and to ask questions. If she cannot answer a question fully, she directs the students to other sources of information available within the classroom and outside the school setting if needed. She does not consider herself the only source of knowledge, nor does she feel that all tasks have immediate solutions.

Notice that the authoritative style is not a democracy (all decisions are not made by majority vote). However, students working with Mrs. Nakato are more actively engaged in their own learning and experience feelings of personal control rather than teacher domination. Though the authoritative style is not a democracy, democratic principles are often promulgated and encouraged. The descriptors *facilitator* and *learner* are two terms that are often used to describe participation in an authoritative classroom (Orlich et al., 1990). Of the three styles outlined, the authoritative is preferable to produce a classroom of active students who are more likely to take responsibility for their learning. When students are given the opportunity to take control of their learning without coercion, with quality tasks to complete and proper guidance by the teacher, student motivation increases, and students work harder on the products they produce (Glasser, 1993, 1992).

The general conclusion is simple yet powerful. Students who have the opportunity to be a part of their own learning in an active decision-making sense are going to learn more and enjoy school more than when they are not able to become an important part of this process. Although much research supports the authoritative, *student-centered classroom* in theory, its application has not been fully adopted in many classrooms. Very few people would argue against the importance of the teacher being able to deliver a motivating, well-organized lecture or presentation, conduct demonstrations or guide student recitations, and these are prime strategies utilized in the *teacher-centered approach* to instruction. Yet, as an overall teaching style in elementary, middle, and secondary classrooms, the student-centered approach to instruction is considered preferable in the majority of teaching situations.

GENERIC CHARACTERISTICS OF EFFECTIVE LESSONS

Educational research has identified a number of lesson characteristics common to effective classroom instruction. While a listing of such characteristics is not intended to be exhaustive, many of the qualities that are frequently found in lessons by successful teachers can be enumerated. Though these generic characteristics of effective lessons are not necessarily found in every lesson, a master teacher has the ability to develop lessons that utilize all of these performance behaviors. The task becomes one of identifying those behaviors that most agree should be included, not necessarily listing all of the characteristics found in everyone's description of a model lesson. Given this premise, the following characteristics are likely to be found on almost any educator's list. Lessons should:

- be *appropriate* to the *developmental level* of the students,
- *address* the *stated objectives* in the lesson,
- have a *motivational aspect* which stimulates the students' desire to attend to the lesson,
- be organized around *a variety of grouping or organizational structures* within the classroom in order to accommodate the students' styles, rates, and abilities,
- have opportunities for all *students to become actively involved* in meaningful learning activities,
- allow students to *apply what they have learned*, and
- be characterized by an ongoing *monitoring of students' progress* with *feedback provided* on a consistent basis.

Appropriate Developmental Level

The concept of grade level often causes misunderstanding when PK–12 teachers prepare for classroom instruction. Historically, the concept grade level has had greater meaning in the elementary grades where self-contained classroom instruction has been the norm. Though students and parents often use the term *grade level*, the grade in which a student is classified in many cases has little meaning in terms of ensuring a distinct level of student ability which often adds a level of complexity in terms of planning for and delivering instruction. Some people too frequently assume that all students at a given grade level are developmentally equal. This antiquated view of human growth and development is inconsistent with the reality of today's classroom. Students at a given chronological age usually will vary substantially in their physical, emotional, social, and intellectual development. For example, students who are highly developed intellectually may be far less developed than their classmates (i.e., age-mates) emotionally. The work of Maslow (1970, 1968) in identifying student needs reinforces this point well. If students' needs are not satisfied, tension is created. This tension may cause students to attempt to achieve goals or to withdraw from the situation to remove the tension. If the tension is too great, students may retreat from the situation or act out against it. If teachers through their behavior create tension, it is critical that they understand the impact of their actions and the resulting impact on students. What causes tension for one student may not for another.

It is essential for teachers to understand the characteristics common to students at a given grade level. And yet, they should be cautious not to allow this information to be used to stereotype students in terms of expectations. Such information should be used as a beginning, diagnostic point for the analysis of individual student needs. The determination of a student's developmental level typically might begin by a consideration of age-group characteristics. Even though there may be great developmental variance within individuals in an age group, there also exists a similarity among students of the same age. Most would agree that the interests, attitudes, habits, and skills of a seven-year-old are usually quite different from those of a fourteen-year-old. However, the same variation can exist between students of the same chronological age. Teachers need to be informed as to the differing interests and characteristics among their students and approach what might be similar topics with different strategies and expectations dependent on the student group. Instruction in curriculum areas such as death education, sex education, and character education, to name obvious examples, must be sensitive to the maturational levels of the students. The selection of strategies for areas such as these should be approached with care and caution. One should not approach the topic of *human reproduction* with eight-year-olds, for example, in the same manner that one would approach the same topic with biologically mature adolescents. Frankly, such care also should be given when addressing the more traditional or core teaching areas of math, science, English, and social studies. As important as age is in helping a teacher determine appropriate levels of subject matter interest and difficulty, psychologists such as J. McVicker Hunt (1964) have also stressed the impact of environmental factors on the developmental process. No teacher can assume that all students in a given group are ready for the same instructional strategies simply because they are all of approximately the same age.

The monumental problem that the classroom teacher faces in seeking to connect material to be learned to student developmental level has been popularly referred to as the *problem of the match* (Hunt, 1961). Given the complexity of the classroom and the society at large, there simply is no one good way to determine a student's developmental level against the myriad of knowledge and skill areas to be addressed. Further, it also is not appropriate to conclude that students at a particular developmental level will perform all of the tasks at that level equally well. Likewise, students will be at different developmental levels in different content areas (Klausmeier, 1988; Klausmeier & Sipple, 1982). Considering this complexity, teachers are advised to use information on child development in a flexible manner when designing instructional experiences and when engaging students in learning tasks. Berlinger and Yates (1993) report that it is appropriate to utilize instructional activities which are within a student's range of capabilities, acknowledging that such a range may be quite broad and could be different for various subject matter areas. In many cases determining the range of a student's capabilities may, in the end, be the result of informed trial and error and nothing more (Ross, Bondy, & Kyle, 1993).

This range of a student's capabilities was identified by the famous Russian psychologist Lev Vygotsky (1962) as the *Zone of Proximal Development*. The zone of proximal development, introduced in Chapter 1, is the way Vygotsky conceptualized the relationship between learning and development. Vygotsky used the term zone because he saw development as a continuum of behaviors or degrees of maturation (Bedrova & Leong, 1996). The word *proximal* means the zone has boundaries that are formed by behaviors that have not yet developed but will soon develop. When providing developmentally appropriate instruction, the teacher's job is to analyze each student's developmental zone to determine what behaviors (skills) form its boundaries and instruct the student in ways that allow for the mastery of those skills forming the boundary. It should be remembered that all students have different zones for different content areas. After determining what skills need to be taught, the teacher provides the students with necessary help that enables each student to perform at a higher level. As the student takes on more of the responsibility for performing the learning task, the teacher can gradually decrease the amount of help provided. This process of providing help and gradually decreasing it as the student begins to function at a higher level is referred to as *scaffolding* within the zone of proximal development (Wood, Bruner, & Ross, 1976). At the beginning of the scaffolding process, the teacher provides greater amounts of help. Eventually, students take on more responsibility for their performance until all scaffolding can be removed. See the following example of a teacher working with a non-reader.

> The teacher reads an enjoyable passage to the student. The teacher uses a finger to point to each word as it is read. After reading the passage several times, the teacher leaves out a word and asks the student to provide the missing word. This process continues with the teacher leaving out more and more words until the student can finally read the passage without help.

However, it must be recognized that a key to the success of this scaffolding procedure is that the student must be interested (i.e., motivated) in learning the task.

It is important to note the aforementioned cautionary points when seeking to apply any theoretical model to the challenge of implementing developmentally appropriate instruction. Piaget (1970), one of the most highly recognized theorists in the area of intellectual development, described in detail the factors that he recognized as determiners of cognitive development and how these factors might apply to the learning process. Knowledge of these factors is helpful to understand more fully the individual developmental differences of a group of students and how best to teach them at a developmentally appropriate level.

Piaget agreed with the traditional maturationists that biological maturation is a determiner of a student's cognitive development. His stages of cognitive development, sensorimotor (ages 0–2), preoperational (ages 2–7), concrete operational (ages 7–11), and formal operational (age 11–adult), are loosely associated with identified age spans. Piaget concluded that children of given age groups are very similar with respect to the way they function when performing certain cognitive tasks. Nevertheless, it is important to keep in mind that Piaget discussed these stages as being several years in duration. He did not suggest that cognitive levels change on a yearly or specifically predetermined basis.

In developing his theory, Piaget also stressed the importance of life experiences in the development of cognitive abilities. Experiences that students have will aid them in cognitive development to the degree that these experiences are rich in variety and easily understood. To the point that students have experiences explained in language that is easily understood, these experiences will be meaningful. It was also Piaget's position that intellectual development is directly related to the amount of oral conversation in which students engage. Not only should students be encouraged to discuss activities, the teacher must also attempt to describe these activities in everyday language that stimulates thinking and furthers understanding.

Piaget stated that students need to expand their conceptual structures in order to develop their cognitive abilities. This expansion takes place when the student has the opportunity to fit, or adapt, new information related to a concept, through accommodation (adjusting schemas to fit new information and experiences) or assimilation (incorporating new information within existing knowledge or schemas), or when the student discovers new characteristics of a concept which must, in some way, alter the existing pattern before it will neatly fit into an existing conceptual structure. (Refer to Chapter 3 for a detailed discussion of the nature of a concept.)

After you as the teacher, through informed observation and through some formal data gathering means, begin to determine the developmental level of your students, it only then will become possible to adjust the curriculum and instruction in such a way as to provide each student with greater opportunities for success. Unfortunately, even after exhaustive diagnosis and preparation, it may still be difficult for even the best diagnostician to accurately match all materials and instruction to the developmental level of a given student guaranteeing both initial and continued success. For those teachers interested in researching best practices based on developmental characteristics of children from birth to age eight, we recommend the careful study of *Developmental Practices in Early Childhood Programs* developed by the National Association for the Education of Young Children (NAEYC) (Bredekamp & Copple, 1997). For those interested in exploring the developmental characteristics and needs of students from ten years of age to early adolescence, we recommend the study of the Carnegie Corporation's *Great Transitions: Preparing Adolescents for a New Century* (Carnegie Council On Adolescent Development, 1995).

The following basic guidelines have been identified to assist teachers in providing instruction appropriate to each student's developmental level.

1. Concepts are developed more easily from the concrete to the abstract. As a result, some students who have difficulty learning an abstraction from a textbook might readily understand the same material when presented in the form of a classroom demonstration.
2. When it is necessary to present certain material in a vicarious manner (e.g., through the use of books, tapes, or DVDs), it often will be necessary to precede the presentation of materials with certain direct, more concrete experiences. Some students may find a unit of instruction more meaningful if it is introduced with such activities as field trips, visits from community experts, or visual presentations. Some may actually need to do the demonstration themselves before fully grasping the concept.
3. The ability of students to use and understand language is central to their developmental level. The length and complexity of sentences are often factors that interfere with student understanding of the directions that they receive from their teachers. Furthermore, some

students function at a developmental level which necessitates their receiving ongoing verbal feedback while they are at work; receiving the teacher's simple explanation will help such students form more complete concepts. It is reasonable to suggest that many students, who have been previously thought of as deficient in their mental abilities, are actually able to learn but unable to understand the language used in schools and classrooms.

4. Another component of a student's developmental maturity is the degree to which it is possible to attend to a learning task over time. This component is usually described as a student's attention span. It is clear that all students do not have the same ability to attend to a learning task for extended periods of time. If a teacher fails to adjust instruction to a student's ability to stay on task, academic difficulty is quite predictable for a student with a short attention span.

5. Finally, because of student differences in emotional development, teachers must pace learning experiences in such a way as to ensure that all students will experience some level of satisfaction in the classroom environment. If the teacher allows too many activities to occur simultaneously for an individual student, the student may become overstimulated resulting in mental confusion and low performance. Another outcome could be that the student becomes emotionally unable to adjust to the dynamics of the environment. This lack of adjustment could cause aggressive behavior problems or withdrawal. The teacher must be aware that some students can become overstimulated and receive inappropriate kinds of reinforcement from the same learning environment which is quite satisfying to other students. Educational research (Wiseman & Hunt, 2008) supports the view that the factors of success and appropriate challenge are key to student motivation. To be motivated, students must have a realistic opportunity for success and that success must be associated with meaningful challenge. Success on tasks that have little or no challenge will not enhance student motivation. Likewise, placing students into learning situations that are unrealistically difficult or which outstrip their abilities will not result in a foundation of motivation either.

Address Stated Objectives

A major emphasis of this text is placed on the importance of using objectives as the foundation of and guide to instruction ensuring that instruction is purposefully designed in order to help students reach the desired learning outcome(s). Teachers who develop lessons without being guided by pre-identified, specific learning outcomes are commonly guilty of *teaching books or sub-*

jects instead of students. Such teachers are, in fact, focusing on the subject matter, not on the students. Before any instruction takes place, the way or ways the lesson is going to benefit the students as they strive to learn should be determined. Chapter 2 provides a detailed overview of objective-driven instruction. As previously noted, state and district content standards guides provide instructional objectives at all grade levels.

Regardless of whether a teacher is teaching the whole class, a small group, or one student an objective with clear learning outcomes needs to guide instruction. During the planning of any lesson, more than one objective may be identified per instructional group. Nevertheless, it is not unusual for the teacher to discover that all objectives listed cannot be addressed in just one lesson. Rather than force something that does not really fit, this simply means that the remaining objectives should be revisited and perhaps addressed in a future instructional period. Because of the need to maintain flexibility in teaching, determined often by individual student needs, talents, and interests, teachers should not force the addressing of all planned objectives in every lesson if they are not naturally accommodated there. To illustrate this point, consider the following objectives related to the study of the concept *democracy*. The student will be able to:

1. from memory, define the terms *republic, representation, democracy, government, constitution*, and *nondemocratic state*,
2. given two different countries, one representing a democratic and one representing a nondemocratic state, compare and contrast the countries in a paragraph discussion pointing out no fewer than three differences,
3. given three separate descriptions of governmental systems, identify the type of governmental structure utilized by each using no fewer than two pieces of supporting evidence for each identification, and
4. using any desired references, create a hypothetical country to include the following: population, geographic region, technological orientation, agricultural orientation, and governmental system using a democratic model.

While all of these objectives may be relevant as desired learning outcomes related to the study of the concept *democracy*, all could not be appropriately addressed in only one or even two class sessions. Even as this is the case, all instruction should be targeted toward at least one or a combination of these stated objectives. If this is not the case, the teacher should adjust the instructional activity to make it relevant to the list of identified objectives. The primary points being made as related to objective-driven instruction are these:

• instruction should not take place without a prior identification of stated objectives or a destination to be reached at the end of the instructional experience;

- instruction observed should be characterized by a clear link between the stated objectives and the instructional activity of the teacher; and
- ultimately, assessment which occurs following instruction should be based on objectives which were established and communicated to students before the start of the instructional sequence.

The Motivational Aspect

A well-planned lesson at any grade level will not be effective if students do not attend to the instruction being provided. Teachers often plan well and present the material to the students in a well-organized format only to have students fail to respond positively because they do not find the lesson interesting. Most teachers feel that students share some responsibility for their own learning, and this is certainly a legitimate position. However, teachers have the greater responsibility to make their lessons interesting and motivating to the degree that students feel excited about learning and are connected to it. Rinne (1998) observes that almost all content or subject matter has the potential to interest students if the teacher has the ability to use a variety of strategies or approaches to relate what is being studied to the students' interests. In order to be effective, teachers must be able to motivate their students by stimulating their interest. This is an essential of best practice in effective instruction.

To help ensure this, instruction should include a communication of the lesson's rationale which provides the teacher with an opportunity to stimulate the group's interest in the subject area. The rationale also serves as a means to stimulate student interest by helping students identify more closely with the reason for and importance of the learning activity. Far too often students are asked, or told, to proceed through learning activities without ever being informed of the value of the study to either their daily lives or their futures. An understanding of the rationale for instruction, or the reason for spending time in the selected area of study, helps assist students in identifying and accepting the importance of the content. Students who see the relevance of study in a particular area will approach their experiences in the classroom with greater energy and positive determination than those who do not see this importance. Regardless of the grade level, this is a most important consideration.

Good and Brophy (2003) state that modeling enthusiasm is a skill necessary for all teachers regardless of the age of their students. Students tend to respond positively to an enthusiastic teacher and become interested in the same things that interest their teacher. As introduced in Chapter 1, enthusiasm is conveyed through the display of a genuine interest in the subject matter and through both vigor and dynamic behavior. Effective teachers, through their enthusiasm, project that they enjoy their work. Rosenshine (1970) reports that enthusiastic teaching promotes greater academic gains for students. This has obvious implications. Teachers who desire to have high-achieving students must make an effort to capture their interest even before instruction begins. Students are not likely to be motivated to learn in a dry, stale classroom with a teacher who seemingly would rather be doing something else.

Probably no other part of the lesson is as important as the lesson's introduction because it is at this point that the teacher is most concerned with establishing high student motivation. If students are not motivated to attend at the beginning of the lesson, it may be difficult for interest to be captured as the instructional sequence develops. Because of this, teachers are advised to plan what may be referred to as *attention grabbers* at the introduction of a lesson for the purpose of stimulating student interest. See Figure 4-1 for examples of several possible attention grabbers. During the course of a lesson, student interest may wane. If this occurs, it will be necessary to implement new motivational strategies to ensure student interest throughout the rest of the instructional period. Teacher dynamics is the key factor in any motivational strategy; teachers can move, touch, show surprise, inflect their voices, and be dramatic. It often has been suggested that teachers need an actor's flare to be successful; there needs to be a bit of Tom Sawyer in all teachers.

Attention-Grabbers

The teacher should:

- use carefully planned introductory questions,
- provide a dramatic demonstration,
- use role playing by the teacher,
- show slides without accompanying narration, and occasionally ask students to guess what the slides are about,
- pose an unpopular argument or point of view,
- ask a riddle or pose a puzzling problem to start a discussion,
- play a record or CD and ask the class to analyze its content,
- use a puppet to introduce a new idea, and
- use an open-ended mystery story.

Figure 4-1. Examples of attention grabbers.

A Variety of Grouping Structures

Chapter 2 emphasized the importance of using a variety of grouping structures to accommodate the rates, styles, and abilities of individual students. Effective teachers, whether in elementary, middle, or secondary school, regardless of the class setting or content being studied, do teach lessons to all students in the class at the same time although it should be stressed that they also often break the class into smaller instructional groups as appropriate. Effective teachers have the ability to teach whole groups, small groups, and individual students in a planned sequence and spontaneously as the need arises. They also frequently vary group size during a given instructional period in order to address the learning needs of their students and to make their instruction more motivating. It is often possible for the teacher to introduce a lesson to the entire group but, after this initial experience, address special learning needs with small group or one-to-one instruction.

To be sure, many teachers feel there are several positive aspects of whole group teaching. Some of these are as follows:

- a greater breadth of content can be covered in a shorter period of time,
- the teacher can be assured that all students have the opportunity to hear the same delivery, which will, perhaps, eliminate possible confusion in direction giving and enhance consistency,
- whole group instruction gives many teachers the feeling of being in control of the instructional scene, thereby affording them the chance to deal with all student questions at one time for the benefit of all students, and
- in a management sense, whole group instruction is seen by many teachers as reinforcing their position of authority which enables them to maintain better classroom control.

While it is not argued that the above list represents unimportant instructional concerns, it is noted that numerous positive characteristics also are associated with both small group and one-to-one organizational formats such as the following:

- many students who feel uncomfortable in a large group setting will participate more readily in small group discussions and activities,
- personal interaction and socialization skills may be addressed in smaller settings where the large group setting makes in-depth attention to these skill development areas less likely,
- independent learning patterns are more easily fostered where students are either working on their own or in small groups, and
- the teacher is provided greater opportunities to work with students on an individual basis and to get to know them personally when small group and one-to-one structures are utilized.

Cooperative learning as both a grouping and teaching strategy has become extremely popular, in particular, as supported by constructivist learning theory. Advocates of this approach argue that students can co-construct more powerful understandings than individuals can construct alone (O'Donnell & O'Kelly, 1994; Linn & Barbules, 1993). Research also supports that cooperative learning benefits the student in the development of cognitive skills (Quinn, Johnson, & Johnson, 1995) and in the development of social skills (Slavin, 1995). Slavin (1996) further notes that students in cooperative learning environments have more positive attitudes about themselves than do students in traditional environments. Chapter 6 provides a more in-depth discussion of cooperative learning strategies.

Active Involvement of Learners

Good teaching allows students an opportunity to take an active part in their own learning and is not characterized by students sitting passively while the teacher assumes the dominant, active role. Putting students actively into the learning process recognizes that the development of understanding is a personal process. Brenner, Mayer, Moseley, Brar, Duran, Reed, and Webb (1997) identify that ensuring individual understanding requires multiple representations of topics. Some approaches will be meaningful for some students while different approaches will be meaningful to others. Offering a variety of representations and approaches recognizes the uniqueness of students and their learning needs. As an example, the use of inquiry instruction (see Chapter 6) represents a powerful approach to ensuring active student involvement in dealing with facts and observations to answer questions and solve problems (Eggen & Kauchak, 2007; Kauchak & Eggen, 1998). While levels of student activity will vary across lessons, with few exceptions, every lesson should provide students the opportunity to do more than passively listen to teachers talk.

At the very least, students should be given the opportunity to engage in some speaking and/or writing activities during the course of every lesson. Even if this may seem minimal to some and excessive to others, providing students an opportunity to speak or write will give them a time to express themselves publicly and to focus their attention on the selected learning task. Allowing students to communicate during the learning experience also will provide the teacher with valuable information about the level of the students' understanding as writing and speaking offer the teacher a basis to provide students feedback concerning their levels of performance.

Active involvement in classroom instruction frequently serves to address the affective portion of the classroom environment as well. Students who feel that they are an important part of the class, and, in actuality through instruction are an important part of the class, in turn seek out higher levels of involvement. Instruction which involves students as active participants in the learning enterprise provides for the most successful instructional climate.

Applying Knowledge Learned

Most teachers are aware of the importance of encouraging students to become actively involved in the learning process. Some of these same teachers, however, do not routinely stress the importance of learning applications in instruction and emphasize higher levels of student cognition. Students too frequently are simply required to answer questions which demand rote memory of information or, at most, a low level comprehension of textbook materials or teacher explanations. While it is true that students may be active in answering questions, it is not the case that they are having an opportunity to apply what they are learning. It is important that students be given the opportunity to demonstrate, not only to the teacher but to themselves, an ability to put their learning to some practical use.

As discussed in Chapter 2, there are six levels of cognitive performance that can take place in any learning environment. Students who are not challenged to extend their cognitive processes often are actually spending valuable learning time engaging in the rather low level mental activities of memorizing or restating the words of their teachers and textbooks. At the very least, students should be encouraged to apply their newly-acquired knowledge on a daily basis.

In order for you to ensure that students have the opportunity to function at least at the applying level, a specific structured sequence of learning activities which allows for the application of knowledge must be planned. The most basic activities will enable the student to develop the required foundation of knowledge upon which higher levels of cognition can be developed. After remembering is developed and students are able to understand the basic concepts of the information studied, they then will be able to apply their new information to *real life* or more novel situations. For example, after the study of internal rhyming techniques, students could be provided the opportunity to write their own poetry. If students appropriately use internal rhyming in their writing without being told precisely to do so, they will be applying their new knowledge and comprehension.

Although teachers may not be able to guarantee that all students will function at the applying level in every area of study, students need to have meaningful learning activities designed to allow them the opportunity to apply what they have learned. While perhaps not possible in each and every teaching situation, application clearly is relevant in most.

Monitoring Instruction and Providing Feedback

One of the most serious mistakes a teacher can make is to assume that learning has taken place simply because instruction has taken place. Good teachers routinely use strategies designed to monitor and reinforce student progress in an ongoing manner. Palincsar and Brown (1984) describe comprehension monitoring as the process of periodically checking to see whether students understand the material they are reading or hearing. Failure to monitor comprehension is a common problem, particularly with low-achieving students. As students are in the process of learning to self-monitor, or to develop their metacognitive abilities, it is the teacher's responsibility to maintain a close watch on their progress and understanding as instruction takes place. While this monitoring and providing of feedback are not always easy to do, guidelines such as those that follow should be of assistance in dealing with this important aspect of instruction.

- Provide some type of evaluation at the end of each learning task in order to identify what students have learned and what they still need to learn before they can master the stated objectives. Bloom (1976) states that this feedback-corrective procedure is one of the most powerful determiners of effective instruction.
- Assess the nonverbal communication of students in order to determine anxiety, stress, confusion, and other factors.
- Ask questions and examine students' work while they are involved in the learning task to determine their level of progress.
- Develop precise learning objectives as guides to instruction and evaluate the attainment of these objectives often and systematically. This assessment does not need to be complex as its purpose is diagnostic not evaluative.
- Summarize or prepare concise statements of the essential meaning of verbal or written passages.
- Move throughout the classroom examining student work and progress in order to identify problems so that, in turn, proper feedback can be given as quickly as possible. When students seem confused or perplexed, ask questions of them in order to determine the source of the confusion and then help them to correct the problem.

For optimum levels of student learning to occur during learning tasks, students need to receive consistent feedback concerning how well they are performing. Weinert and Helmke (1995) document the importance of feedback in promoting learning. Effective feedback increases student learning by providing immediate, specific, and corrective information as well as having a positive emotional tone (Murphy, Weil, & McGreal, 1986). Providing quality feedback is a complex and difficult task to master though it may very well be one of the most important determiners of effective teaching. Research has noted that feedback is most effective when students are confident in their response even if the response is incorrect (Snowman, McCown, & Biehler, 2009). That is, before students can benefit from being told that they have made an incorrect response, they must have enough self-confidence in their abilities to perform the task. Feedback has little positive effect on students if they have little or no self-confidence. This is true even if the correct response is being provided. The list of considerations provided in Figure 4-2 is designed to help ensure that you make proper use of feedback in instruction.

---

1. Feedback should not be used to promote a lack of confidence in students (i.e., to promote a negative self-concept). If students are told of their mistakes too often, they are likely to form a negative self-image which will then result in poor performance in the future.

2. Feedback should be immediate and positive in order to build slow learners' self-confidence in the learning task.

3. Accelerated students seem to benefit from being told when they have made mistakes. Actually, telling students of high self-confidence that they have correct answers has been found to have minimal positive effect on their performance because it simply confirms what was already known or what they already perceived.

4. Immediate feedback functions best when a student is working with factual information or learning a specific task such as the appropriate procedure to do something.

5. When accelerated students are involved in complex, higher level thinking, it is often more productive to momentarily delay feedback. Such students are likely to think about the task at a later time and then give themselves internal feedback concerning the correctness of their responses. This is especially true after formal thought processes have been developed.

Figure 4-2. Considerations involving the proper use of feedback.

QUESTIONING: A CRITICAL TEACHING PERFORMANCE

It should be evident from the preceding discussion that a variety of teaching skills is needed to carry out effective classroom instruction. Some teaching behaviors are basic to virtually any lesson. One such behavior is teacher questioning. Teachers need to understand the classifications of questions and the techniques for using all types of questioning because of the critical importance of this behavior.

A widely accepted goal of education is the development of higher thinking abilities in students. Since questions used by teachers long have played an important role in guiding the performance of students, it follows that the strategic use of questions is one of the basic means available to teachers for stimulating student thinking. The use of questioning sometimes consumes as much as 80 percent of all school time (Borich, 2007). Depending upon the skill of the instructor, teacher questioning can shape the learning environment by setting the students' expectation levels and by guiding their study toward deeper levels of understanding.

Questioning Practices

Teachers at all levels ask many questions each day, although research indicates that the emphasis of most of these questions is on the lower levels of cognition. Hoetker and Ahlbrand (1969), in a review of studies spanning a half century, concluded that the dominant mode of thinking as exemplified by teacher questions is the memorization and recall of facts. There seems to be little or no change in the predominant use of lower-level questions today. Current research indicates that most teacher questions solicit recall type student responses and few require high levels of thought to answer (Borich, 2007; Chuska, 2003).

The following classroom scene reflects a typical questioning practice. Consider the questioning approach used by Mr. Smith in his fourth grade classroom.

Mr. Smith: "Today, class, we are going to continue our study of dental health. I hope that you read the chapter for today. Jaime, did you?"

Jaime: "Sort of – I got as far as I could."

Mr. Smith: "Well, you must study hard to keep up. Maybe Carrie has done her work. Carrie, what can happen if people don't brush their teeth?"

Carrie: "They get cavities."

Mr. Smith: "Right! Now who can tell me how to avoid cavities? Robert?"

Robert: "Brush your teeth after every meal."

Mr. Smith: "And what else did the book say to do? Jaime?"

Jaime: "Floss your teeth."

Mr. Smith: "What did the text say about the food you eat? Harry?"

Harry: "Don't eat sweets."

Mr. Smith: "Why, Harry?"

Harry: "They cause cavities."

Mr. Smith: "Anything else?"

Harry: "I think that's all."

Now analyze the following class discussion of Mrs. Howard's second grade class.

Mrs. Howard: "Class, today let's explore what we know about the people in our community. What kinds of people who work in our community help to make it a good place to live, Latrice, can you name one?"

Latrice: "The police officer, I think."

Mrs. Howard: "Yes, you're right. Joe, what are some of the things that police officers do to help our community?"

Joe: "Well, they help stop robbers; they help you if you get lost, and they help people if something bad happens to them."

Mrs. Howard: "On target! Who else in our community helps us? Billy?"

Billy: "The people at the post office."

Mrs. Howard: "What do they do to help us?"

Billy: "They make sure that we get our mail. They also help us get our mail taken to other people."

Mrs. Howard: "Those are good answers. Denise, what do you think things would be like if there were no police officers or postal workers?"

Denise: "I don't think it would be very good. There probably would be a lot of people who would hurt other people."

Mrs. Howard: "That's too bad isn't it? You may be right. But what about postal workers? Jamal?"

Jamal: "Well, for one thing, we wouldn't ever get any letters or packages. There would be no way to send things."

Mrs. Howard: "Good ideas! Beatrice, this might be kind of a hard question, but, who do you think helps our community the most? The police officer or the postal worker?"

Beatrice: "I think the police officer."

Mrs. Howard: "Why?"

You may have noticed that in the first illustration of questioning practices presented that Mr. Smith jumped from subtopic to subtopic requesting factual information without ever going into depth on any one aspect of the major topic. Some students probably were not particularly motivated by the discussion and their answers were correspondingly narrow and brief. Mr.

Smith would be advised to structure his questions so that students are challenged to think about relevant points and build upon them.

Mrs. Howard, on the other hand, is more systematic in her style of questioning. She initially asks students for factual information and for descriptions (explanations). But, Mrs. Howard also seeks out student ideas using hypothetical, *what if* questions. Student judgments are also requested. Mr. Smith and Mrs. Howard clearly are quite different in their styles of questioning.

Teachers like Mr. Smith traditionally have developed low cognitive (remembering level) thinking while openly stating the value of higher level mental performances; the inconsistency is evident. If students are to understand what is taught at a variety of levels of thought, questions at a variety of cognitive levels must be used. Teachers like Mrs. Howard, who use higher level questions in their instruction, are able to elicit higher level questions and responses in return from their students. Mrs. Howard is actually modeling desired student behavior. Since many studies have shown that most teachers use primarily remembering and understanding level questions, it is expected that student understanding of the subject matter will more than likely remain at these lower levels of cognition. In order to aid students in performance at the higher cognitive levels, questions must be frequently used at these levels. If teachers incorporate questions at a variety of cognitive levels, students, in turn, will be aided in thinking and performing at a variety of levels. Perhaps Mr. Smith's students would have an opportunity to perform at higher levels if he would provide greater structure and development in some of his questions and questioning style.

While reading through the next section on classifying teacher questions, recall some of the questions used by Mr. Smith and Mrs. Howard. By learning more about the classification of teacher questions you will come to appreciate the skills displayed by Mrs. Howard. The ability to ask good questions does not develop naturally. Mrs. Howard obviously has done a great deal of preparation in developing this aspect of her instructional style.

Classifying Teacher Questions

Numerous attempts have been made to develop a classification system for teacher questions which accurately characterizes the thought level required of the student answering the question and, at the same time, gives the classroom teacher guidance in the framing of orally stated questions. One of the most functional systems available was developed a number of years ago by Gallagher and Aschner (1963). This observation system, based on Guilford's classic model for the structure of the intellect (Guilford, 1959), is used for analyzing what is termed the quality of thinking in classrooms. The major categories of this observation system are (1) cognitive-memory, (2) convergent, (3) divergent, (4) evaluative, and (5) routine. The question classification system recommended in this text is a modification of those categories generated by Gallagher and Aschner. It is recommended not as a panacea for solving all question-asking problems of teachers but as a means of studying and analyzing one's own questions and improving the quality of questions asked in the classroom. In this modification, only the levels, or types, of questions dealing with the cognitive domain are considered: *Cognitive-Memory, Convergent, Divergent,* and *Evaluative.* The four questioning levels constitute a thinking hierarchy. That is, they are ranked with cognitive-memory being the lowest and evaluative being the highest. A basic assumption of this classification system is that a question asked at a given level will produce thought and subsequent response at the same level. The teacher who asks a cognitive-memory question will get a cognitive-memory response. Too, a teacher who asks a divergent question will get a response at the divergent level, yet the response will reflect the incorporation of cognitive-memory and convergent thinking elements. Each of the four major categories is discussed in the following paragraphs.

Cognitive-Memory Questions

By definition, cognitive-memory questions require a recall of previously learned and memorized knowledge. Cognitive-memory questions represent such a low level of thought involved in responding to the question that responses often require only single-word answers, and student answers tend to sound alike and are predictable. Even more lengthy responses to this type of question, however, may not require creative thought. Cognitive-memory questions typically require such behaviors as *recalling, recognizing,* and *reporting.* The following examples illustrate questions at this level of cognition.

- What is the atomic number of zinc?
- Why did we say that Indians are sometimes called Native Americans?
- Who painted the Mona Lisa?
- What is the oldest city in the United States?

Convergent Questions

As the previous examples indicate, cognitive-memory questions involve the recall of factual knowledge or the reporting of a past experience or observation. Convergent questions, on the other hand, refer to a broader type of question which requires the respondent to put facts or concepts together in order to obtain the single correct answer. To classify a question correctly as convergent, it must be assumed that the respondent has not merely provided a memorized response. Many convergent questions expect the student to put the response in his or her own words. In so doing, the student provides the single correct answer resulting from the interrelating of different facts or concepts. Convergent questions may require students to *make comparisons, explain facts or concepts, state or describe relationships,* or *solve problems* using learned procedures. The following examples illustrate convergent questions:

- How many sandwiches would you have left at the end of the day if you came to school with three and only ate one?
- What is the relationship between crude oil and plastic?
- How are amphibians and reptiles alike?
- How are present methods of communication different from those used in the past?

Divergent Questions

The third category of this classification system describes those questions which expand on the convergent category by allowing more than one possible correct answer. In other words, the respondent is expected to engage in a divergence of thought and produce a response which is original for that respondent. Students answering such questions carry on higher levels of thought by organizing elements into new patterns. As teachers enter this broader questioning level, predictability in student responses is reduced. Student responses, by the very nature of this level, should be unique and novel. Questions classified as divergent may require students to *predict, hypothesize,* or *infer.* An expression such as *what if* is common to questions classified as divergent. The following examples illustrate divergent questions.

- What do you think our society will be like in one hundred years?
- If Darwin were incorrect about evolution, how could we explain the diversity of life on our planet?
- What kinds of problems might occur if Spanish was not allowed to be used in the United States?
- If the last act of *Hamlet* were eliminated, how would you finish the play?

Evaluative Questions

The highest category of thought is termed evaluative. In responding to evaluative questions, the student must make judgments based on logically derived evidence. The evidence is derived from the use of the levels of thought described in the other three categories. Additionally, students must defend their judgments based upon criteria that they designate or which have been established by others. In either case, reasons for judgments must be implied or explicitly stated. Responses to evaluative level questions represent a two-part intellectual procedure. First, a decision must be made or a stance identified. Second, the reason supporting the decision or stance must be communicated. Evaluative questions require students to *make judgments* as well as *defend their positions*. The following examples illustrate evaluative level questions.

- Should we change to electric cars in this country? Why?
- Which is the better numeration system – the Roman or Arabic system? Why do you think this?
- Which is the best nursery rhyme we have heard? Why?
- Do you think that people are more inquisitive today than in the past? Why do you think this?

It is recommended that teachers occasionally classify their questions according to their appropriate cognitive levels using the classification system introduced here. An audio tape made during a classroom discussion will reveal valuable information that can be of great assistance when analyzing questions at the different levels. Analyzing questions in such a manner certainly is not the only means of improving instructional efforts, but the reward in doing so, in terms of better planning and increased student achievement, will be well worth the effort.

To determine if you are prepared to effectively analyze your own questions, classify each of the following questions as cognitive-memory (CM), convergent (C), divergent (D), or evaluative (E).

1. What is four times two?
2. Which do you think is more important to life, clean water or clean air? Explain.
3. Suppose that from this point on all poets were men, how might poetry be different in the future?
4. Who discovered the vaccine for polio?
5. What is one primary color?
6. In what ways are living in a big city and going to a big school the same?
7. How do you think our country would be different if there were three major political parties instead of two?
8. If you could go anywhere on a vacation, where would you go? Why?
9. What do you think it would be like to live under a dictator rather than a president?
10. What is the difference between soccer and rugby?

ANSWERS: (1) CM, (2) E, (3) D, (4) CM, (5) CM, (6) C, (7) D, (8) E, (9) D, (10) C

Hopefully, you got at least eight of the ten questions correct. If you did not, it would be beneficial to review the definitions and examples which were provided. If by chance you are still having difficulties, study the definitions and examples once more and keep in mind that the goal is to learn to plan as well as use questions at the various cognitive levels. The ability to classify the questions of others in isolated situations is perhaps not as crucial.

Planning Questions

Merely asking students who are unfamiliar with a topic large numbers of divergent and evaluative questions actually could prove to be fruitless because, in order to reach these thinking levels, careful preparation is needed. Students must have experiences with the topic at the lower cognitive levels before they will have the necessary background experiences and knowledge to really profit from higher-level questioning. To reach the greatest levels of effectiveness, teachers should plan a variety of questions in advance of class discussion.

For example, if you were to plan a model lesson on *ecology*, it would be a good idea to plan questions at each cognitive level to help guide your presentation and interaction with the students. It would be unwise, however, to try to plan all questions in advance because this could lead to an inflexible, stilted approach where you would merely be recalling your own questions to ensure that you are asking each one of them, pausing only long enough for student responses. Opportunities should be made for complete student responses which can be built upon as the lesson progresses. All that is needed in advance are a few questions at the various levels to stimulate your thinking as the discussion progresses so that a logical questioning sequence may be followed. For the topic *ecology*, you could plan questions such as those that follow.

Cognitive Memory

- In what year was the first federal legislation passed to protect our environment?

Convergent

- What is the difference between ecology and conservation?

Divergent

- What might happen to the world if people stopped being concerned about ecology?

Evaluative

- Which do you think is more important, our environment or our industrial growth? Why?

Good and Brophy (1997) report that when quizzing students it is important that most questions, at least 75 percent, should elicit correct answers. Asking questions that 75 percent or more of the students can answer correctly may accomplish two important goals. First, students will become confident because they are successful. Second, simpler questions can actually enhance attainment of higher-level learning objectives (Brophy & Good, 1986) as these responses build the students' foundational knowledge in the area.

GUIDELINES FOR EFFECTIVE QUESTIONING

Planning questions according to cognitive levels is only one aid in improving the quality of classroom questions. A teacher should also consider such characteristics of questions as clarity, sequence, and frequency. Henson (1996) offers a number of important guidelines for the use of questions in the classroom.

- Avoid using a long series of questions to introduce a lesson.
- Delay questions about content until a knowledge base has been established.
- Use a combination of levels of questions, extending from recall to evaluation.
- Pause for at least three seconds following a thoughtful question.
- Do not expect students to be able to guess what the teacher means.
- Address questions to individual students, using student names.
- Keep content-oriented questions specific.
- Help students develop skills in answering questions.
- Encourage students to ask questions.
- Help students develop skills in asking questions.
- Listen carefully to student questions and respond, using their content.
- Prior to making a reading assignment, showing a video, or taking a field trip, pose questions relative to the major concepts or objectives of that experience.

To supplement the suggestions offered by Henson (1996), Figure 4-3 presents some specific do's and don'ts of good questions and questioning strategies as an aid in developing effective questioning practices. An examination of these important points will provide further help in developing successful questioning strategies.

Do's

Write out beforehand, in a logical sequence, the key questions to be asked during the lesson.

Listen to student answers carefully and phrase subsequent questions accordingly. Be flexible and deviate from the planned sequence as necessary.

Ask questions at a variety of cognitive levels, not just low (cognitive-memory, convergent) or high (divergent, evaluative). In addition, strive to include variety in the phrasing of questions.

Provide ample time for students to respond, especially to those questions requiring higher levels of thought. As noted in Chapter 1, Rowe (1969) studied the problem of giving students enough *wait-time* to answer questions and found that the average wait-time before the teacher rephrased the question, asked another student to answer, or answered the question for the student was *less than one second*. This is clearly not long enough to develop quality answers.

Consider the ability and maturity levels of students in deciding what questions to ask. Students with lesser ability will only be frustrated by a question which is far above their ability. However, challenging questions can sometimes provide the necessary motivation for able students to encourage them to achieve at higher cognitive levels.

On occasion, repeat or rephrase students' responses. Such behavior serves to reinforce their efforts. However, avoid overdoing this; students may begin to ignore listening to one another while expecting the teacher to repeat all important information.

Systematically record classroom questions; use these recordings to analyze and develop questioning skills. Such recording and analysis encourages the development of this essential skill for effective instruction.

Don'ts

Do not ask questions which encourage a choral response such as: "Why did the President order an embargo, class?" It is often better to address a single student by name following a question to avoid a choral response.

Do not make extensive use of rhetorical or leading questions. Such questions serve little purpose, and they occasionally confuse the students.

Do not ask fill-in-the-blank type questions such as "The formula for density is *what*? These questions tend to catch students unaware and create confusion. It is much better to initially phrase the question clearly and unambiguously; for example, "What is the formula for density?"

Do not make frequent use of questions which call for a *yes* or *no* answer such as "Was Sitting Bull an Apache chief?" Such questions allow students a fifty-fifty chance of arriving at the correct response; these responses could provide the teacher with inappropriate feedback concerning the student's progress.

Do not ask questions using complex language which causes ambiguities.

Do not ask questions which are actually two questions in one such as "Who discovered America and where was he from?"

Do not use questions which actually allow a variety of correct responses when only one correct response is desired. Such a question as "Which is our largest state?" might be confusing in that either geographic size or population could be thought of by the student.

Figure 4-3. Do's and don'ts of effective questioning.

Chapter 5

THE TEACHER AS AN INSTRUCTIONAL STRATEGIST: DIRECT INSTRUCTION

Planning the procedures portion of any lesson, regardless of the type of information to be communicated, requires that teachers select or develop appropriate strategies to meet identified lesson objectives. This chapter examines several specific direct instructional strategies from which teachers might develop learning experiences that are both varied and stimulating. While there are many strategies that can be used in instruction, each strategy has identifiable characteristics which may make it more effective for some lesson purposes than for others. Strategy selection should be based, primarily, on the correlation of the objectives of the lesson, i.e., desired student learning outcomes, with the readiness of the students. Readiness may be thought of in a broad sense to include mastery of prerequisite knowledge or skills, motivation level, and developmental stage. The teacher also must consider such factors as time requirements, resources available, and cost of materials required for each strategy. In order to choose an instructional strategy for a given objective or set of objectives, the teacher needs to be knowledgeable of the salient characteristics of each strategy as well as its most appropriate area of application.

Teaching strategies are often classified into two broad categories: those which are characterized by a greater level of teacher direction, i.e., direct instructional strategies; and those characterized by a greater emphasis on active student self-learning, i.e., indirect instructional strategies. This chapter will focus specifically on those strategies identified as direct. Such strategies also are often referred to as teacher-centered strategies (Eggen & Kauchak, 2007). Direct instructional strategies are frequently considered to be teacher-centered because, in many ways, these strategies are focused on what the teacher does, i.e., the behavior and actions of the teacher, more so than the students. This distinction, however, is actually quite artificial as, when the strategy is used effectively, students definitely are engaged during direct instructional activities. If they are not engaged correctly or properly, the potential for their learning is diminished. Consequently, there is student engagement and involvement when a teacher is using a direct instructional strategy even though the strategy may be referred to as teacher-centered. Regardless of the categorization of the strategy, the purpose of any strategy remains the same: to aid students in the mastery of stated objectives. Figure 5-1 provides a helpful comparison that identifies key differences between direct and indirect approaches to instruction.

Many educators have contributed professional articles, chapters, and entire books on the topic of teaching strategies. Although most educators agree as to what a teaching strategy or an instructional method is, there

Direct Instruction	Indirect Instruction
Objective: To teach facts, rules, and action sequences.	*Objective:* To teach concepts, patterns, and abstractions.
Teacher begins the lesson with a review of the previous day's work.	Teacher begins the lesson with advance organizers that provide an overall picture and allow for concept expansion.
Teacher presents new content in small steps with explanations and examples.	
Teacher provides an opportunity for guided practice on a small number of sample problems. Prompts and models when necessary to attain 60% to 80% accuracy.	Teacher focuses student responses using induction and/or deduction to refine and focus generalizations.
Teacher provides feedback and corrections according to whether the answer was correct, quick, and firm; correct, but hesitant; careless, or incorrect.	Teacher presents examples and nonexamples of the generalization, identifying critical and noncritical attributes.
	Teacher draws additional examples from students' own experiences, interests, and problems.
Teacher provides an opportunity for independent practice with seatwork. Strives for automatic responses that are 95% correct or higher.	Teacher uses questions to guide discovery and articulation of the generalization.
	Teacher involves students in evaluating their own responses.
Teacher provides weekly and monthly (cumulative) reviews and reteaches unlearned content.	Teacher promotes and moderates discussion to firm up and extend generalizations when necessary.

Figure 5-1. Characteristics of direct instruction as compared to indirect instruction (Borich, 2007, p. 292).

remains some debate as to the identification and classification of a basic set of best strategies. Beck (1998) suggests that a primary mission of educators should be the development of a taxonomy for identifying, classifying, and interrelating teaching strategies. The identification of best strategy may, in fact, not be all that complicated. It is actually determined by (1) how well the strategy matches the learning objective(s) that the teacher has identified for the students; (2) the teacher's ability to use the strategy; (3) the resources, including time, available to the teacher; and (4) the students' understanding of what is expected of them and their ability or potential to reach the teacher's desired level of performance.

In this chapter, you will learn more about direct teaching strategies through study of the following topics:

1. the major strategies that teachers use that are referred to or categorized as direct instructional strategies, and
2. the major characteristics, including both strengths and limitations, of direct instructional strategies.

DIRECT INSTRUCTION

Direct instructional strategies are those teaching approaches or methods that are designed to allow teachers to organize and present material to students, e.g., subject matter content, rules, procedures, skills, etc., in the form in which the students are expected to learn or show understanding. There is an important place for such instruction in any classroom. Many teachers enjoy using direct instructional strategies because they are characterized by a level of predictability in terms of anticipated student responses that is not present to the same degree when indirect instructional strategies are used. This level of predictability applies to what may be anticipated as student responses, but it may also apply to time management needed to coordinate the strategy with the classroom schedule.

Research suggests that, when teaching low-achieving and at-risk students, a highly structured approach may be the most effective. Direct instruction is such an approach. Direct instruction, however, often is less effective for high-achieving and independent students who prefer instruction to be less structured and more flexible where they can apply their more individual learning skills and be more creative (Ornstein & Lasley, 2000).

Direct teaching, also referred to as systematic or explicit instruction, is best used to impart information and help students learn procedures and skills. When using direct instructional strategies, teachers do not typically ask students to create, discover new information, or think independently. When using direct instruction, teachers present information, students apply knowledge or practice a skill, and teachers give feedback. Borich (2007) defines direct instruction as a teacher-centered strategy where the teacher is the major information provider. The teacher's role is to pass facts, rules, or action sequences on to students in the most direct way possible. This usually involves a presentation and recitation format with explanations, examples, and opportunities for practice and feedback. Burden and Byrd (2007) define direct teaching strategies as approaches where the teacher structures lessons in a straightforward, sequential manner. The teacher is in control of the content or skill to be learned and the pace and rhythm of the lesson. The approach may be seen as having the following four features:

1. clear determination and articulation of goals,
2. teacher-directed instruction,
3. careful monitoring of students' outcomes, and
4. consistent use of effective classroom organization and management methods.

Silver, Strong, and Perini (2007) comment that the recent popularity that has been achieved by instructional approaches such as inquiry, discovery, and constructivist learning have served to diminish the view held toward direct instruction and that this is an unfortunate occurrence. This is, in particular, as direct instructional strategies have an important place in the teacher's repertoire of strategies, especially when the teacher is emphasizing content or skill mastery where inquiry, discovery, and constructivist learning approaches are less effective. The following four-step process has been identified by Silver, Strong, and Perini as comprising the direct instruction process.

1. **Modeling** – the skill is modeled by the teacher, who thinks aloud while performing the skill;
2. **Direct Practice** – the teacher uses questions to lead students through the steps and to help them see the reasons behind the steps;
3. **Guided Practice** – students generate their own leading questions while working through the steps. The teacher observes, coaches, and provides feedback; and
4. **Independent Practice** – finally, students work through more examples on their own.

Direct instruction is a structured, teacher-centered approach to teaching characterized by teacher direction and control, high teacher expectations for student progress, maximum time spent by students on academic tasks, and efforts by the teacher to keep negative effect to a minimum (Santrock, 2008). A strong emphasis is given to using time wisely and maximizing student learning time. Direct instruction can be the most effective and efficient approach to use in some situations.

Direct instruction is often "whole group" or "teacher led" instruction that has its foundation in behavioral principles (Orlich, Harder, Callahan, Trevisan, & Brown, 2007). The technique involves academic focus, provides few optional choices for student-initiated activities, tends to be used when large-group instruction takes place, and often emphasizes factual knowledge. Strengths of the direct instruction approach include (Orlich et al., 2007; Kozloff, LaNunziata, Cowardin, & Besellieu, 2001):

1. content is delivered to the entire class,
2. the teacher controls the focus of attention,
3. the process maximizes available time,
4. feedback assesses class understanding of learning,
5. the teacher focuses on class objectives,
6. the teacher provides clarity through explanations,
7. less teacher preparation is required, and
8. all students work on the same task.

Standard and systematic steps for the teacher to follow when using direct instruction are:

1. review and check previous work,
2. present new material in small units,
3. provide for guided practice,
4. provide for feedback and correctives,
5. supervise independent seat work, and
6. review concepts every week and every month.

Direct instruction is seen as a time-efficient approach to teaching designed to teach well-defined knowledge and skills that will be needed for later learning (Eggen & Kauchak, 2006). It can range from a highly structured, scripted, and somewhat behaviorist approach to one that is more flexible and cognitive in its direction (Eggen & Kauchak, 2007).

As can be seen by the various descriptions of direct instruction presented here, common elements are apparent in any of the sequenced approaches taken. Direct instruction typically begins with an introduction and review of the content and needed prior learning which is followed by a presentation of information and culminates with practice and feedback.

Borich (2007) identifies that direct instruction strategies are appropriate when the teacher's purpose is to (1) disseminate information not readily available from texts or workbooks; (2) arouse or heighten student interest; and (3) achieve content mastery and overlearning of fundamental facts, rules, and action sequences that may be important to subsequent learning. To be most effective, instructional strategies should be selected as they best address the desired learning outcomes of the teacher's lesson. In this regard, student learning outcomes have been organized into the following two broad classifications.

Classification 1: Facts, rules, and action sequences
Classification 2: Concepts, patterns, and abstractions

Direct instructional strategies are best suited to meet those learning outcomes associated with the first classification. Figure 5-2 offers the following examples of these types of outcomes.

Facts	Rules	Action Sequences
1. Recognize multiplication with two-digit numbers	Carrying with two-digit numbers	Multiplying to "1,000"
2. Identify apostrophe "s"	Finding words with apostrophe "s"	Using apostrophe "s" in a sentence
3. Select multisyllable words from a list	Pronouncing multisyllable words	Reading stories with multisyllable words
4. State chemical composition of water	Combining 2 parts hydrogen with 1 part oxygen	Writing the expression for water

Figure 5-2: Examples of learner outcomes for facts, rules, and action sequences (Borich, 2007, p. 223).

Direct Instruction: Pros and Cons

Direct instructional strategies have come to be viewed less positively by some educators as well as students. As noted earlier, their decline in popularity is directly related to the rise in popularity of such strategies as inquiry, project-based learning, discovery and constructivist learning, and the focus on student problem solving and creative thinking. Direct instructional strategies, however, have an important place in the teacher's portfolio of strategies. Such strategies can be very important, if not essential, when the teacher's purpose in the lesson is for students to achieve content mastery and an understanding of fundamental facts, rules, and procedures. Today's focus on increasing student achievement and standardized testing argue for the value of direct instruction. Direct instructional strategies are efficient and effective for these purposes. Well-organized, clear presentations, the use of explanatory links, and reviews all can help students better understand connections among ideas. Guided practice can also provide the teacher with an important view of student progress. Direct instruction has an especially important purpose for the development of student understanding of foundational information, sometimes identified as low cognitive information, and skill development. When done properly, direct instruction lessons can be an important resource that students use to develop understanding (Hoy & Hoy, 2009).

However, there are valid criticisms of direct instruction. Direct instruction has its limitations as do virtually all instructional approaches. Students are often more passive and less active when direct instruction is used. Direct instructional approaches are considered more traditional than innovative by nature. These characteristics can lead to greater levels of student motivation and management problems. Too, when teachers break subject matter into small segments, this may not portray the content as it really should be viewed for best understanding. When the focus of the approach is on what the teacher does, students may not think to ask questions or to become deeply involved in the really important ideas of the teacher's lesson (Freiberg & Driscoll, 2005). To make direct instructional strategies as dynamic as possible, teachers should seek to involve students, as appropriate, through direct as well as open-ended questioning that will elicit their engagement and critical thinking (Stowell, Rios, McDaniel, & Christopher, 1996).

As with any strategy, a direct instructional strategy is at its best when it is used well, with the right student audience, and for the right instructional purpose. While students may be more passive than active during direct instruction, this does not mean that they are destined to be bored and disinterested. The strategy should be used where its strengths lie, that being when the teacher is focusing on the student's acquisition of factual information, the understanding of rules and/or procedures, and the mastery of skills.

Five popular direct instructional strategies are *Explicit Teaching, Lecture Presentation, Demonstration, Drill,* and *Teacher-led Guided Discussion.* An effective teacher knows when and how to use each to ensure maximum student learning.

Explicit Teaching

Being explicit is generally thought of as being fully and clearly expressed, defined or formulated, forthright, unreserved in expression, and readily observable. It is easy to see how explicit teaching as an instructional strategy follows this definition. Explicit teaching is a very direct form of teaching where the teacher begins by gaining student attention, presents information, provides students with opportunities to practice and/or use what is being presented, reinforces correct responses, provides feedback to students on their progress, and emphasizes the amount of time that students spend actively engaged in learning course content (Burden & Byrd, 2007).

Six teaching functions are commonly associated with explicit teaching (Burden & Byrd, 2007; Rosenshine, 1987; Rosenshine & Stevens, 1986).

1. **Review Daily:** The review is to determine whether or not students have the necessary prerequisite knowledge or skills for the lesson. This often involves going over previously covered material, correcting homework, or reviewing prior knowledge.
2. **Present New Material:** The presentation of new material needs to be well organized, clear and concise, focused on stated lesson goals, addressed in a step-by-step manner, and attended to one point at a time.
3. **Conduct Guided Practice:** Students need to have the opportunity to practice what the teacher has just presented. It is important that guided practice is a frequent event in all lessons.
4. **Provide Feedback and Correctives:** Providing feedback and correctives is an important part of or follow-up to guided practice. Nothing is gained by allowing students to continue to make errors that could be corrected.
5. **Conduct Independent Practice:** Independent practice follows guided practice and offers the opportunity for the student to work on his or her own on the material covered during the teacher's presentation.
6. **Review Weekly and Monthly:** As guided and independent practice are important to explicit teaching, so to is regular and ongoing review. Regular review ensures that student learning is maintained and monitored and that the teacher clearly understands the status of the student's learning.

Homework, used commonly in schools today, and often misused, is a type of independent practice. When used properly, homework can help students achieve automaticity. This is learning and understanding to the level where the student's performance response, reflecting understanding and/or ability, is automatic. For this to occur, teachers should assign homework that is an extension of what the students have studied and practiced in class and that is aligned with the teacher's learning objectives and activities. Homework can be particularly positive in the middle and high school and frequency and consistency in homework are important (Cooper, Lindsay, Nye, & Greathouse, 1998). It tends to be less effective with younger children. This is partially because younger children have less well-developed study and attention skills. Additionally, those students who are having difficulty in learning something at school can have even greater problems at home without proper monitoring and guidance. Teachers of young children who assign homework should monitor their students' progress closely to ensure that it is having the positive effect they desire (Cooper & Valentine, 2001).

Consider the following characteristics of effective homework (Figure 5-3).

Characteristic	Rationale
Extension of classwork	The teacher teaches; homework reinforces.
High success rates	Success is motivating. Success leads to automaticity. (Although, no one may be available to help if students encounter problems.)
Part of class routines	Becomes a part of student expectations; increases likelihood of students completing assignments.
Graded	Increases accountability and provides feedback.

Figure 5-3. From Cooper, H., and Valentine, J. (2001). Using research to answer practical questions about homework. *Educational Psychologist, 36*(3), 143–153.

Burden and Byrd (2007, pp. 133–134) note that there are basically four types of homework assignments: (1) *practice*, to help students master specific skills and to reinforce material presented in class; (2) *preparation*, to prepare students for upcoming lessons; (3) *extension*, to go beyond information obtained in the classroom and to transfer new skills and ideas to new situations; and (4) *creative*, to offer students the opportunity to think critically and engage in problem-solving activities. The following guidelines for teachers should be considered when making decisions about homework assignments.

1. *Recognize that homework serves different purposes at different grade levels.* For younger students, homework should be used to foster positive attitudes toward school and better academic-related behaviors and character traits, not to measurably improve subject matter achievement. For older students, the purpose of homework should change toward facilitating the acquisition of knowledge in specific subject areas.

2. *Have a mixture of mandatory and voluntary homework.* Some homework should be mandatory at each grade level. A mixture of mandatory and voluntary assignments may be most beneficial to students.

3. *Use homework to address topics previously covered, those covered on the day of the assignment, and those yet to be covered.* In this way, students are reinforced for topics that have been covered, address topics covered on the day of the assignment, and are familiarized with topics to be covered in the future.

4. *Have homework focus on simple skills and material or on the integration of skills already possessed by the student.* Do not use homework to teach complex knowledge and skills. Assignments and directions should be very clear as students will be working on the homework independently.

5. *Select an appropriate amount of homework for the grade level.* While much will depend on the individual teacher, student, and even community, general guidelines can be offered, such as: grades 1 to 3 – one to three mandatory assignments each week, each lasting no more than 15 minutes. Each week, grades 4 to 6 – two to four mandatory assignments; grades 7 to 9 – three to five assignments; and grades 10 to 12 – four to five assignments.

6. *Select a process for providing feedback and grading homework.* The practice of grading homework should be kept to a minimum, especially if the purpose is to foster positive attitudes toward the subject matter. The greater purpose of homework should be to diagnose individual learning problems and provide feedback. Homework should be collected and checked for completeness with ongoing instructional feedback.

7. *Do not use homework as punishment.* If a student misbehaves and punishment is needed, nonacademic consequences should be selected. Using homework as punishment conveys the wrong message about the value of academic work.

8. *Clearly communicate the homework policy to students.* Students need to know the procedure and policy for homework. The importance of homework must be carefully explained. Motivation is enhanced when students recognize the value of the homework and its place in the academic program.

9. *Show students ways to overcome distractions.* The main disturbances for students studying and doing homework at home are the phone, television, family members, and the radio. Guidance should be given for ways to minimize and overcome these distractions. These could include selecting a quiet study place and using a regular study time.

10. *Teach homework skills to students.* Students can improve homework skills by establishing appropriate places and times for studying, previewing the material, focusing attention, reading carefully and thinking about the concepts covered, self-testing, and taking notes effectively.

Teachers should keep a number of important points in mind when preparing to use the explicit teaching strategy. The following considerations (Figure 5-4) are recommended when using explicit teaching (Burden & Byrd, 2007, p. 120; Rosenshine, 1988, p. 76).

In using the explicit teaching strategy, the teacher should:

1. begin the lesson with a short statement of goals,
2. allow for a short review of prior learning,
3. present new material in small steps, with student practice after each step,
4. give clear and detailed instructions and explanations,
5. provide a high level of active practice for all students,
6. guide students during initial practice,
7. ask many questions, check for student understanding, and obtain responses from all students,
8. provide systematic feedback and corrections,
9. obtain a student success rate of 80 percent or higher during initial practice,
10. provide explicit instruction and practice for seatwork exercises and, when necessary, monitor students during seatwork, and
11. continue practice until students are independent and confident.

Figure 5-4 Suggestions for developing explicit teaching lessons.

Lecture Presentation

The lecture approach, also referred to as expository teaching, is the most direct instructional strategy of all. Lectures have fallen into some disrepute simply because there have been too many lectures that were poorly done by too many teachers. A good lecture that is well planned and delivered smoothly with conviction, however, can be an exciting learning experience that is well received by students. Pierce and Lorber (1977) observe that the line between such a lecture and an artistic performance is a very fine line. Nevertheless, the extensive use of lectures should be reserved for the teacher with the personality and ability to conduct them effectively.

Lectures are most appropriately used to (1) quickly and concisely present to students a body of new and integrated information, (2) clarify relationships among general points or between specific causes and effects, (3) explain procedures, and (4) summarize information. Rather than just distributing information to students in handout form, the lecture allows for spontaneous student response and questions, making it possible for points to be clarified as they are raised by students. Lectures generally do not follow the specific systematic steps introduced earlier with explicit teaching.

Lecture involves telling or presenting to students information the teacher wishes them to learn; this information is often presented in what is considered to be its final form. Whether it is a first grade teacher telling students about the zoo, or a high school teacher explaining the relationship between proper punctuation and effective communication, the emphasis is on the teacher telling students what they need to know. Students are to learn the information as it is presented to them.

The lecture typically involves the teacher making a formal presentation to the entire class with minimal involvement by the students. Though the teacher is the main focus of attention in the lecture, lectures need not be boring. Informative lecturers often illustrate their lectures through the use of varied electronic aids such as the Internet and PowerPoint. Such pictorial displays add vividness to the presentation. Some teachers also make extensive use of the whiteboard or presentation board. Illustrating the lecture serves the important purposes of aiding in the maintenance of student interest and providing students with additional reference points by which they may associate the newly-learned material. The most effective lecturers are very well organized; show enthusiasm in their delivery; are animated to some degree; use good voice tone and inflection; and, through their own verbal and nonverbal communication, keep the students' attention throughout the lecture period.

The following lesson characteristics or features are recommended for improving lectures and explanations in class (Ornstein & Lasley, 2000). The teacher's lecture approach may be evaluated against these guidelines for progress and improvement.

1. Maintain eye contact with the class.
2. Use handouts and overheads to help students follow the presentation and focus on important ideas.
3. Avoid detail unless supplemented by graphs, tables, or illustrations.
4. Write important information on the white board or presentation board.
5. Define new terms and concepts.
6. Provide an outline for note taking.
7. Present relevant examples to explain major ideas.
8. Relate new information to prior information.
9. Occasionally summarize important ideas.
10. Go slowly when discussing difficult concepts.
11. Be willing to repeat or elaborate when necessary.
12. Use alternative explanations when necessary.
13. Develop internal connections by helping students see relationships, compare or contrast, analyze, etc.
14. Include questions to clarify information being presented.
15. Try not to digress; be aware of time and pace yourself accordingly.

Most teachers can plan and organize the content of a good lecture. To ensure effectiveness, however, they also must have the content firmly understood and organized to such a degree as to be intelligible and interesting to all students in the class when the lecture is given. Teacher clarity, personal dynamics, and the teacher's ability to develop a personal relationship with the students during the lecture become of vital importance. A primary strength of the lecture strategy lies in the fact that large amounts of material can be delivered uniformly to all students in a short period of time. Occasions exist, at all grade levels, when this may be both necessary and desirable, although, such occasions are fewer in number with young children.

When preparing a lecture presentation, a number of important considerations should be kept in mind. Most authorities agree that the following teacher behaviors are important when presenting a lecture (Figure 5-5).

In using the lecture strategy, the teacher should:

1. relate the presentation of new information to that which the students have already learned or experienced,
2. begin the lesson with an "attention grabber,"
3. use audio or visual aids to provide stimulus variation,
4. use concrete and descriptive language in order to "paint verbal pictures,"
5. present the selected content for instruction in a logically ordered sequence,
6. solicit verbal feedback through questioning,
7. monitor student nonverbal behavior to determine receptivity,
8. use voice inflections and animated body movements,
9. be receptive to student questions during the presentation, and
10. project confidence in understanding the material.

Figure 5-5. Suggestions for presenting an effective lecture.

If poorly planned or inappropriately used, the lecture strategy definitely can lack stimulation for students. This is an important consideration when preparing to use this teaching method. Students at all levels, particularly those in the elementary and middle grades, prefer and need active involvement. Of possible concern is that the lecture strategy can relegate the student to a distinctively passive role. If this occurs, it limits the amount of teacher-student interaction which is needed for a complete evaluation of the instructive process. In general, the lecture approach, certainly the longer lecture, is

more appropriate for older students pursuing larger amounts of lower level
cognitive material. This observation reinforces a very important characteristic of the lecture strategy; it is best used for the remembering and understanding levels of cognition. Only infrequently do students develop higher
levels of cognition through lecture. If inappropriately used, a lecture may go
from the teacher's notes to the students' notebook without ever passing
through the *mind* of either individual. However, when used properly, some
educators (e.g., Ausubel & Robinson, 1969; Ausubel, 1968) have suggested
that lecture is the most efficient method of instruction with abstract thinkers
if the teacher can clearly tie the new information being presented to information the students have already learned or are already familiar with. The
lecture can be effective if thoroughly planned for and implemented with clarity and enthusiasm. If not, lectures can lack stimulation as well as effectiveness.

Demonstration

Unlike a lecture, which essentially is telling students that which the teacher
wishes them to learn, a demonstration primarily involves showing. The
kindergarten teacher demonstrating how to tie the laces on a shoe, the elementary teacher demonstrating proper subtraction procedures on the whiteboard, or the high school teacher demonstrating how to mix a chemical com-
pound are all instances of teachers using the demonstration or showing
approach. Demonstrations have the advantage of enabling students to
observe the demonstrator engaged in the learning task rather than simply
talking about it. Whether of some laboratory procedure, physical skill, or
other action, the demonstration can be a stimulating instructional experience
because it offers a living model. A good demonstration can be like a picture
– worth a thousand words. In a demonstration, students are afforded the
opportunity of looking at something instead of merely talking or hearing
about it. This helps to take the experience from the abstract to the concrete.
Demonstration is what often takes place when teachers actually intend to
conduct an experiment. True experiments require the guided inquiry strategy, not the demonstration approach. Regrettably, few real experiments are
done in public schools. Most are classroom demonstrations where the
expected outcomes are already known by the teacher and often by the students in advance. Regardless, students are often better able to make a visual
analysis in route to understanding a particular concept or modeling an
expected behavior after watching a demonstration.

Effective demonstrations require very careful planning and preparation
that should include the teacher practicing the demonstration prior to making
the actual classroom presentation. Such practice of the demonstration serves

to determine if the procedure actually works and provides the expected end results. The teacher also has an opportunity, during the practice session, to compose an appropriate narrative and set of questions to guide the students through the lesson. Although demonstrations are mostly showing, verbal communication by the teacher during the demonstration is important. Most effective demonstrations include extensive guiding questions which accompany a narrative produced by the teacher. It may even be necessary and appropriate in some demonstrations, particularly those dealing with abstract concepts, to include written guide sheets or other materials to be used by the students.

Teacher demonstrations fall into two basic categories: (1) those concerning the demonstration of phenomena or events which students are unable to do or experience for themselves, and (2) those which are of an explanatory-directive nature which require students, at a later time, to complete the demonstrated task themselves resulting in a product or an improvement in a process or skill.

One strength of an effective demonstration is that it provides a concrete example. Facts may be illustrated and verified for students. Some abstract concepts can be made more meaningful (e.g., molecular structure, appropriate telephone manners, or factoring) and thus understandable by demonstrating concrete instances of the concept. Students may also sharpen observational and listening skills through illustrative demonstrations. The demonstration has the quality of being a strategy which may substitute for students actively doing something themselves. In this instance, the teacher may choose to provide a demonstration of an activity which may be too dangerous or time consuming for students to do for themselves or for which sufficient materials are lacking. Through demonstrations teachers may more expediently help build concepts for students rather than letting them, alone, acquire the information. All points considered, demonstrations are usually very economical in terms of time, materials, and effort.

A key consideration when selecting the demonstration strategy, as with the lecture strategy, is the somewhat passive role assumed by students. As mentioned previously, many students prefer and need active involvement in their learning and there is evidence that more meaningful learning does take place when students are actively involved. Another concern about demonstrations is that clear viewing for all students can sometimes be a problem. All students must be able to see the demonstration for the demonstration to be its most effective. This is not always easy in a classroom of twenty to thirty students. This disadvantage may be alleviated somewhat by the use of instructional technology such as the overhead projector, document camera, or video recorder. If facilities and equipment are available, the teacher may wish to record a demonstration that is difficult to see. This technique has the advantage of providing the means for individual student viewing, or review-ing of the demonstration, and of keeping a successful demonstration for future classes as well as for students who missed the initial presentation. A further limitation of a demonstration becomes evident if the strategy is poor-ly correlated with the teacher's ongoing instruction. Students may, in this case, perceive the demonstration as merely a *show* or diversion. It is impor-tant that teachers deal with this potential problem and, through effective planning and explanation, ensure for students the relevance of all demon-strations. Even when this is done, the best-planned demonstrations can sometimes fail and not communicate the intended results. This is particular-ly true of the classroom *experiment* type of demonstration. The intended event simply may not occur as expected. Creative teachers usually take advantage of this type of situation, however, because if this happens opportunities are now generated for student inquiry by asking the question, "Why did it not work out as we expected?"

Demonstrations that can be followed by immediate student practice have the maximum effectiveness. If this is not possible, a review of the demon-stration is important before practice eventually begins. If time or conditions do not permit student practice, it may be possible that an alternative experi-ence would be as effective as a fully prepared demonstration.

One effective way to conclude a demonstration is to conduct a short ques-tioning session that covers specific procedures, terms, labels, and cause-effect relationships (Pierce & Lorber, 1977). If the demonstrated skill or procedure is to result in some product, as opposed to the understanding of some process, examples of satisfactory and unsatisfactory products should be avail-able so that students can compare and contrast their own products with the demonstrated model.

Figure 5-6 presents an outline of the major responsibilities of a teacher conducting a demonstration.

Drill

Drill perhaps should not be thought of as a separate instructional strategy at all but as a component of virtually any strategy for students at all grade levels. If the teacher expects students to learn, not only must the stimulus material be presented, sufficient opportunities for appropriate practice also must be provided. Practice was also an important component of explicit teaching. Drill refers to actually repeating the performances described in the objectives after they have been demonstrated by the teacher. This strategy provides an opportunity for the student to obtain feedback – a necessary component of effective instruction (Biehler & Snowman, 2006; Good & Brophy, 1986). Feedback has been described as an essential event of effec-

In using the demonstration strategy, the teacher should:

1. practice the demonstration before using it in class,
2. arrange seating so that everyone can see and hear,
3. develop an outline to guide the demonstration,
4. begin with a short overview,
5. outline the main points in handouts, on the whiteboard, the overhead projector, or document camera,
6. describe the procedure at the same time that it is being demonstrated. Repeat as needed.
7. elicit verbal or physical participation by students,
8. conclude with a question/answer session to clarify main points,
9. provide immediate practice opportunities for maximum effect, and
10. plan a follow-up to the demonstration.

Figure 5-6. Major responsibilities of a teacher conducting a demonstration.

tive instruction (Gagne, 1985) and, as such, should be incorporated as an integral part of all strategies. Analysis of homework assignments, a common practice, can provide teachers and students with necessary feedback concerning their progress. Or, a portion of class time may be set aside for an organized drill session in order that students, as well as the teacher, may obtain more immediate feedback.

The drill strategy has the important advantage of aiding in retention through the provision of immediate feedback to the student. If students understand a concept and are able to apply it through appropriate drill, the material will be remembered longer and more completely than if they are not afforded the drill opportunity for feedback. Numerous educators take the position that drills can provide an *overlearning* which eventually aids in the retention of factual material.

Ornstein and Lasley (2000, p. 197) offer eight recommendations for improving practice and drill with students. Research suggests that these approaches can improve practice and drill activities and other seatwork and enhance student learning.

1. *Have a clear system of rules and procedures for general behavior.* Rules and procedures for behavior allow students to deal with personal needs, e.g., going to the restroom, and procedural routines, e.g., sharpening a pencil, without disturbing other students in the class.
2. *Move around the room to monitor students' seatwork.* Students need to feel that the teacher is aware of their behavior and the difficulties they

may encounter. The extent of teacher monitoring correlates with the students' academic ability and need for teacher attention.

3. *Provide comments, explanations, and feedback.* The more recognition/ attention students receive, the more they are willing to pursue seat-work activities. The teacher should watch for signs of student confusion and respond quickly. This increases the students' willingness to persist and helps the teacher to know how students are doing in order to plan the next instructional task.

4. *Spend more time teaching and reteaching the basic skills.* Elementary and low-achieving students should be exposed to concentrated skills learning, which requires practice and drill. When students have difficulty, it is important to instruct in small steps to the point of over-learning.

5. *Use practice during and after learning.* Practice and drill should be used only sparingly for initiating new learning. It is most effective mixed with other activities as learning progresses, such as demonstrations, explanations, and questioning, depending on the age and abilities of the students.

6. *Provide variety and challenge in practice and drill.* Practice can easily drift into busywork and frustrate or bore students if it is too easy, too difficult, or too monotonous.

7. *Keep students alert and focused on the task.* The teacher needs to keep students on task – periodically questioning them, calling on volunteers and non-volunteers, elaborating on incorrect answers, etc.

8. *Maintain a brisk pace.* There should be little confusion about what to do during practice and drill; activities should not be interrupted by minor disturbances. A snap of the finger or other signal procedure should help deal with inattentive or disruptive students without stopping the lesson.

It may be difficult for teachers to decide when drill in a particular area is appropriate. Drill is being used inappropriately if its main purpose is only to keep students occupied (i.e., *busywork*) or when what is being drilled has already been learned. This is not an efficient use of instructional time. An appropriate use of drill is to provide students with an opportunity to develop competencies identified in a lesson's instructional objectives. An additional consideration for the teacher is the readiness level of the students to engage in a drill activity. The teacher runs the risk that students may be practicing their errors of understanding if they lack the proper background to prepare them to do the drill exercises. Figure 5-7 provides guidelines to help ensure a successful use of the drill strategy.

In using the drill strategy, the teacher should:

1. ensure that students have an understanding of the significant concepts or skills before drill is begun,
2. clarify for students why the drill activity is important,
3. match the practice with individual student attention spans,
4. match the practice with learning abilities,
5. use short drills frequently,
6. make certain that students do not see the drill as punitive,
7. when possible, move through the classroom in order to monitor progress and answer questions,
8. provide corrective feedback as soon as possible,
9. maintain focus on instructional objectives as students practice, and
10. have a closing out component to the lesson following the drill activity.

Figure 5-7. Guidelines for using the drill strategy.

Teacher-Led or Guided Discussion

The teacher-led or guided discussion is among the most commonly used strategies at all levels of elementary, middle, and secondary education. A directed discussion is appropriate if students are to be guided through a series of questions to the discovery of some principle, formula, relationship, or other predetermined result (Pierce & Lorber, 1977). For optimum effectiveness, discussion sessions need to be planned carefully to complement other strategies. Although some class discussions are essentially off-task conversations, effective discussions provide a purposeful interaction designed to achieve stated objectives and are characterized by active student verbal, though guided, participation. While the strategy may contain elements of both inquiry and lecture, extensive student-initiated interaction and participation are its defining characteristics. Discussion sessions work best if students feel free to participate and believe that their input is valued by their teacher and classmates. Such feelings are engendered by teachers who acknowledge the importance of differing views, who refer to others during the discussion, and who are overtly authoritative.

Teachers often select the guided discussion strategy because it aids in the development of certain positive learner attributes: objectivity, listening, open-mindedness, and flexibility of thinking. A good discussion session has several other advantages. It can quickly tie student interests and personal experiences to the subject under discussion. This serves not only to increase the value of student experiences, but also to enhance interest in the academic subject and encourage participation. An additional strength of guided discussion is that it potentially allows for the development of higher level thought processes by students. When students are encouraged to publicly present their ideas, understanding of information, or feelings, they then can receive the feedback necessary for effective analysis of their own thinking processes. Teachers can facilitate this development by carefully planning their questions in advance in order to move students from lower to higher levels of thinking. Reflective analysis of one's thought processes leads to the improvement of these processes. The more a student's thought processes are constructively analyzed, the more sophisticated they become. While considerable student participation is desired and needed for the strategy to work well, it is considered a direct instructional strategy as the direction, focus, and, to some extent, the end result, has been previously determined by the teacher. As the discussion is teacher-led, i.e., guided, student participation is more a reaction to the direction given by the teacher through the teacher's planning and preparation for the strategy. Figure 5-8 presents the responsibilities of the teacher when planning for effective instruction during a class discussion.

In using the discussion strategy, the teacher should:

1. prepare objectives and organize content to structure the discussion,
2. provide background information and resources,
3. use key preplanned questions as a guide,
4. encourage student-to-student interaction (e.g., arrange seating in a circle),
5. accept student contributions as worthwhile,
6. expand upon student contributions and use praise as appropriate,
7. encourage non-volunteers to participate (without them feeling threatened),
8. keep digressions to a minimum (return to the topic as soon as possible),
9. use short summaries throughout to maintain focus, and
10. ask questions at the end of the lesson to help determine its success.

Figure 5-8. Guidelines for effective discussions.

Brainstorming is a procedure often used to facilitate guided discussion sessions. The purpose of brainstorming is to generate a large variety of ideas concerning a specific problem or situation in a short time period which are then typically used in the discussion. In using brainstorming procedures, the

teacher acts as a facilitator by making sure that certain basic procedures are followed as outlined below.
The teacher:

- identifies a problem/situation (perhaps with the help of the students),
- clearly explains the purpose of the session and encourages everyone to participate,
- states that ideas are not to be discussed or evaluated during the session,
- writes student contributions on the whiteboard or presentation board as they are made, and
- encourages a brisk pace and completes the session in a short time period (usually less than ten minutes).

After the brainstorming session, the teacher helps the students organize and clarify the ideas and contributions for the discussion to follow.

When using the guided discussion strategy, it should be remembered that it is a strategy that may become time consuming. The discussion is thought by many to be more time consuming than most other strategies, with the exception of inquiry. Consequently, the teacher must decide, while considering lesson objectives and other parameters of the classroom, if the time spent is worth the anticipated gains in student motivation and learning. Following this decision, it is felt that effective teachers will frequently involve their students in some guided discussion episodes.

Overview: Direct Instructional Strategies

To be effective, teachers must analyze each strategy to decide which strategies will be most appropriate in the given classroom setting and use those that are projected to have the greatest promise based on the nature of the material to be taught, time available, and the learning styles, rates, and abilities of the students involved. Figure 5-9 will aid in completing this analysis by providing a summary of the major considerations of the direct instructional strategies that have been presented in this section.

Instructional Strategy	Major Considerations
Explicit Teaching	• is systematic and procedurally coordinated throughout.
	• has as its primary objective the teaching of skills or the mastery of a specific body of knowledge.
	• is dependent on the teacher being well prepared and organized in delivery.

Continued on next page

• has the ability to assist students in developing positive organizational skills and learning habits.
• gives students the opportunity to actually use and apply their learning through guided practice and independent practice procedures.
• ensures feedback from the teacher to the student in terms of the quality of the student's performance.

Lecture Presentation
• adapts easily to all areas,
• delivers large amounts of information quickly and uniformly to all students,
• depends upon high levels of clarity in the presentation for effectiveness,
• requires a basic "performing" talent on the part of the teacher,
• focuses on the knowledge and comprehension levels of thinking,
• can lack motivation if poorly done,
• limits active student involvement but can sharpen listening skills.

Demonstration
• capitalizes on the visual modality of learning,
• results in occasional viewing problems,
• is economical in terms of time, material, and effort,
• replaces a student's direct experiences with dangerous materials,
• sharpens listening and observational skills,
• provides concrete examples, and
• relegates students to a somewhat passive role.

Drill
• provides practice opportunities,
• aids in retention through the provision of immediate feedback,
• can contribute to overlearning,
• risks the practicing of errors, and
• is conducive to over use.

Teacher-led or Guided Discussion
• complements all other strategies,
• allows extensive student interaction and participation,
• aids in development of positive student characteristics,
• aids in development of higher level thought,
• may be time consuming, and
• reduces the breadth of material which may be explored.

Figure 5-9. Synopsis of direct instructional strategies.

As can be seen from the examples of direct instructional strategies included in this chapter, the ability to conduct direct instruction should be an important part of the skill-set of any classroom teacher. Direct instructional strategies have an important place throughout the PK–12 grade continuum. Such strategies represent effective approaches to teach procedures, skills, sequences, rules, and subject matter at the lower levels of the cognitive domain. To be effective, they require that teachers be well organized, well planned, knowledgeable in the areas that they are teaching, keen observers of their students to determine attentiveness and understanding, and sensitive to learning difficulties that their students may encounter. The ultimate effectiveness of direct instructional strategies comes with their appropriate match to the desired learning outcomes that the teacher has identified and the degree to which the teacher effectively uses them in the classroom. Direct instruction can be purposeful, stimulating, motivational, and an effective means by which to establish a systematic way of achieving those learning objectives that are more suitable to direct instructional strategies. Not done well, as with any teaching approach, the opposite outcomes will be the end result.

TECHNOLOGY AND INSTRUCTION

The utilization of instructional technology in public school classrooms has created major innovations in instruction. While the impact of the use of technology has been felt across the entire curriculum and instructional program, and is not specific to any one content area or instructional approach, the discussion of technology and instruction has been included with direct instructional strategies as its use often is associated as a supplement to these types of instructional approaches more so than any other. As with any instructional resource that may be available, teachers need to determine just how, or if, a particular resource may be advantageous for them to use. Technology such as VCRs, audiotapes, cable television, computers, CDs, DVDs, and the Internet provide multisensory learning and in-depth ways for students to acquire knowledge (Ornstein & Lasley, 2000). Four assumptions need to be considered with respect to the merits of using technology in instruction: (1) information in school can be independently learned from electronic media and data sources other than the teacher or text; (2) students are capable of assuming responsibility for their own learning, especially if the material presented is visually and auditorally stimulating; (3) students learn best when they control their rate of learning; and (4) teachers can be assisted to successfully employ technology-based instruction. Each of these points is important in the teacher's search for improved instruction in the classroom.

One significant way that technology is being advanced in the field of education is through the national efforts of professional organizations and such programs as the Educational Technology Initiative: Technology for the 21st Century originated during the Clinton Administration. This program was designed specifically to provide all teachers and students with modern computers and access to the Internet (President's Educational Technology Initiative, 1999). The Initiative calls for the following:

1. modern computer and learning devices will be accessible to every student,
2. classrooms will be connected to one another and to the outside world,
3. educational software will be an integral part of the curriculum, and as engaging as the best video game, and
4. teachers will be ready to use and teach with technology.

While honest debate continues as to what extent computers will actually be involved in meaningful instruction as the twenty-first century unfolds, it is obvious that the computer will be a major instructional tool of the future. Computers, however, are only one aspect of instructional technology. Available instructional technology must be analyzed for its potential to assist students and teachers in the learning process. Technology should be viewed as a tool or resource that educators have available to use in their teaching strategies to better communicate with and provide unique learning opportunities for their students rather than as a discretely separate instructional strategy. The computer and other forms of technology can and should be utilized as instructional aids with many existing strategies. Teachers are encouraged to incorporate computerized instructional techniques into the strategies they now use as opposed to selecting an activity simply because it focuses on computer usage. Resources such as Grabe and Grabe's *Integrating Technology for Meaningful Learning* (2007) can be helpful as teachers analyze available technology and compare this to their own instructional purposes.

Teachers need not become programming experts or even have programming expertise to effectively use instructional technology. Teachers do need to become familiar with the basic operation of the technology while keeping abreast of advancements in instructional software. The rapid changes in the computer market make it impossible to predict just what levels technology may reach in the near future. However, it is clear that computers will continue to play an increasingly important role for educators.

Above all, teachers need to learn to use computers and other technologies in their teaching in ways that are most advantageous and meaningful to their students. For example, it is obvious that computers can be used for drill and practice. Computers certainly never *get tired* of repeatedly asking the same questions over and over. Using the computer only as an electronic workbook, however, is an example of underutilization of this technology. It is desirable that teachers also use existing software packages to incorporate inquiry strategies and simulation and nonsimulation games into their instruction. It may be possible that the most significant use of the technology is one that allows students to be creative and reflect on their own thoughts and to develop their research abilities. All teachers need to become familiar with the varied instructional uses of the computer, in particular as these apply to their own individual disciplines.

There are many obvious advantages to the use of computers to complement instructional strategies. As presented in Chapter 2, the Internet provides rapid access to a vast amount of information and avenues for investigation. However, the use of computer technology by school-age students requires a strong level of adult supervision and guidance because, especially with less mature learners, students may have difficulty assessing the validity, reliability, and bias of information sources that they encounter (Passe, 1999).

At least three major ways have been identified where teachers must be prepared to use computers instructionally. Teachers (1) must be able to teach the basic technical skills students need to operate the computers, (2) need to master strategies that focus on using computers to assist in concept development and problem solving in various content areas, and (3) must have an understanding of the social and ethical consequences associated with the widespread use of computer technology. These understandings will allow teachers to convey to their students the importance of human rights in a world becoming more and more dominated by technology (Jarolimek & Foster, 1997).

There is no reason to doubt that technology will continue to change the way teachers teach and create learning environments throughout the twenty-first century. Researchers are aggressively studying the impact of technology on teaching and learning in classrooms across the country. It is a reasonable supposition that many of the traditional functions that have characterized classroom teaching in the past will be carried out, or at least assisted by computers, in the future (Wiles, 2004). It should be remembered, however, that many of these functions involve planning, monitoring student performance, and record keeping which will make time available to teachers to focus greater efforts on specific instructional needs of students (Jacobsen, Eggen, & Kauchak, 1999).

To reinforce the national impact that technology and its applications are having in the field of education, one need only turn to the work of the International Society for Technology in Education (ISTE), the leading national organization for professional development, knowledge generation, advocacy, and leadership for innovation in technology in education. ISTE has developed technology standards for students as well as teachers and has had tremendous impact, not only in the behavior of teachers in classrooms, but on the improved level of technology use by students in their learning as well.

The following represents ISTE's National Educational Technology Standards (NETS) for Students (ISTE, 2007).

1. Creativity and Innovation

   Students demonstrate creative thinking, construct knowledge, and develop innovative products and processes using technology. Students:

   a. apply existing knowledge to generate new ideas, products, or processes.
   b. create original works as a means of personal or group expression.
   c. use models and simulations to explore complex systems and issues.
   d. identify trends and forecast possibilities.

2. Communication and Collaboration

   Students use digital media and environments to communicate and work collaboratively, including at a distance, to support individual learning and contribute to the learning of others. Students:

   a. interact, collaborate, and publish with peers, experts, or others employing a variety of digital environments and media.
   b. communicate information and ideas effectively to multiple audiences using a variety of media and formats.
   c. develop cultural understanding and global awareness by engaging with learners of other cultures.
   d. contribute to project teams to produce original works or solve problems.

3. Research and Information Fluency

   Students apply digital tools to gather, evaluate, and use information. Students:

   a. plan strategies to guide inquiry.
   b. locate, organize, analyze, evaluate, synthesize, and ethically use information from a variety of sources and media.
   c. evaluate and select information sources and digital tools based on the appropriateness to specific tasks.
   d. process data and report results.

4. Critical Thinking, Problem Solving and Decision Making

   Students use critical thinking skills to plan and conduct research, manage projects, solve problems, and make informed decisions using appropriate digital tools and resources. Students:

    a. identify and define authentic problems and significant questions for investigation.
    b. plan and manage activities to develop a solution or complete a project.
    c. collect and analyze data to identify solutions and/or make informed decisions.
    d. use multiple processes and diverse perspectives to explore alternative solutions.

5. Digital Citizenship

Students understand human, cultural, and societal issues related to technology and practice legal and ethical behavior. Students:

    a. advocate and practice safe, legal, and responsible use of information and technology.
    b. exhibit a positive attitude toward using technology that supports collaboration, learning, and productivity.
    c. demonstrate personal responsibility for lifelong learning.
    d. exhibit leadership for digital citizenship.

6. Technology Operations and Concepts

Students demonstrate a sound understanding of technology concepts, systems, and operations. Students:

    a. understand and use technology systems.
    b. select and use applications effectively and productively.
    c. troubleshoot systems and applications.
    d. transfer current knowledge to learning of new technologies.

In addition to developing NETS for Students 2007, ISTE has also developed National Educational Technology Standards (NETS) for Teachers (ISTE, 2008). Standards for teachers were initially released in 2000 and most recently updated with thousands of educators participating and providing feedback. Based on the 2008 standards, all classroom teachers should be prepared to meet the following technology performances.

1. Facilitate and Inspire Student Learning and Creativity

Teachers use their knowledge of subject matter, teaching and learning, and technology to facilitate experiences that advance student learning, creativity, and innovation in both face-to-face and virtual environments. Teachers:

    a. promote, support, and model creative and innovative thinking and inventiveness.
    b. engage students in exploring real-world issues and solving authentic problems using digital tools and resources.
    c. promote student reflection using collaborative tools to reveal and clarify students' conceptual understanding and thinking, planning, and creative processes.

d. model collaborative knowledge construction by engaging in learning with students, colleagues, and others in face-to-face and virtual environments.

2. Design and Develop Digital-Age Learning Experiences and Assessments

   Teachers design, develop, and evaluate authentic learning experiences and assessment incorporating contemporary tools and resources to maximize content learning in context and to develop the knowledge, skills, and attitudes identified in the NETS-S. Teachers:

   a. design or adapt relevant learning experiences that incorporate digital tools and resources to promote student learning and creativity.
   b. develop technology-enriched learning environments that enable all students to pursue their individual curiosities and become active participants in setting their own educational goals, managing their own learning, and assessing their own progress.
   c. customize and personalize learning activities to address students' diverse learning styles, working strategies, and abilities using digital tools and resources.
   d. provide students with multiple and varied formative and summative assessments aligned with content and technology standards and use resulting data to inform learning and teaching.

3. Model Digital-Age Work and Learning

   Teachers exhibit knowledge, skills, and work processes representative of an innovative professional in a global and digital society. Teachers:

   a. demonstrate fluency in technology systems and the transfer of current knowledge to new technologies and situations.
   b. collaborate with students, peers, parents, and community members using digital tools and resources to support student success and innovation.
   c. communicate relevant information and ideas effectively to students, parents, and peers using a variety of digital-age media and formats.
   d. model and facilitate effective use of current and emerging digital tools to locate, analyze, evaluate, and use information resources to support research and learning.

4. Promote and Model Digital Citizenship and Responsibility

   Teachers understand local and global societal issues and responsibilities in an evolving digital culture and exhibit legal and ethical behavior in their professional practices. Teachers:

   a. advocate, model, and teach safe, legal, and ethical use of digital information and technology, including respect for copyright, intellectual property, and the appropriate documentation of sources.

b. address the diverse needs of all learners by using learner-centered strategies providing equitable access to appropriate digital tools and resources.

c. promote and model digital etiquette and responsible social interactions related to the use of technology and information.

d. develop and model cultural understanding and global awareness by engaging with colleagues and students of other cultures using digital-age communication and collaboration tools.

5. Engage in Professional Growth and Leadership

Teachers continuously improve their professional practice, model life-long learning, and exhibit leadership in their school and professional community by promoting and demonstrating the effective use of digital tools and resources. Teachers:

a. participate in local and global learning communities to explore creative applications of technology to improve student learning.

b. exhibit leadership by demonstrating a vision of technology infusion, participating in shared decision making and community building, and developing the leadership and technology skills of others.

c. evaluate and reflect on current research and professional practice on a regular basis to make effective use of existing and emerging digital tools and resources in support of student learning.

d. contribute to the effectiveness, vitality, and self-renewal of the teaching profession and of their school and community.

There is no doubt that technology has emerged as an additional essential knowledge-base for teachers as they continue to enhance their effectiveness with students in the twenty-first century. The impact of technology on teaching clearly will continue far into the future.

Chapter 6

THE TEACHER AS AN INSTRUCTIONAL STRATEGIST: INDIRECT INSTRUCTION

Educators today are keenly aware of the need to provide students with opportunities to develop new ideas and concepts as they explore their world. Student exploration should characterize many of the learning activities conducted at all grade levels. Indirect instruction was briefly introduced in Chapter 5 as it relates to direct instruction which was the primary focus of the chapter.

INDIRECT INSTRUCTION

Indirect teaching strategies emphasize student exploration and self-learning. In using indirect instructional strategies, the teacher's role as a guide and facilitator is stressed, as opposed to the notion that teachers should directly provide information in its final form. Some educators observe that indirect instructional strategies are more focused on depth of study whereas direct instructional strategies are more focused on breadth. In this regard, teachers traditionally cover larger amounts of lower cognitive and/or skill information through the use of direct instructional approaches and smaller amounts of information, though much more deeply, through the use of indirect instructional approaches.

As noted in Chapter 5, instructional strategies need to be selected as they best meet the purpose of the teacher's lesson (Borich, 2007), i.e., the learning outcomes that the teacher has identified for the students. The teacher's desired student learning outcomes may be placed into one of two broad classifications.

Classification 1: Facts, rules, and action sequences

Classification 2: Concepts, patterns, and abstractions

Indirect instructional strategies are best suited to meet those learning outcomes associated with the second classification. These strategies are popularly referred to as student- or learner-centered strategies, whereas direct instructional strategies are often referred to as teacher-centered. Indirect instructional strategies are designed to have students involved in higher order, independent, and participatory learning experiences. As such, their purpose is distinctly different from those strategies classified as direct. When the teacher's purpose is for students to develop a deeper understanding of concepts, inquire, problem solve, and think more independently, indirect instructional strategies will be needed. In these experiences, students are seeking resolutions to questions, issues, and explaining ideas.

In this chapter, you will learn more about indirect instructional strategies through study of the following topics:

1. the major strategies that teachers use that are referred to or categorized as indirect instructional strategies, and
2. the major characteristics, including both strengths and limitations, of indirect instructional strategies.

Nine indirect instructional strategies which focus on providing student-centered instruction are discussed as follows: *Guided Inquiry, Panel Discussion, Laboratory, Field Trip, Instructional Game, Instructional Contract, Learning Center or Station, Independent Study,* and *Cooperative Learning.*

Guided Inquiry

Instructional approaches referred to as inquiry, discovery, and problem-solving are designed so that students become involved in the process of investigation by enabling them to collect data and test hypotheses (Burden & Byrd, 2007). In guided inquiry instruction, students identify problems, brainstorm solutions, formulate questions, investigate, analyze and interpret results, discuss, reflect, make conclusions, and present results (Bruner, 2004). As a strategy relevant for students of all ages, guided inquiry is the only strategy considered here that may best be defined in terms of what the students do rather than specific teacher behaviors. When used with very young children, care should be given to adjust expectations to the intellectual levels and attention spans of individual students as well as the learning group; that is, instruction should be developmentally appropriate. In this approach, the role of students is to engage in problem solving: beginning and conducting investigations of phenomena. While doing so, students not only learn about the topic being investigated, but, at the same time, learn how to learn on their own. Through guided inquiry, students develop the ability to be reflective problem solvers and to logically address situations that they will encounter in the future. The inquiry process, also referred to as the scientific method, is often described as being made up of the following procedural steps: (1) statement of the problem, (2) development of hypotheses, (3) collection of relevant data, (4) analysis and interpretation of data, and (5) reporting of conclusions and generalizations. The teacher's role in inquiry instruction is primarily that of a guide using effective questioning techniques, giving good directions, and providing quality resource assistance. The teacher is also responsible for helping students, when appropriate, with the investigation, selection, or development of problems and/or situations to investigate. Teaching through inquiry is a process of developing and testing ideas and, as such, must be approached systematically to be successful. Figure 6-1 presents an outline of the major steps of the guided inquiry strategy and indicates the associated teacher responsibilities.

Steps	Teacher Responsibilities
1. Statement of the Problem	Aid in problem selection, clarify problem(s) through a question/answer session, help make problem(s) meaningful and manageable.
2. Development of Hypotheses	Elicit hypotheses through questioning, accept all relevant hypotheses, help clarify hypotheses, aid students in focusing on a manageable number of hypotheses.
3. Collection of Relevant Data	Serve as a resource for the development of data collection methods, guide students to sources of data, provide references to the extent possible, allow classroom time for students to collect data if necessary.
4. Analysis and Interpretation of Data	Use questions to clarify data, investigate the different sources of data utilized, organize all data collected, identify relationships among data collected.
5. Reporting of Conclusions and Generalizations	Provide a system of reporting (e.g., data gathering committees present oral reports) or help students determine what types of conclusions and generalizations can be made related to the original hypotheses.

Figure 6-1. Steps in the guided inquiry strategy.

The following is an example of how a teacher might incorporate the steps outlined in Figure 6-1 into the introductory lesson of a unit of instruction which incorporates the guided inquiry strategy. Mrs. Perez often uses a guided inquiry method in her fourth grade classroom. One of her favorite lessons is based on the problem: "What are the French people like?"

> Mrs. Perez gives the students an opportunity to form hypotheses then gives them French coins and stamps to examine. Her first eliciting question – "What do you see?" – encourages the students to enumerate the data. The students then write down everything they see on the stamps and coins.
>
> Mrs. Perez then asks the students: "How would you group or organize this information?" The students then look at their data and put them into categories, after which she leads the students to label the categories (e.g., symbols, people, and buildings). Finally, the students are encouraged to form generalizations and conclusions about the French people. Mrs. Perez asks the students to tell the class what they think the French people are like based solely on the data found on their national currency and postage stamps.
>
> Following such an introductory lesson, Mrs. Perez' students develop tentative hypotheses as to what the French people are like. Either as groups or individuals, Mrs. Perez sends the students into further areas of investigation, using such out-of-class resources as the library, the Internet, and possibly individual interviews, to include such subtopics as religion, education, politics, family life, and industry. Once the investigation is complete, Mrs. Perez brings the students back together and assists them in testing their hypotheses and in forming more in-depth conclusions and generalizations.

Young people are natural inquirers; they wish to learn. While the preceding statement is true, all too frequently formal schooling can have a negative effect on some students' natural inquiry. The classical rote memory approach to education (e.g., "Who discovered America?") tends to stifle the natural curiosity of most students. What is needed are strategies such as guided inquiry that embrace students' natural tendencies and utilize them to the advantage of the student. Teachers like Mrs. Perez incorporate the guided inquiry approach into their teaching and move beyond the *facts* to work with *bigger ideas* providing students with an opportunity to display and further develop their natural tendencies to inquire. The modeling of a systematic approach to the solution of problems through guided inquiry provides valuable experiences for students. Such experiences enable students to become better at solving problems and making related decisions. If students become involved with something that interests and challenges them, they then will be motivated to deal with other problem situations in the future particularly if the guided inquiry procedures used by the teacher are designed to produce success.

Guided inquiry may be used when the lesson's goal is to have students investigate a particular situation, form generalizations, and think and work at higher levels. It also may be used to encourage interest in the subject matter. The strategy is not appropriate when content mastery is desired only at the remembering and understanding levels of cognition. Lessons which expect students to apply, analyze, evaluate, or create are lessons which should be used to foster inquiry behavior in students. An inquiry lesson is best thought of as an experience in the subject matter, rather than an experience about the subject matter. Therein lies its greatest strength as students, through their inquiry, will develop a much more realistic conceptualization of the subject matter being studied. An additional strength of guided inquiry is the development of thinking skills which are transferable to other subject matter areas. Finally, guided inquiry has the quality of building student understanding in the subject matter as well as interest in learning in general. Inquiry motivates the student to think, an often rewarding and always necessary process.

A consideration not to be taken lightly when using this strategy is that it is demanding. Teachers may find it much easier and more convenient simply to go into the classroom and page through the adopted textbook, predeveloped curriculum, or set of worksheets with their students while concentrating on factual material. This is not possible in guided inquiry. Teachers must develop effective questions and directions to guide students through the lesson since, in inquiry instruction, students are active learners, not passive participants. Problems and situations to be investigated must be selected with care and attention given to the level of cognitive development of the students (i.e., cognitive readiness) and the abstract nature of the information to be learned. Teacher questions must be preplanned in the same manner. While teachers may find it easy to ask many questions, the object in guided inquiry is to ask questions which aid the student in understanding, applying, and internalizing the inquiry process along with the content. Questions at all cognitive levels are needed, not just at the lower or even the higher levels.

An additional characteristic that makes guided inquiry a complex approach is that it is not intended for the delivery of large amounts of material normally emphasized at the remembering and understanding levels of cognition. Such material, however, is often necessary to provide the foundation for future inquiry and learning. Accordingly, inquiry must allow time for the assimilation of facts and concepts for the development of new thoughts. If time is needed in class to review large amounts of material, then guided inquiry would not be the most appropriate strategy. A more efficient means of accomplishing such a task might be an expository presentation such as the lecture strategy. The teacher will have more control over the amount of information that each student is exposed to and the rate at which the information is delivered when the lecture approach is used as opposed to guided inquiry.

The following checklist, adapted from Sugrue and Sweeney (1969), may be helpful in analyzing the teacher's approach to guided inquiry teaching.

Am I An Inquiry Teacher?

	Always	Frequently	Sometimes	Never
I focus on lessons involving exploration of significant ideas, concepts, or problem areas that can be investigated at many levels of sophistication.	___	___	___	___
I prepare for a broad range of alternative ideas which the students may raise related to a central topic.	___	___	___	___
I select materials and learning experiences to stimulate student curiosity and support student investigation.	___	___	___	___
I make available a wide variety of resources and materials for student use.	___	___	___	___
My introductory lessons present some problem, question, contradiction, or unknown element that will maximize student thinking and interest.	___	___	___	___
My aim is for students to react freely to the introductory stimulus with little direction from me.	___	___	___	___
I encourage many different responses to a given introductory stimulus and am prepared to deal with alternative patterns of exploration.	___	___	___	___
The students talk more than I do.	___	___	___	___
Students are free to discuss and exchange their ideas.	___	___	___	___
When I talk, I "question," not "tell."	___	___	___	___
I consciously use students' ideas and base my statements and questions on their ideas.	___	___	___	___
I redirect student questions in such a way that students are encouraged to arrive at their own answers.	___	___	___	___
My questions are intended to lead the students to explore, explain, support, and evaluate their ideas.	___	___	___	___

Panel Discussion

Panel discussions are particularly useful for enabling a small group of students to delve deeply into an area of interest and then to act as a source of information for the rest of the students in the class (Pierce & Lorber, 1977). A panel discussion frequently involves four to five students (one of whom generally serves as chair of the panel) who have completed study on a topic and who share their information with the remainder of the class. The role of the teacher in using this strategy has similarity to the one assumed when using guided inquiry in that the teacher assists with establishing and communicating guidelines in the research process and assigns various responsibilities to individual students. After guidelines have been established, individual students then gather information and later present it, as members of a panel, to their classmates. Panel members usually make a short presentation concerning their assigned areas of study after which the panel, as individuals or a group, responds to questions through the guidance of the chairing member and the teacher. Due to the fact that some younger students may lack the necessary communication, thinking, and study skills to participate successfully in a panel discussion, this strategy may be more appropriate for the intermediate elementary, middle and secondary levels.

To use this strategy well, it is necessary to consider incorporating procedures which will prevent the panel from aimlessly meandering from one member's opinion to another's. Since students often lack extensive experience in conducting and participating in well-organized discussions, they need to be well prepared so that their ideas are properly specified and structured. A prepanel orientation session can help with this and be conducted by the teacher so that all panel members will have carefully identified their problems, the time available and how it should be spent, and selected and organized all important information. The teacher also should carefully choose a leader for the panel who has definite leadership qualities, not just a popular student, and cue the leader to questions that either should be anticipated from nonpanel students in the class or should be posed to other panel members. After the panel members have concluded their remarks, the teacher, as a skillful guide, should follow up on the discussion by highlighting the salient points presented ensuring closure through enumerating all important items. Figure 6-2 outlines suggestions for planning and conducting a successful panel discussion.

Panel discussions are particularly useful for current events or issues topics such as political campaigns, the environment, and other areas where differing opinions can be identified. They also are very suitable for any topic that lends itself to any type of investigation or research activity. Selected topics may not only be complex, requiring considerable out-of-class preparation,

In using the panel discussion strategy, the teacher should:
1. identify three to five students for the panel,
2. clarify the purpose of the study,
3. select and assign responsibilities for the chairperson and others according to abilities and interests,
4. suggest and guide the development of a major topic,
5. assist students in dividing their research efforts,
6. suggest appropriate time schedules and how the research conducted should be reported,
7. regularly monitor students during the time they are doing their research,
8. ensure time for a pre-panel orientation in preparation for the panel discussion, and
9. provide summary remarks which relate to the instructional objectives.

Figure 6-2. Suggestions for planning and implementing panel discussions.

but they may be topics where differences of opinion exist. By dividing responsibilities among several panel members, complex topics where opinions will differ can be discussed more effectively and in a more balanced way. A limitation of the panel discussion lies in the number of students involved at one time. Without careful planning, the teacher may find that the panel plus three or four verbal students represent the only students actually involved in the activity. In such circumstances, it is the teacher's role, as a guide and facilitator, to encourage more active involvement of the remaining students in the class through skillful questioning. Lack of involvement may be avoided if the teacher closely adheres to the suggested guidelines previously identified.

In planning to use panels as debate teams, it is useful to consider two types of debates: *formal* and *informal*. The formal procedure uses the same basic team makeup as two panels. There are two chairpersons, one on each debate team, i.e., panel, who coordinate the research on the selected topic. During the debate, the teacher serves as moderator allowing equal time for presentation of views and rebuttals. The student chairperson leads the team and directs members to make presentations and rebuttals. The informal debate can involve larger numbers of students and, perhaps, allow the entire class to participate. Once a debate topic is selected, all individuals may be assigned to opposing viewpoints after researching the topic. In this approach, one-half of the class would present one viewpoint and the other half of the class another. During the debate, students volunteer to speak on the topic from the lectern with each team taking turns. The teacher serves as moderator and allows each team equal time for presenting and responding to questions from the other team. Like the panel discussion, the use of debates, whether formal or informal, requires considerable planning and preparation by the students and the teacher and frequently will involve prior direct instruction.

Laboratory

With the laboratory strategy, students manipulate objects or equipment under the direction of the teacher. Manipulation may also refer to calculations wherein concrete materials are manipulated to solve mathematical problems as is frequently the case in the elementary classroom. The laboratory strategy is appropriate at all levels of schooling and is not limited to high school science and mathematics classrooms. The laboratory strategy, for example, is being used when kindergarten students are working in small groups using manipulatives. One need not think of a laboratory as a *physical* place except perhaps in computer or middle and secondary level science classes. A laboratory is better thought of as a process rather than a place; it may be best to think of it as a verb rather than a noun. Laboratories represent a hands-on, learn-by-doing teaching strategy which generates exciting, student-involved instruction. In the laboratory approach, the amount of structure will vary from grade level to grade level, but, by utilizing the strategy, students learn by doing with the teacher serving as the director of the concrete experience which is the focal point of the strategy.

A laboratory is sometimes defined to include demonstrations as well. But, a useful distinction between the two strategies is that a laboratory usually involves several small groups (e.g., teams or lab partners) working on an activity, while a demonstration, as presented in Chapter 5 as a direct instructional strategy, is typically presented by the teacher to all of the students at the same time. The two strategies may be combined, however, in that the teacher may choose to demonstrate effective laboratory techniques prior to the students using them.

A typical laboratory activity may serve to address one or more purposes such as the following:

- to gain new information and knowledge,
- to apply previously learned concepts,
- to develop new skills and processes,
- to serve as reinforcement or verification of previously learned knowledge, and
- to serve as appropriate practice to reinforce skills or objectives already mastered.

Some laboratory sessions aid in clarifying the nature of the subject matter in a manner that would be possible with no other strategy. For example, science may be more realistically approached as inquiry through the effective use of laboratory experiences in which data are organized and conceptualized into unique concepts and generalizations.

The role of the teacher in using the laboratory strategy is one of monitoring and questioning in order to help students focus on and accomplish the task(s) at hand. This would be a more powerful learning experience than one where the teacher only lectures on the information to be learned. In guiding the process, the teacher is able to maintain emphasis on the accomplishment of stated instructional objectives. The teacher's assessment of progress must, in fact, be ongoing and informal during the laboratory with laboratory reports and similar student products entering into the teacher's assessment after the completion of the laboratory session. Figure 6-3 outlines suggestions for the teacher in planning and implementing a successful laboratory strategy.

Pre-laboratory Activities	• plan activities to correlate with instructional goals and objectives, • use demonstrations of techniques or equipment utilization as necessary, • provide necessary content background, • delineate roles and expectations for students, and • select or develop laboratory procedures/guides.
Laboratory Experience	• allow students to work in teams of two or three, • serve as a facilitator and guide, monitoring the classroom and answering questions as needed, • provide adequate time for completion of the laboratory, and • direct students to maintain records of their activities.
Post-laboratory Activities	• correlate the laboratory experience with instructional objectives once again, • conduct follow-up discussions, • allot time for the presentation of reports/findings as necessary, and • evaluate the objectives if this was not built into the laboratory exercise itself.

Figure 6-3. Suggestions for planning and implementing a successful laboratory strategy.

An advantage of the laboratory strategy lies in its versatility. It can serve a variety of important functions as outlined above as well as various subject matter areas (e.g., science, English, mathematics, physical education, social studies, and foreign language). Students usually are motivated by laboratory work because it is often a change from the typical class routine and provides an opportunity for them to work with each other and to participate more fully in their own learning.

A disadvantage in the laboratory strategy, however, may be cost. If multiple copies of expensive equipment are needed, the cost of the laboratory activity may become prohibitive. Space requirements can also be a deciding factor when considering the use of a laboratory activity. In order to properly conduct laboratory activities, adequate equipment and space are needed to ensure active and safe student involvement. In those circumstances where adequate space and materials cannot be provided, it may be advisable to purchase only one piece of apparatus and utilize the demonstration strategy rather than deleting the experience from the students' curriculum entirely.

Field Trip

While strategies such as demonstrations and laboratories are intended to bring a portion of the *real* world into the classroom, the field trip strategy is designed to take students out of the classroom and into the real world to see things for themselves. Mackenzie and White (1996) report that active field-trip participants learn more than students who have not gone on field trips. Falk and Balling (1996) note that well-designed field trips can lead to new learning, reinforce what has been already learned, and aid greatly in the retention of information. Some field trip destinations are deeply educational beyond the accepted value of traveling and observing. Many museums, for example, are not just for traditional trips any longer but offer curriculum links and staff development. Museums and cultural institutions like the aquarium often provide a crucial resource for students and teachers in science classes (Lessons at the Museum, 2008). Shorter, closer-to-home field trips are recommended for young students, whereas trips that are more novel, possibly to some place unfamiliar, and extensive are recommended for older students. Field trips require the teacher and students to leave the classroom in order to become fully involved in the learning experience. Trips may merely be to the school grounds outside the classroom and school or may be more extended and involve transportation to areas far removed from the immediate school facility. The length of the trip can vary from ten to fifteen minutes on the school grounds to an all-day or, perhaps, overnight excursion to other locales.

Since field trips can serve to introduce or conclude a unit of study and motivate students, they require extensive planning well in advance of the actual trip itself. In elementary classes, where students are not as able to grasp abstract concepts, it is recommended that the teacher plan concrete experiences, such as field trips, to introduce units of instruction. Pre- and post-trip activities also must be well planned in order to fully capitalize on the educational significance of the trip. Other factors, such as cost, transportation, scheduling, and supervision must be considered, along with appropriate measures to evaluate student outcomes and the success of the experience. As with any other strategy, the use of the field trip should be based on its relationship to the attainment of identified student learning outcomes or objectives in the lesson. Figure 6-4 outlines important teacher responsibilities in planning and implementing a successful field trip.

Pre-trip Activities

Plan Instructional Components:
- Correlate the field trip with goals and objectives.
- Develop necessary background information.
- Decide on safety information.
- Define role expectations.

Plan Noninstructional Components:
- Calculate cost.
- Secure sanction of school.
- Secure transportation.
- Secure adult supervision.
- Coordinate with on-site personnel.
- Develop schedule.
- Secure permission of parents.

Trip Activities

- Serve as guide and director.
- Assist students in gathering information.
- Provide new information as needed.

Post-trip Activities

- Conduct a follow-up discussion or other activity to correlate the field trip experience with goals and objectives.
- Evaluate instructional objectives using student reports or a more formal testing situation.

Figure 6-4. Responsibilities in planning and implementing a field trip.

Like demonstrations, field trips have the advantage of providing concrete, real-world experiences not usually available in the classroom. In addition, field trips typically generate high student interest. It is hoped that this level of motivation has not been precipitated by a strategy viewed only as an opportunity to escape formal classroom instruction but as a result of an opportunity to experience a relevant, concrete learning activity of high interest. An important characteristic of field trips is that they provide experiences which students may not have otherwise. A tour of a power plant to learn, firsthand, how electricity is produced is an example of such an experience. While such visits usually are not available to the general public, school group visitations are often encouraged. Some field trips share a disadvantage with certain laboratory sessions in that they may be costly. If students are to be transported over fairly long distances, for example, the expense may become prohibitive. Extended (at least one-half day) trips have another disadvantage, particularly in secondary school settings, of interfering with ongoing instruction in other classes. A field trip in one class may necessitate a student being absent in another. The amount of time devoted to planning a successful trip also must be considered. For the trip to be successful, the teacher must plan carefully to ensure the safety and proper supervision of all students. Some of the noninstructional components of the field trip strategy that need careful consideration include: transportation, adult supervision, food/refreshments, advance scheduling, and on-site arrangements.

Instructional Game

Instructional games, role playing, simulations, and non-simulations can play important roles in some classrooms and insignificant roles in others. Role playing, in particular, can be useful in helping students to understand the views and feelings of others especially concerning personal and social issues. Role playing is a student-directed activity where students act out or dramatize a specific situation, circumstance, or idea (Burden & Byrd, 2007). The strategy can be time consuming and, in some cases, getting all students to take the activity seriously can be a challenge. Unless the teacher and the students are well prepared, the teacher may not get the most out of the time invested. A nine-step process has been identified to maximize the benefits of the role playing strategy (Joyce, Weil, & Calhoun, 2004).

1. *Warm up the group:* The warm-up introduces the students to the activity and makes sure that the problem/activity and its purpose are understood. An example of what is to follow is given and ample time is provided for questions and answers.
2. *Select the participants:* The various roles are identified and explained. The teacher needs to make sure that students are matched well to their roles.
3. *Set the stage:* The teacher should ask the students to review the scene and set aside a place for the action to take place.

4. *Prepare the observers:* Typically, the non role playing students are observers. The teacher should ask them to analyze what they see and be ready to discuss the role playing after it has concluded.

5. *Enact:* The role play takes place. It should be kept fairly short and end after the main points/purpose have been addressed.

6. *Discuss and evaluate:* Students should discuss what they saw, including those role playing, and evaluate the impact of the activity.

7. *Reenact:* A reenactment can be held to make sure that the role play achieved its purpose in terms of what students learned and/or to explore different ways that the role play might have ended.

In addition to role play, Perry and Conroy (1994) assert that instructional games have an enormous potential for developing concepts and skills, not only because of the active involvement of the participants, but also because of the thinking that is stimulated. They explain that playing games results in students using their imagination, thinking creatively, showing curiosity, investigating concepts, and concentrating on important ideas. Such higher order thinking should be the goal of all teachers. These goals can be difficult to attain using more traditional instructional strategies. The use of games can facilitate the accomplishment of these goals and make it easier for teachers to involve students in significant and meaningful thought.

Instructional games may be classified into two major categories: simulation and non-simulation. In simulation games, students simulate, i.e., pretend, authentic roles and experiences through role play. Other games require following simple rules to accomplish the goal of the game. Regardless of the type of game, people have played and enjoyed games for centuries because they are a fun and psychologically important activity (Huzinga, 1970). Playing games offers students a challenge to figure out or solve a simple task and to succeed at a task, both of which can be motivating.

Instructional games of all kinds, but particularly those of a simulation nature, provide extensive opportunities for students to practice and improve their communication and decision-making skills. Students are often required to communicate their viewpoints and listen to the ideas of others during simulations. The use of well-planned games may also be a successful strategy to help clarify abstract concepts. For example, if a student is required to simulate through role play the values of another person, abstract values such as love and hate may be clarified further for that student as well as for others participating in the simulation or even viewing the simulation. Students could also, for example, be asked to simulate the main participants in a court trial, the negotiations between a salesman and a prospective customer at a car dealership, proper manners in a fine restaurant, or appropriate ways to ask a friend for a favor. The possibilities for meaningful simulation activities are virtually endless.

Many non-simulation games are available commercially such as *Monopoly*, *Candyland*, and *Jeopardy*. These and many other games can be easily adapted for academic use but also require careful planning. Simulation games, because of their extensive sets of rules and roles to consider, can require substantial planning time. Games should not be used just to fill time or simply to have fun, but they should assist students in attaining important teacher-identified objectives. Used properly, games can be among the most satisfying strategies for teachers as well as students.

Instructional games likely will be unsuccessful if their implementation is poorly planned, including the degree to which students are introduced to and fully understand the concept of the strategy. To be effective, the teacher must plan both pre- and post-game activities to facilitate the best learning. Such activities, before and after the game, can be as important as playing the game itself. Figure 6-5 provides guidelines for teachers to follow when using instructional games.

Pre-game Stage	• Relate the game to instructional goals and objectives. Students must realize that the game is a part of their ongoing instruction. • Outline the game, whether it is a simulation (role-play) or non-simulation (e.g., board) game, explaining its purpose and procedures.
During the Game	• Firmly establish ground rules at the beginning of the game in order to avoid confusion at a later point. Duplicated copies of the ground rules are very useful. • Serve as a monitor and source of directions for the game or actively participate in the game. The latter is recommended whenever possible.
Post-game Stage	• Serve as a discussion leader in relating the game experience back to its original goals and objectives. • Conduct formal or informal evaluation keyed to the instructional objectives if it was not built into the game.

Figure 6-5. Guidelines for conducting instructional games.

Instructional Contract

Burden and Byrd (2007) identify that learning contracts provide a structure that allows a student and teacher to agree on a series of learning tasks to be completed in a given period of time. Most contracts are designed to offer students the opportunity to work independently through a body of required subject matter or to carry out individual projects. An instructional contract is an agreement between two or more parties, usually one teacher and one student, formed to bring about specific learning outcomes (Wiseman, 1983). In the instructional contract, the student may agree to complete contract activities as the teacher has designed them, or negotiate with the teacher certain portions of the contract with alternatives being suggested. The teacher may even be presented with a student-prepared contract to approve, disapprove, or modify through discussion.

Contracts generally involve student consideration of what may be called learning alternatives, i.e., choices. Alternatives are learning experiences which the teacher feels represent the contract subject area to be studied. The student typically is given the opportunity to make selections of alternatives to complete. Following a grading formula previously established, the student may actually contract for a specified grade. This depends upon how many, or perhaps which, alternatives are selected. The contract approach does not limit the leadership role of the teacher, but it provides an alternative form of instruction which is accompanied by a high level of student participation. Whether teacher-, student-, or jointly-designed, the teacher gives final approval before any contract is accepted for use.

Instructional contracts are characterized by a set of basic elements which cover the entire learning procedure. Common elements, together with their purpose or content, are as follows:

- *Title:* An exciting and intriguing inducement to capture the students' attention and draw the students into the experience.
- *Introduction:* An explanation of what may be found in the contract and an overview of the content.
- *Instructional Objectives:* A list of what is to be known, performed, or accomplished through the contract activities.
- *Learning Alternatives:* Varied choices should be provided which include opportunities for active participation in the learning experience.
- *Resources and Materials:* Materials necessary for the successful completion of the contract should be listed.
- *Reporting Procedures:* An identification of how the student will show what has been accomplished.
- *Closing Agreement:* A clear indication of what grade is being contracted for, which alternatives will be completed and any other conditions. The grade contract portion is typically omitted in early childhood settings.

In a very real sense, the use of contracts in teaching represents an effort toward individualization. Teachers should carefully analyze the major factors related to the use of this strategy prior to classroom implementation. When considering the use of instructional contracts, the following questions should be reviewed.

- *Who should be given a learning contract?* Adding variety to the traditional classroom, getting to know all of the students in a more personal way, thinking of students as individuals, and involving students in decision-making activities are all worthwhile outcomes, regardless of the academic level of the class. Instructional contracts can be used with virtually all students, particularly from the intermediate grades and above, provided that individual learning style and student maturity are taken into consideration.
- *How long should a contract last?* A basic guideline to follow is that, if the contract approach is new to both the teacher and students, the length of time devoted to the contract should be relatively short. As a starting point, allow perhaps a two-week maximum length for contracts to be completed, or even less for elementary students (e.g., one week).
- *Can contracts be broken?* The contract must allow for decision-making on the student's part. As this is the case, changes are possible. The time will come in the contracting activity, however, where changes are no longer practical nor profitable. At some point, decisions made should be considered final.
- *If contracts are used in some subjects, should they be used in all subjects?* There is no need for a teacher who chooses to use contracts in one class or subject to feel that all other classes or subjects must use contracts. All content or perhaps even student groups do not lend themselves to the contract strategy.
- *Who determines the guidelines for the instructional contract?* Student ideas must be considered since the contract is presented as a means of increasing student involvement in the learning process, although the teacher has the final decision to make regarding the guidelines.

The contract is an endeavor wherein student success in an engaging form of instruction is desired and clearly possible. Learning alternatives should represent assignments or expectations which nearly all students can complete. If the contract has a hidden agenda, it is in providing relevant decision-making and confidence-building experiences for students. Consider the following contract designed for the upper elementary level for further analysis in preparation for developing other instructional contracts.

Title: Why Eskimos Don't Wear Flip-Flops

Introduction:

Have you ever wondered what it might be like to live in an igloo? Would you like to live in a climate where it rains every day? What causes climates to be different? This contract is designed to acquaint you with different climates and how they affect human lives.

Instructional Objectives:

1. Following independent investigation, describe the influence of climate on the human life-style.
2. Given reading, writing, and participating activities, identify the relationships among temperature, precipitation, and climate.

Learning Alternatives:

The following learning alternatives relate to the objectives for this contract. Those alternatives marked with an asterisk (*) must be completed. You will be graded according to the number of alternatives you select (A = 6; B = 5; C = 4; D = 3) and successfully complete.

1. Pretend you are taking a trip to Greenland. Make a list of the following: (a) the items you might take with you, (b) what you would expect to see during your visit, (c) the countries you will travel through on your trip.
2. Look at the slides on geographic areas. Write a paragraph telling how you think people living in each of the areas might make their living. Support your answers.
3. *Choose one of the world climate regions and make a poster or collage depicting that region.
4. Find pictures of people who live in different climates and make a scrapbook. Label the climate region in which they live.
5. *Make a diagram of the sequence of mild, severe, and polar regions in relation to the equator.
6. Find and read a short story about Eskimos, nomads, or natives who live in the tropics. Make a report to the class using PowerPoint or put your report on a cassette tape or CD.
7. Write a two-page paper identifying the world climate region in which you would like to live. Tell why you would like to live in this particular region.
8. *Write a paragraph describing the relationship of temperature and precipitation to climate.

Resources and Materials:

National Geographic, newspapers and magazines, slides (geographic areas), maps, globes, World Wide Web, textbooks, and encyclopedia.

Reporting Procedures:

Your teacher will check the items you have selected and enter the date you complete them on a checklist. This will be done on conference days. At the beginning of a conference day, arrange a time to meet with the teacher.

Closing Agreement:

I agree to fulfill the requirements for the following learning alternatives: _____. It is my understanding that by successfully completing these alternatives I will receive the grade of _____ for my work on this learning contract. Number of learning alternatives selected:_____

Contract Due Date: _____   Signed:
                                        Teacher _____
                                        Student _____
                                        Date   _____

Two strengths of the contract approach are that the teacher can readily provide opportunities for student choices and a rather high degree of individualization. In addition, contracts provide opportunities for independent student activities with the teacher serving more as a planner and facilitator and less as the fountain from which all knowledge springs. Finally, students using instructional contracts are allowed to work at different rates; to this degree, contracts are self-paced.

Contracts, however, require more and different resources than some of the more traditional forms of instruction. This could prove to be costly if teachers choose to include expensive materials in each contract. Increased teacher planning and organizational efforts are also important considerations in using the contracting procedure. The planning and organizing required represents increased teacher responsibilities. Furthermore, some students may have difficulty in using their time wisely due to their inability to function without close supervision. The teacher must remember that the ability to be self-paced does not develop naturally in all students. For this reason, it is suggested that time be spent, before individualizing is attempted, to develop the students' abilities to stay on task and to pace themselves in their work. Figure 6-6 outlines the basic steps and responsibilities of the teacher using the contract strategy.

Introduction	Present the contract to all students while establishing procedural rules and delineating student responsibilities.
Student Interview/Conference Session I	Set aside time to meet individually with each student to discuss which learning alternatives are to be selected and for which grade the student is contracting.
Student Exploration Period	Provide a period of student exploration to allow the student to get into the contract and see what is there.
Student Interview/Conference Session II	Continue to monitor student progress closely and make final decisions regarding learning alternatives and grading procedures.
Student Work Period	Allow for a larger segment of time during which the student completes most of the work on the learning activities selected.
Contracts Handed In/Wrap-Up	Provide a closing counterpart to the introduction that allows the entire class a chance to meet for the purpose of reacting to the contract experience.

Figure 6-6. Basic steps and responsibilities for a teacher using a contract strategy.

Learning Center or Station

The use of a learning center (or learning station) can be an extremely productive strategy for the student as well as the teacher. A learning center is defined as an area designated and designed by the teacher, sometimes with the help of students, for the purpose of providing students with an opportunity to participate in individualized, student-centered instruction so that differing styles and rates of learning can be accommodated. It typically is a place designated within the classroom where a student may go to pursue either required or optional learning activities (Burden & Byrd, 2007). Learning centers create situations where students become active participants in their own education. Santrock (2008) comments that learning centers can be especially good alternatives to paper-and-pencil seatwork. They are applicable to virtually any content area including study with and of computers.

A learning center is a place where one or more students at a time can complete activities and objectives using materials provided by the teacher. Because active involvement is required, the use of centers increases the possibility that more students will achieve the desired learning objective(s) and, at the same time, demands that they accept a greater responsibility in the learning process. Learning centers typically are of two types: (1) those that promote and reinforce skill and content development, and (2) those that provide content enrichment. Each type has its own appropriate place in the classroom.

Skill and content development centers are useful because they are designed for use after initial instruction by the teacher and reinforce the skill or content that the teacher is seeking to develop. Once the teacher has introduced the skill(s) or content to be learned, students proceed to the center to practice at their own rates and, eventually, to master the material. The teacher should provide a diverse selection of materials to aid students as they work on their tasks. These centers often develop concepts through stages. For example, a concept may be developed from concrete to abstract (i.e., simple to complex).

Enrichment centers, as the name implies, are designed to expand and enrich the student's knowledge and interest about a particular area of study. These centers provide a number of alternatives that may stimulate an individual student's curiosity and allow for the various interests that exist to be pursued and expanded. While skill and content centers provide many effective ways for students to demonstrate various levels of competency of learning, the activities there are generally prescribed as being essential. As such, each student is expected to demonstrate competence with respect to the material being studied. Enrichment centers, on the other hand, provide for more variability in student achievement because there is ample opportunity for students to proceed in any number of directions. Enrichment centers generally are less prescribed in their organization.

Centers can be set up in any area of a classroom and can range from a very elaborate design to one that is extremely simple. They can be arranged in a variety of ways and in a variety of places (e.g., tables, walls, and open alcoves). While often believed to require wide, spacious facilities, they can be quite functional in limited physical areas. There actually can be numerous centers in any one classroom each promoting different skills or interests that reinforce and expand upon the material presented in the text, class lecture, or discussion.

In order to prepare a learning center, regardless of type, it is helpful for the teacher to follow a systematic procedure such as the following:

- decide purpose/topic based on current needs of students and the curriculum;
- prepare objectives to be posted in the center;
- assemble or create activities to help students achieve stated objectives;
- collect or create materials to be used in the activities and place them on a table or in a designated area of the room. There may be several activities in one area on different facets of the topic being studied;
- develop activity cards, worksheets, and/or directions for students to follow in completing the activities. Post directions for activities in the center on "starter cards." Audio tapes can be used for students who are non-readers;
- prepare an evaluation to let students know when the objectives have been met. For example, an answer key may be provided on the back of the directions for the center. This provides needed feedback quickly and enables the student and teacher to assess progress. In this way the materials are self-correcting;
- try out and revise as needed. Be sure to encourage students to add to the center, especially enrichment centers. Such centers are best if started by the teacher and expanded by the students. For example, students may wish to add to a leaf collection initiated by the teacher; and
- change the materials often enough to provide appropriate learning and stimulation.

In considering the use of this strategy, the teacher should keep in mind a number of important responsibilities (Figure 6-7).

Learning centers provide the teacher with the opportunity to (1) expand the curriculum, (2) foster active learning for the students, (3) make content more relevant to student concerns and interests, and (4) provide increased alternatives for learning. The implementation of learning centers in some

In using the learning center or learning station strategy, the teacher should:

1. orient the students thoroughly to the concept of learning centers or stations before they begin,

2. have complete instructions and objectives in each center or station that complement a captivating title which is used to generate student interest,

3. establish a set of clearly designed learning activities,

4. provide learning activities that are diverse in terms of varying student abilities, rates, and learning modalities,

5. develop activities which follow a logical sequence (e.g., concrete to abstract, familiar to unfamiliar),

6. create activities that provide the opportunity for students to clarify and/or expand on what they have learned by applying what they know to new situations,

7. establish and communicate procedures for assessment prior to student work, and

8. plan such management details as:
   a) how many students may be in a center/station at one time,
   b) how long students may stay in a center/station,
   c) who decides which center/station a student may be in, and
   d) what students should do when not working in a center/station.

Figure 6-7. Teacher responsibilities in planning and implementing learning centers.

ways requires more work and organization than a traditional approach to teaching. For this reason, teachers who already feel overburdened in their work may not be immediately receptive to this strategy. While the initial effort may seem Herculean, the hard work eventually pays off in terms of providing more time for instruction and requiring less time for busywork. In addition, the teacher may be assured that, when implemented properly, students are learning more, probably having a more enjoyable time doing it, and, above all, are learning to learn on their own.

Independent Study Project

Independent study projects have long been used by teachers in a variety of ways and for many purposes. Good and Brophy (2003) report that about one-third of teachers at the elementary level and about one-fifth at the secondary level attempt to individualize their instruction through some form of independent work. An entire unit of instruction often can be presented through the use of independent study projects. Independent study projects are those activities, initiated by the student with the teacher's guidance or assigned by the teacher, which culminate in a student-prepared product. This product, or exhibition, usually consists of a student report (written and/or oral) which is often accompanied by an example of the student's creative efforts (e.g., models, illustrations, and collections). Regardless of the type of product prepared, an important feature of this strategy is that students have an opportunity to display the results of their work. This provides positive rewards for those doing the projects and illustrates numerous individual learning possibilities available for other students in the classroom. Blumenfeld, Soloway, Marx, Krajcik, Guzdial, and Palincsar (1996) report that individual projects have the capacity to motivate and teach at the same time and are typically characterized by three features: (1) a project requires a question or a problem; (2) activities in which the students are involved should have a real-world quality; and (3) activities that are a part of the project should result in some product such as a presentation, written report, etc. Borich (2007) expands on this when adding that project-based learning must (1) present a real-world challenge; (2) allow for some student choice and control; (3) be doable, i.e., achievable; (4) require some level of collaboration, i.e., students working with other students; and (5) result in a concrete, tangible product.

To plan for such a strategy as the independent study project, the teacher might begin by developing a menu of project ideas which correlate directly with planned instructional objectives. The purpose is to aid the student in the selection of worthwhile, relevant projects that will help in mastering stated objectives. If a project topic or idea does not relate clearly to the teacher's instructional objectives, it should not be pursued. The teacher must also prepare evaluation measures for these objectives to determine if or when they are mastered by the students. Consider the following examples.

Mrs. Brown, a fifth grade teacher, teaches a unit using a grouping of objectives related to the study of the *family*. Mrs. Brown has identified five potential independent study projects available for study in this unit. They may be thought of as constituting Mrs. Brown's menu of projects from which students may select.

1. Design a family mobile with no fewer than five parts and display it in class for at least one week.
2. Cut at least twenty pictures from magazines and make a family collage poster. Display the poster in class for at least one week.
3. Interview at least three family members (brothers, sisters, cousins, aunts, uncles, parents, grandparents) about what things they like to do best as a family. Prepare a written report on your findings.
4. Do research in your text, from the library or the Internet and compare families found in a foreign country (e.g., China, Japan, Russia,

Germany, Sweden, or Brazil) with your own family. Write a report of your findings, and give an oral report to the class.

5. Prepare a diorama depicting families in different periods in history. Use *the frontier family, the modern family,* and *the family of the future* as three periods to illustrate how families change over time.

Mr. Stottlemeyer's tenth grade math class is studying the topic *measurement.* The following are some independent study projects which he has made available to his students.

1. Prepare a scale model of the basketball court using a one inch to thirty-six inch scale.
2. Make a growth chart using both standard and metric units for the growth of a bean seedling over a two-week period.
3. Make a drawing comparing the size of the gym to the size of your classroom using measures to the nearest square foot.
4. Observe the numbers of cars, SUVs, pickup trucks, and semi-trailer trucks passing through the intersection in front of the school from 3:00 pm to 4:00 pm for a one-week period. Make a bar graph to illustrate the results of your observations.
5. Prepare a line graph based on one week of observation in the school lunchroom during your lunch period. Graph your observations of the relationship of students purchasing their lunch from the fast food service to those purchasing from the full meal service.

An important feature of this teaching approach is that it permits students, because of the unique interest developed, to become more fully involved in their own learning. Students who sometimes do poorly in traditional classroom assignments produce excellent projects because of their increased interest in an activity that they have been able to pick themselves. Independent projects may be very motivating in as much as students are necessarily active in their work. Figure 6-8 outlines major teacher responsibilities in planning and using independent study projects.

Although student projects do not consume as much of the teacher's planning time as contracts and some other strategies, a characteristic of this strategy is that it frequently requires a great deal of class time for the completion and reporting of project activities. Additionally, if they have had no prior experience with the strategy, some students may tend to feel unsure that they do not know exactly what to do, at least during the early stages of the strategy, and need considerable individual direction and assistance from the teacher.

A problem that some teachers have faced when selecting this strategy relates to the originality of the student product. Some teachers report having received projects that appeared to be the result of efforts of an individual

In using the independent study project strategy, the teacher should:

1. identify instructional objectives related to the goals of the unit being studied,
2. prepare evaluation measures based on the objectives,
3. develop a menu of project possibilities,
4. guide students in selecting their projects,
5. clearly delineate expectations for student products and evaluation criteria to be used,
6. provide students with guidance and assistance while they develop their projects,
7. monitor students closely as they work on their projects,
8. collect written reports and/or hear oral reports,
9. lead a discussion on the major points developed in each report or project, and
10. evaluate all aspects of each project as related to desired student learning outcomes.

Figure 6-8. Teacher responsibilities in planning and implementing independent study projects.

other than the student. Teachers should be concerned with legitimate content considerations for the given quality of the product. This may help the teacher avoid such problems which arise when student projects are evaluated. To help ensure quality and originality in the student-developed project, the teacher should make available adequate class time for the monitoring and guiding of the students' work.

Cooperative Learning

Cooperative learning is an indirect instructional strategy that promotes students working together for the benefit of each individual as well as the entire group. This method of instruction became very popular in the 1980s, especially through the research of Slavin (1994) and Johnson and Johnson (1992) and their associates. Research (Slavin, 1995) suggests that cooperative learning can be an effective strategy for improving student achievement where two conditions are met: (1) group rewards are included where some type of recognition is given to the group allowing the members to see that it is in their best interest to help each other, and (2) individuals are held accountable to include some method of evaluation that reflects each member's contribution.

Johnson and Johnson (1999) suggest that each cooperative learning lesson should have the following five basic elements:

1. *Positive interdependence:* Students believe that they are responsible for their learning and the learning of other group members.
2. *Face-to-face interaction:* Students work in groups and interact together on a regular, planned basis.
3. *Individual accountability:* Each student is accountable for mastery of the work that is assigned.
4. *Interpersonal and small-group skills:* Each student must be able to communicate effectively, be respectful of other group members, and work with others to resolve problems.
5. *Group processing:* Each group must be assessed to see how well the members work together and how they can improve.

Student Team Learning, the name given to Slavin's model for cooperative learning, is based on three central principles: team rewards, individual accountability, and equal opportunities for success. In using this strategy, students are first divided into teams, and each team has its own specific achievement goals. Team members receive rewards if team achievement goals are met or exceeded. All or none of the teams may receive rewards because the teams are not in competition with each other. Each student is held accountable in this process, and the team's success is dependent upon the individual performance of all team members. When assessments are given, each student works without help from teammates, and all students are given grades based on their own work. Grades are not given to the group as a whole. Consequently, students are encouraged to help teammates through peer tutoring or study groups prior to assessment.

Many educators prefer the advantages of this cooperative learning model over classical group work (Hunt, Wiseman, & Bowden, 2003) where students work together on an assignment leading to the same grade for each group member. Many feel that giving one grade to all group members is a poor practice since some students may do much more and better work than others.

Cooperative learning groups should, under optimal conditions, be comprised of approximately four students with different ability levels, genders, and ethnic backgrounds. This type of diversity among team members optimizes the opportunities for success for all students. Because all students are competing against their own previous performance, or against the standard that the teacher has set, each student should have an equal opportunity for success. Cooperative learning has been found to be a highly successful procedure when teaching students of varying abilities (Stowell, Rios, McDaniel, & Christopher, 1996).

Slavin (1994, 1990) developed *Student Teams Achievement Divisions* (STAD) that has become a popular method for structuring cooperative learning lessons. STAD involves four-member teams. The teacher begins by teaching a lesson to the students who, in turn, study the new material in their cooperative groups helping one another learn as effectively as possible. After the study period ends, the teacher individually quizzes the students on the material without help from their peers. Each student receives an individual grade on the quiz which allows the teacher to compare each student's score with that student's previous performance in order to determine if improvement/progress is being made. The members of each team earn rewards based on the degree that team members equaled or exceeded the criteria based on their prior performance.

All cooperative learning models, however, are not based upon students receiving grades. Johnson and Johnson (1989), for example, developed the *circle of knowledge* as a brainstorming type activity where the team is given a question or a prompt to which team members are to respond. The brainstorming lasts five to seven minutes, allowing each group member time to respond in any fashion he or she feels appropriate. One student, called the recorder, takes notes, writing down the comments of each team member. These notes are then signed by each group member and returned to the teacher who may react to the work but not grade it. Later, the teacher can put each team's response on a chart, PowerPoint, or overhead transparency as a focal point for class discussion.

In using the cooperative learning strategy, the teacher should:

1. clearly review the rules for group learning with the students before the activity begins. For example, students should be responsible for their own work, help one another when needed, and refrain from using put-downs,

2. place students in heterogeneous groups comprising teams of approximately four students,

3. assign roles to each team member such as *facilitator* (keeps the group on task), *reporter* (informs the teacher or class about group activities), *timer* (keeps track of time), *artist* (illustrator of displays), and *recorder* (keeps notes on group processes),

4. provide each group with a clearly defined learning task to perform,

5. move around the classroom frequently from group to group observing and providing help where needed,

6. ask students questions to help them evaluate their performance when the activity is complete,

7. evaluate each student's learning, and

8. assign grades to individuals and rewards to teams as appropriate.

Figure 6-9. Major responsibilities of a teacher conducting cooperative learning lessons as adapted from Hunt, Wiseman and Bowden (2003).

Considerable interest has been shown by teachers over the past few years in the cooperative learning strategy as a way of getting students more involved in their own learning through the use of a more indirect teaching strategy. Figure 6-9 provides a list of the major responsibilities of a teacher conducting cooperative learning lessons.

Overview: Indirect Instructional Strategies

Effective teachers are able to use any of the indirect instructional strategies presented here as determined by the purpose of the lesson, time constraints, student readiness, and circumstances of the learning environment. Strategies should not be used at random but only after careful analysis of lesson purposes, student characteristics, and instructional constraints or parameters (e.g., time, room environment, cost, and availability of materials). Most teachers prefer to use an eclectic approach which requires the use of multiple strategies. Figure 6-10 provides a summary of the major considerations of those indirect strategies that have been presented.

Instructional Strategy	Major Considerations
Guided Inquiry	• provides an opportunity for students to display natural tendencies to inquire, • interests and challenges students, • develops higher level thinking, • requires considerable planning time and expertise, and • does not deliver large amounts of information quickly.
Panel Discussion	• leads to stimulating coverage of current events, issues topics, and other research-oriented topics, • typically involves only a limited number of students, • enables students to share information with one another, and • aids in the development of student research skills.
Laboratory	• capitalizes on active student involvement, • encourages group sharing of ideas, • clarifies the nature of the inquiry process, • can be very motivating for students, • requires extended teacher preparation and organization time, • is versatile in adapting to various instructional objectives, and • can be costly.

Continued on next page

Field Trip	• brings a portion of the real world to the student's learning,
	• provides experiences that may not normally be available to the student,
	• requires extensive planning,
	• offers concrete experiences,
	• generates high interest, and
	• can be costly.
Instructional Game	• may simulate authentic roles and experiences,
	• motivates through active student involvement,
	• enhances communication skills,
	• encourages student creativity
	• can oversimplify reality, and
	• may require considerable planning and instructional time.
Instructional Contract	• provides an opportunity to develop independent study habits,
	• provides extensive opportunities for student choice,
	• generates high interest and involvement,
	• creates an environment where students may not use study time wisely,
	• requires extensive and varied resources,
	• requires considerable teacher planning and organizational skills, and
	• may create difficulties in the identification of suitable resources.
Learning Center and Station	• encourages movement and interaction,
	• adapts to limited space requirements,
	• provides an opportunity to develop independent study habits,
	• offers teachers an opportunity to expand the curriculum,
	• fosters active involvement and increases relevance,
	• provides alternatives for learning, and
	• requires considerable teacher planning and organizational skills.
Independent Study Project	• gives students an opportunity to display their work,
	• provides an opportunity to develop independent study habits and research skills,
	• expects students to become meaningfully involved in their own learning,
	• requires extended class time for task completion and reporting,

Continued on next page

- creates the possibility that teachers may encounter unoriginal work,
- can make objective evaluation challenging, and
- requires considerable teacher organizational skills.

Cooperative Learning
- capitalizes on students working together,
- promotes peer tutoring and learning,
- students can be graded on their own work while receiving rewards for helping others,
- works well with students of various ability levels,
- requires considerable planning, and
- can be time consuming.

Figure 6-10. Considerations in using indirect instructional strategies.

As has been emphasized in Chapter 6, indirect instructional strategies are important to the effective teacher's skill-set of instructional strategies as such strategies are designed to focus on learning experiences that expect students to inquire, investigate, problem solve, work independently and cooperatively, and, generally, extend their understanding of the universe to the higher cognitive levels. Direct instructional strategies, discussed in Chapter 5, are not designed with these purposes in mind. Consequently, they serve an entirely different purpose in the teacher's repertoire of instructional strategies. As with either approach to instruction, effective instruction will only be achieved if the teacher is well planned and well prepared, knowledgeable in his or her subject matter area, well versed in terms of how certain strategies match to certain instructional objectives and how others do not, and sensitive to the learning needs and individual characteristics of the students in the classroom. Without this understanding on the part of the teacher, any instructional approach used will fall short of its ultimate potential to advance the learning of students.

Chapter 7

THE TEACHER AS A MANAGER OF STUDENT BEHAVIOR

While it is not suggested that classroom management skills are the most important competencies a teacher can possess, it is readily acknowledged that teachers who cannot control the behavior of their students are certain to find much unhappiness in their work, are less effective in advancing the instructional process, and are likely to have a short tenure in the teaching profession. Moreover, there is a genuine desire on the part of parents and the public in general to ensure that students are provided with a safe, optimal learning environment. Because of this, educational leaders simply cannot afford the poor public relations typically associated with classrooms that are constantly in a state of disruption, where teachers have difficulty teaching, and learning is too frequently disrupted.

Much has happened that has changed public schooling since the first edition of *Effective Teaching* was published twenty-five years ago. Some of this change has come about because of changes taking place in American society. As Weinstein and Mignano (2003) note, America's classrooms are more heterogeneous today than ever before. The need for teachers to be able to relate to and communicate with students who do not use English as their primary language has become commonplace in school districts all over the nation. Students with disabilities are now frequently mainstreamed with their nondisabled classmates. This type of diversity has many dividends for students at all grade levels, but diversity can create a more complex environment, an environment that often brings challenges for teachers who try to manage student behavior, instructional time, and academic attainment within public school classrooms. However, even with these changes, some fundamentals have remained constant. Classrooms should be seen as social groupings where one person's behavior may have an effect on the behavior of all other group members, and teaching must be viewed, in part, as leading the group.

Thus, the teacher as classroom manager should be thought of as a leader within a complex society. To study teaching, one, of necessity, must examine "life in the classroom."

We agree with Zabel and Zabel (1996) that classroom management involves much more than classroom discipline. The concept *classroom discipline* tends to have a connotation of being after the fact. *Classroom management*, on the other hand, implies not only the ability to deal with problems that arise but, also, the ability to organize the classroom environment in such a way as to actually prevent the occurrence of deviant behavior. The ability to avoid behavior problems is one of the most important competencies which can be possessed by any teacher. Regardless of how adept the teacher may be at getting a group of students under control after a disturbance has arisen, that teacher is running a risk of losing overall control of the class simply because the disturbance has been allowed to take place. This risk would not have occurred if the teacher had been able to prevent the disturbance from happening. Good and Brophy (2003) appropriately note that successful classroom management is primarily a matter of preventing problems before they occur. It would be erroneous, however, to assume that behavior problems will never emerge in an effective teacher's classroom. Behavior problems will occur because, if for no other reason, some students have trouble adjusting to the social dynamics of the schooling environment. Because of the importance of preventing problems before they occur and the need to effectively solve behavior problems after they emerge, this chapter is organized to examine both of these important areas.

After careful study of this chapter, readers will learn more about the following topics:

1. the characteristics of effective classroom managers,
2. three major control strategies and their effects on students,
3. the classroom as both a psychological and sociological environment,
4. three major theoretical models of classroom management, and
5. the causes and prevention of the most common unwanted student behaviors.

CHARACTERISTICS OF EFFECTIVE CLASSROOM MANAGERS

Good classroom managers represent a relatively heterogeneous group of teachers. That is to say, it is difficult to develop a list of very specific characteristics common to all effective managers. This difficulty is due partly to the fact that many ineffective managers also exhibit some of these same effective management behaviors. It is possible, however, after analyzing both effective and ineffective managers, to develop a listing of broad categories of behaviors which are characteristic of teachers who have the ability to control the behavior of their students. Nonetheless, it must be noted that effective classroom managers will vary in the degrees to which they exhibit any one or all of these behaviors. It is suggested that you examine each category of behavior carefully in order to rate yourself in terms of whether or not you can model the behavior identified. Figure 7-1 will facilitate this rating process after an examination of each of the characteristics.

EFFECTIVE MANAGEMENT CHECKLIST			
Characteristics	**Exists Satisfactorily**	**Needs to be Improved**	**Personal Notes**
Thorough Preparation			
Development of Routines			
Calm and Confident Behavior			
Professional Demeanor			
Recognizing Inappropriate Behavior			
Avoidance of Retreating			
Communication with Families			
Preventing Problems			

Figure 7-1. A checklist for classroom managers.

Thorough Preparation

An effective classroom manager is aware of the fact that most deviant student behavior emerges when students are not on task. Students who have nothing meaningful to do because they have finished their work early are frustrated because the work they have been given is beyond their ability level, or who have to wait idly for long periods of time because the teacher has not given them an assignment, may tend to exhibit some type of unwanted behavior. Conversely, students who are meaningfully occupied with their studies have less opportunity to become involved in misconduct. Good managers, knowing this, exhibit behaviors which keep students on task and purposefully involved in some aspect of the learning enterprise. Effective managers plan ahead of time exactly what will happen throughout the entire instructional period. As a result, time is not wasted at the beginning of the lesson, the lesson itself is engaging, and it is not likely that students will be left with nothing to do at its end.

Until the teacher is confident in planning adequately for a given time allotment, it is advisable for that teacher to plan more than could possibly be accomplished. It is, by far, better to overplan than to underplan for instruction. A teacher who has left students without anything meaningful to do is creating an environment conducive to student misconduct.

Developmental Routines

Another important aspect of effective organization is the ability to develop a comfortable, customary procedure for handling the daily, ongoing affairs of the classroom. Students are much less likely to exhibit misconduct when they know exactly what to do and can, in effect, function almost by habit. Good managers structure the classroom environment through established routines in such a way as to lessen the opportunity for confusion. These routines must take place at all grade levels. One example might be the biology teacher who has set procedures for the distribution and collection of laboratory equipment and manuals. Another example might be the kindergarten teacher who has structured the manner in which children wash their hands and line up before leaving for lunch. The classroom is an interesting, exciting social arena. Teachers can expect and need to plan for student loss of self-control when the student either does not know what is about to take place or what is expected. Through this development of routines, effective managers structure daily activities to promote both a positive predictability and a calming effect on students.

Calm and Confident Behavior

The teacher's own behavior is an essential feature of the development of a calming social environment. Effective managers exhibit leadership styles characterized by calm, confident behavior. As teachers lose confidence in themselves as managers and come to feel that they cannot control their classes, panic is a typical end result. Often becoming defensive, such teachers frequently are unable to think rationally when confronted with misconduct. Teachers who are not calm and confident are apt themselves to exhibit behaviors that destroy the productive atmosphere of the classroom.

Effective teachers rarely display loss of temper because they know that this behavior could lead to arguing and bickering with students. Teachers who seem out-of-control appear weak and insecure in the eyes of students. But, teachers who maintain an air of confidence are less vulnerable and more likely to be in charge. They also are less likely to make mistakes in judgment because they do not panic when confronted by the unexpected. Students have greater respect for teachers who seem calm and confident than those who have emotions which are easily manipulated.

Professional Demeanor

A professional demeanor is one of the most important attributes of the teacher who desires to command the respect of students. Conduct in a professional manner is a somewhat abstract idea, and *professionalism* is, no doubt, defined in several acceptable ways. A professional in the classroom, regardless of the definition, is one who accepts the role of leader seriously. A teacher must gain and maintain the respect of all students through consistent and fair treatment. Such a teacher treats all students with respect and never holds grudges against students for past misbehaviors.

Beyond the rather obvious characteristics of fair play and respect for students, professional conduct also implies that teachers are aware of their overall duties and responsibilities and carry them out in a dignified fashion. Teachers, additionally, must have respect for the profession. For example, they should dress, speak, and act professionally as they are guided by the expectations of society and colleagues. Effective managers develop relationships with their students which could be characterized as being similar, in a sense, to parent-child relationships. Rarely is it found that an effective manager will have developed a peer-like relationship with students. Teachers who want to have the respect of their students must consistently put themselves in positions where students look to them for leadership. This is not to imply that teachers should be inflexible, despotic leaders. On the contrary, teachers should lead with concern and respect for students while, at the same time, remembering that they are the adults in charge. Finally, a professional is one who continually strives to develop greater competency in teaching skills and is willing to make changes directed toward personal improvement without feeling threatened.

Recognizing Inappropriate Behavior

One of the most important skills a good classroom manager can possess is the ability to determine when student behavior is truly inappropriate at the time and place that it occurs. Behavior that is inappropriate and which should be responded to at one time, may be best ignored at another. An effective manager realizes the importance of analyzing each situation to determine the best course of action to take. Many teachers often disrupt class by stopping instruction in order to reprimand a student for doing something which, in fact, is not causing a serious disturbance or interfering with anyone's learning. This is a mistake in management. The teacher who is involved in a stimulating lesson, for example, should not interrupt such a positive learning environment by focusing everyone's attention on two students who briefly whisper in the rear of the classroom. A good manager does not react to everything that occurs. It may be best for the teacher to *pretend* not to see everything that happens. This is not to imply that teachers can ignore true disturbances and hope they soon will go away. When left alone, real disturbances tend to worsen, not diminish. The important point to be remembered is that teachers must not treat innocuous student behavior as if it were truly inappropriate and of major importance. Such action on the teacher's part can frustrate students and have the effect of disturbing the flow of an effective lesson, and this, in turn, will result in the distracting of all students and potentially causing even more misbehavior. When correcting student misbehavior, effective managers react only to behavior which clearly impedes learning, endangers one or more students, is socially unacceptable, or violates established school rules.

The ability to recognize innocuous behavior only solves part of the perplexity of identifying inappropriate behavior. Effective leadership also necessitates the ability to determine which student behaviors require an immediate corrective response from the teacher. Teachers who have problems with classroom control typically make the mistake of assuming that they need do little or nothing about classroom disturbances and still can be effective leaders. In reality, teachers cannot afford to ignore true disturbances in the learning environment. Those who fail to successfully meet such disturbances with determination and corrective measures are likely to find themselves surrounded by chaos.

When infractions are minor in nature, ignoring the inappropriate behavior may be best. As infractions become more serious, the teacher will then find it necessary to become more assertive. Before they become serious, it is most effective to stop the behavior by reminding the students involved of the rules established for conduct. As Nucci (1987) notes, this is more effective than simply saying, "Stop that," because it provides an opportunity for students to think about their behavior and link that behavior to existing classroom rules or consequences. However, when infractions are truly serious, consequences should be applied immediately at that time.

Avoidance of Retreating

Although it has been illustrated that some teachers are guilty of creating disturbances by reacting unnecessarily to certain student behaviors, too often other teachers allow real disturbances to continue and, in turn, destroy their credibility as leaders. At no other time do teachers seem so incompetent and weak as when they stand before a chaotic group of students trying to teach when few, if any, are paying attention to the instruction. Such teachers usually leave the profession due to their own anxieties or are relieved of their positions by administrators whose evaluations document their inability to demonstrate competence in this critical area. Sadly too, many remain in the profession continuing to provide ineffective instruction for students. Perhaps no other characteristic can be more damaging to a teacher's reputation than the inability to control undesirable student behavior. Hunt and Bedwell (1982) state that a single behavior seems to be common to teachers who have trouble controlling their students; this behavior is referred to as retreating. It is important to note that, while retreating is characteristic of poor leaders, it is rarely a behavior exhibited by teachers who control their classes skillfully.

As described by Schlechty (1976), retreating is a complex social behavior common to small groups where the leadership of the person in charge is being undermined by one or more group members. Retreating occurs in the classroom when the teacher backs down from student rebellion or misbehavior. The retreating sequence takes place when the teacher issues a directive intended to influence the behavior of one or more students with the result being that the students ignore the teacher in such a fashion as to let it be known that they are not going to comply. At this time, if the teacher ignores the rebellious behavior of the students, the teacher is, in fact, retreating. Consequently, retreating occurs when the teacher does not respond to the fact that students are continuing to exhibit unwanted behavior after they have been asked to stop. A critical point occurs in the management episode immediately after the teacher gives a directive to change the deviant behavior of one or more students. The teacher must follow through on the established directive to students.

No other behavior so clearly separates the effective from the ineffective manager as does retreating. The teacher who avoids retreating is more likely to avoid management problems before they reach a critical stage. Teachers whose behaviors are characterized by a series of retreating patterns are likely to find themselves in situations where control is lost, never to be regained. Once the teacher retreats, the rebellious effects of a few students are likely to run through the entire group. The teacher, who has already demonstrated weakness in leadership, is now in a situation that the best of teachers would find difficult to remedy.

Obviously, the best plan of action is to avoid retreating. The avoidance of such behavior is likely to result in the teacher's being able to prevent future classroom disruptions. Hunt and Bedwell (1982) offer the following suggestions to help teachers avoid such management problems.

1. Give directives to students only when necessary (i.e., only when student behavior is harmful or disturbing).
2. Observe student behavior immediately after a directive has been given since this is the most critical instant during the management episode.
3. Know what will follow if the students choose not to follow the directives – this helps the teacher feel prepared and less threatened.
4. Remember that leaders must enforce their authority – do not become involved in a confrontation unless it is known that the leadership position can be sustained.
5. Deal with rebellious students outside of the total group – the chance of negatively affecting the group is thereby lessened.
6. Stay calm and confident when dealing with a control problem – the poised teacher is much less likely to retreat.

The teacher who follows these rules and avoids retreating is well on the way to preventing many classroom management problems before they ever occur.

Communication with Families

The ability to develop strong communication networks with parents is a characteristic of effective teachers especially as it affects classroom management (Weinstein & Mignano, 2003, 1993; Epstein, 1990). Positive parent communication results in an increase in parental participation, more positive parental attitudes about the schooling process, and improved social and academic behavior on the part of students (Eggen & Kauchak, 2007).

Though there may be certain barriers or at least challenges to parental communication, it is the teacher's responsibility to make every effort to bridge these barriers and meet these challenges. Ellis, Dowdy, Graham, and Jones (1992) report that employment concerns prevent some parents from getting involved in their youngster's schooling. Because of this, teachers need to be flexible when arranging conferences remembering that some parents work difficult hours and cannot afford to miss work. There also may be cultural barriers to parental communication. Delgado-Gaiton (1992) and Harry (1992) note that some parents have experienced school in a form very different from the one their children are experiencing. Also, some parents have had very negative school experiences themselves which makes it more difficult for them to approach teachers. These cultural and experiential barriers are greatly augmented when the parents have an inability or difficulty in speaking English (Eggen & Kauchak, 2007).

It is obvious that teachers must take the lead in developing communication with parents, especially where barriers exist. Many teachers, unfortunately, have a negative perception of parental involvement and underestimate its importance (Zirpoli & Melloy, 2004). However, effective teachers are aware that research has shown that teachers can help parents become better able to help students in the home which can greatly increase the teacher's ability to make progress with the students at school (Hoover-Dempsey, Bassler, & Burow, 1995).

Preventing Problems

Unless problems occur in the classroom, the teacher will never have to be concerned about confrontations and retreating. Because of this, the ability to avoid problems before they occur is the most important leadership quality a teacher can possess. It is far better for the teacher to be proactive than reactive. Due to the complexity and importance of this characteristic, the prevention of behavior problems will be discussed at length in this and subsequent sections.

Above all else, teachers who desire to prevent management problems must consistently conduct themselves in a controlled fashion and model the types of behaviors described earlier in this section. Being a good, effective leader requires much forethought. Teachers simply cannot *leave it to chance* that they will be able to control students and function successfully in the classroom. Management problems are contagious; a few problems today tend to balloon into excessive problems in the future. Conversely, the absence of behavior problems today increases the likelihood that there will be fewer behavior problems in the future. The avoidance of behavior problems becomes, in itself, a measure of prevention.

Under the best of conditions, it is unrealistic to expect that all behavior problems are preventable. Problems do arise for all teachers. However, some teachers have many more management problems than should be expected. Charles (1981) suggests seven key steps to be taken in the prevention of behavior problems. These steps are concerned with the (1) *physical setting*, (2) *curriculum*, (3) *attitude of the teacher*, (4) *expectations of the teacher*, (5) *support systems*, (6) *plans for the unexpected*, and (7) *performance of teaching*.

The *physical setting* definitely influences the behavior of students. Students who are too hot, overcrowded, unable to see or hear the teacher well, or in some other way uncomfortable are more likely to become inattentive and create disturbances. The physical setting of the classroom should be arranged to diminish the number of possible distractions that might occur due to noise or movement outside of the room. A wise teacher is even aware that some students are likely to become distracted if they sit too close to one another. Making a formal seating arrangement can become crucial. Many teachers also find it best to seat easily distracted and inattentive students near the teacher's desk in order that the teacher's nearness will decrease the probability of a disturbance (additional attention was given to this topic in Chapter 2 as related to learning styles; see also Emmer, Evertson, Clements, & Worsham, 1996 as well as Evertson, Emmer, Clements, Sanford, & Worsham, 1994).

The *curriculum* must match the needs, abilities, and interests of each of the students if they are all expected to remain task-oriented throughout instruction. When the curriculum becomes so difficult that a student becomes fatigued or, even worse, begins to fail at most or all tasks, that student is apt to become disenchanted with learning, and the teacher, and become a behavior problem. The student who meets learning endeavors with success is much more likely to remain on task. Industrious and active students rarely disrupt the classroom. On the other hand, the student who faces a curriculum that is too easy or lacks relevance is likely to talk or move around disturbing other students.

The *attitude* with which a teacher enters the classroom is most important to good management. If a teacher feels that controlling a class will be impossible, that teacher very likely will fail. However, teachers who enter the classroom feeling that they are the leaders in charge typically are able to communicate this feeling to the students with the result being a prevention of control problems. Good and Brophy (2003) note that the essential attitudes of an effective manager are (1) respect and affection for students, (2) consistency which leads to credibility, (3) responsibility for all students' learning, and (4) enjoyment of learning which leads to the students valuing education.

Expectations for behavior should be decided upon and delineated from the beginning of the school year (Eggen & Kauchek, 2007; Evertson, Emmer, Clements, Sanford, & Worsham, 1994). Charles (2008) suggests that many teachers have used a system of rules over a great many years; his example stresses having a few rules (e.g., three to five) that are nonnegotiable. It is the teacher's responsibility to determine how behavior will be rewarded or corrected, with possible input from students, in relation to these rules. Charles emphasizes that it is important to have criteria for rewarding good behavior in relation to rules. Expectations should not be thought of only in terms of negative consequences associated with nonconformity. Again, it is important that rules are established at the beginning of the school year and consistently followed thereafter.

Effective teachers, in order to prevent behavior problems, also consider the development of a *support system* to help sustain their management plans. The principal, as an example of a support, must be aware of the teacher's plan, and the teacher should fully understand the extent to which the school administration is willing to offer support or backing. Parents also must be fully aware of the teacher's intentions. And, the teacher must be aware of the extent to which each parent is willing to cooperate with the established plan and the administration. Individual parents often will vary in the extent to which they will actively support a management plan.

Teachers must be *prepared for unexpected events* that can take place during the school year. Students should know how to conduct themselves if, for example, a substitute teacher replaces the regular teacher or if the classroom has unexpected visitors. When teachers try to enumerate all of the possible unexpected events which could take place and prepare the class for them, it is less likely that the students will show confusion at an inopportune moment.

Charles' steps for prevention also consider the actual *performance of teaching*. He further divides teaching performance into four categories: (1) management of teaching, (2) *the golden tongue*, (3) teacher on stage, and (4) acceptance for everyone.

Management of teaching refers to two unique concepts: classroom routines and the delivery of lessons. Classroom routines, as discussed earlier, act as parameters for structuring student movement and behavior in the classroom environment. The routines are the organized, consistent procedures that take place in the school setting. When students know there is one accepted way to ask permission to leave the room, sharpen pencils, hand in papers, or line up, much less confusion is likely to occur during such events. A lesson which is delivered in an interesting fashion and which has no large time lapses is one which keeps the students' attention on task. As a result, this type of lesson delivery helps to prevent control problems.

The teacher who has a *golden tongue* is one who speaks to students with respect, not with sarcasm or disdain. The importance of communicating with clear, supportive messages was discussed in Chapter 3 in great detail. Students are more likely to exhibit courteous behavior when the teacher makes a practice of speaking to them with respect.

Stage presence deals with the teacher's ability to form a close relationship with the students by holding their interest through the use of dramatic and novel gestures and voice inflections. A dry, unexciting teacher will not be able to hold the interest or the attention of students for an extended length of time. When this is the case, students may be more interested in nonacademic endeavors (i.e., disruptive behavior) than in the content of the lesson being presented.

Many educators have pointed out the importance of accepting all students so that they, the students, feel important and valued within the group. Students obviously have a need to feel accepted. Students who see themselves as existing at the fringe of the social group or, worse yet, as isolates from the group are less likely to follow the rules and expectations for behaviors within the classroom. Teachers must draw such students into the mainstream of the social and academic activities of the classroom.

Charles' thoughts on prevention of management problems are worthy of any teacher's scrutiny. Good and Brophy (2003), in their discussion of the prevention of management problems, add one further suggestion concerning how a teacher can improve classroom management through effective delivery. These authors note the importance of variation in questioning patterns (see Chapter 4). The teacher who randomly calls upon students, never allowing the students to know who will be called upon next, is better able to hold certain students' attention and keep them on task. This is to say that, while routines are important, too strict routines in questioning styles can lead to undue predictability resulting in a greater possibility of management problems.

Waller (1932), in his classic analysis of the classroom social system, notes that a student having feelings of inferiority is more likely to exhibit disruptive behavior than a student with a positive self-concept. Teachers must be aware of the fact that, in many cases, those students who are academically unsuccessful are often the same students who frequently behave in ways that disrupt the classroom. The student who has a low self-concept typically is unhappy at school, especially when academic activities are being conducted. While the teacher must show acceptance for all students, the notion that all students should be treated equally is erroneous. Some students are very successful in the learning environment of the classroom, and their success leads to reinforcement from teachers and acceptance and respect from peers. Other students cannot share this envious position. School can become a hated place for students who constantly fail and are ridiculed by their peers for their ineptness. There is little wonder why some students rebel against the school, its curriculum, and its authority figures. Rebellion, in this sense, is a type of defense mechanism used to maintain sanity. Not to rebel would mean to accept a system which daily crushes self-worth. Students must be treated with patience and understanding, even when it seems they are doing everything in their power to disrupt classroom activities. To treat these students negatively is to provide a poor model of behavior which results in an augmented feeling of inferiority and an increased likelihood of continued defiant behavior.

Teachers who go into the classroom with a plan for preventing problems before they occur, i.e., being proactive, are well on their way to becoming effective classroom managers who not only communicate confidence but develop in their students the characteristics of well-behaved learners who know what to do and expect in their classrooms. Figure 7-2 summarizes some of the major ideas that a teacher must remember to prevent behavior problems.

Personal Considerations	Instructional Considerations	Environmental Considerations
Conduct one's self in a calm, confident fashion.	Able students must be challenged.	The classroom must be a clean, comfortable setting.
Be prepared for unexpected events.	Low ability students should not be placed in unduly frustrating situations.	The classroom should be void of major distractions to learning.
Praise positive behavior.	Instruction should be both exciting and enjoyable.	A few rules for acceptable conduct should exist.
Show respect and affection for students.	A variety of questioning patterns should be utilized.	Parents and administrators must offer support.
Treat students in a consistent fashion.	All students should experience success.	The atmosphere should be one of acceptance.

Figure 7-2. Considerations for the prevention of management problems.

CONTROLLING DISRUPTIVE BEHAVIOR

There are three main categories of leadership strategies which can be used to control the behavior of others: *normative, remunerative,* and *coercive* (Schlechty, 1976). The type of strategy chosen will, to a significant degree, affect the learning environment of the classroom. There is also reason to believe that all teachers cannot use each strategy with equal success. A given teacher may be able to control students by using coercive strategies while being unable to establish control through the use of either normative or remunerative strategies. Too, a given student may comply to the influence of normative and remunerative strategies but not readily comply to coercive strategies. It is important for the teacher to be cognizant of both his or her own personal characteristics as a leader as well as the characteristics of his or her students as followers. Each of the three strategies will be discussed at some length in this section, with special attention given to the topic of punishment.

Normative Strategy

The normative strategy develops naturally as a result of the teacher having the characteristics of an effective manager as discussed earlier in this chapter. When teachers use this strategy of control, students are expected to conform due to respect for the teacher's role as a professional leader. When normative control is applied, all are expected to comply to the teacher's directives because it is expected that, when teachers give directions, students will follow them. Obviously, this is an ideal type of leadership. When students comply to normative control, the group is relatively easy to manage. If a disruptive situation arises, the teacher simply makes a request for the unwanted behavior to stop. As a result of the teacher's request, students are influenced to comply and they stop the unwanted behavior.

Normative control is based upon the students' respect for the teacher or the teaching position. This type of respect, gained through interaction, is earned by the teacher, it does not come automatically. Unfortunately, some teachers do not understand the relationship between their own actions and levels of ability to influence students through the normative strategy. Teachers who are not well prepared, not well organized, not calm and confident, not characterized by a professional demeanor, not able to recognize inappropriate behavior, not able to avoid retreating, and not able to prevent problems before they occur will have trouble influencing student behavior through the normative strategy. Teachers who take their leadership roles seriously and strive to conduct themselves in a manner conducive to effective classroom control, however, will find that students are much more frequently influenced normatively.

For an assortment of reasons, the normative strategy does not work for every teacher in every situation. Due to their inability to adjust to the social complexity of the classroom group, some students find it virtually impossible to comply to normative control in a consistent manner. Normative compliance requires students to be well adjusted to their roles, just as normative control requires that teachers be well adjusted to theirs.

Remunerative Strategies

Control through remunerative strategies is used to influence the behavior of students by the manipulation of a reward system. Rewards are those things which are reinforcing and not normally systematically received. For example, if students typically receive a fifteen-minute break during the day, it is not a reward when the teacher allows students to go on their break because they have finished all of the assigned work. But, if the teacher increases the break time to twenty-five minutes because all the students finished their work, the reward for everyone finishing would be the extra ten minutes. Remunerative strategies are viewed as positive in that the teacher concentrates on and reinforces desired behavior.

The operant conditioning theory of B. F. Skinner has been applied to the shaping of desirable behavior in the classroom (Zirpoli & Melloy, 2004). *Applied behavior analysis* is the name given to the systematic application of operant conditioning as used in the classroom setting. Since the latter part of the 1960s, applied behavior analysis has been a major part of many teacher training programs. Applied behavior analysis is based on the assumption that only observable behaviors are significant. Teachers should carefully observe the behaviors of given students and record the frequency that they exhibit deviant behaviors. The goal becomes to lessen the frequency of the unwanted behaviors. Teachers, taking each unwanted behavior separately, design a schedule of reinforcement to reward the student for exhibiting proper behavior. In theory, the frequency of proper behavior will increase because it has been reinforced, while, at the same time, the frequency of unwanted behavior will diminish because of the lack of reinforcement.

The concept of applied behavior analysis is based upon a principle of conditioning which has a long history of supportive research. The principle is that behaviors recur to the degree that they are reinforced. Although numerous behavioristic psychologists recommend the use of applied behavior analysis as a remunerative control strategy, other social scientists and educators have been critical of its use. Travers (1977) has taken the position that the stated values of applied behavior analysis have dubious validity and that the many commercial training kits available are too expensive and often lacking in a substantive base to validate their worth. Kounin (1970), who seemed to analyze the classroom more from the sociological viewpoint, warned that such remunerative strategies can be ineffective when overly used and may have negative effects on the students not receiving rewards.

This is not to suggest that applied behavior analysis is an ineffective method of control. When used properly in a systematic routine, it is a very powerful method of management. Many teachers, as noted by Charles (1981), have found it to be the answer to their management problems. Through its successful use, the emphasis on reward instead of punishment and on *good behavior* instead of *bad behavior* makes life in the classroom more enjoyable for teachers as well as students.

An important point for all teachers to remember is that leaders often inappropriately use remuneration to reinforce behaviors because they actually are not aware that they are giving rewards. A teacher, for example, may allow a disruptive student to go on an errand in order to get the student out of the classroom. This strategy may gain the teacher a few minutes of peace and tranquility, but more problems will be caused in the long run. Without being aware of it, the teacher has used a remunerative strategy. The student received a reward (being allowed to go on an errand) for exhibiting something the teacher did not mean to reinforce – disruptive behavior. If the theory is sound, the student is likely to relate such disruptive behavior to being allowed to leave the room. This then would result in the augmentation of similar disruptions in the future. Teachers must constantly and systematically analyze their own behavior to determine if the reinforcements they provide are really for those behaviors they want to see repeated.

All instructional leaders, at some point, use certain remunerative strategies to control the behaviors of their students. As noted here, teachers at times actually reward behaviors that they would like to see extinguished. Since remuneration is such a powerful tool in the management of behavior, teachers must use it carefully and systematically, not randomly. When rewards are given in an unsystematic manner, they lose their effectiveness and tend to have a negative impact on the total group.

Coercive Strategies

Coercive strategies are punitive in nature and are designed to react directly to the disruptive behavior being exhibited. Coercive strategies are being used, for example, when a teacher does one of the following: (1) strikes a student, (2) takes away a student's belongings or privileges, or (3) threatens to do either of the preceding. Coercion is leadership by force. When a teacher decides to use coercion in order to influence the behavior of students, that teacher is telling the students they must do what they are told to do because the teacher is a powerful person whose strength and influence must be feared. Coercive strategies rest upon a power base which must be sustained. The degree to which a teacher appears strong and in control is the degree to which that teacher can expect to influence students through coercion.

One is reminded, when thinking of threats and their effects, of the analogy of the town marshal and the gunfighter in movies about the *Old West*. In this analogy, the marshal's ability to control the town is based on his strength and skill with a gun. On one particular day an outlaw comes to town and the marshal's ability to maintain order is based upon the fact that he must be able to either scare the deviant away or defeat him in a contest of strength. The marshal begins by issuing a threat to the gunfighter (these threats often work on less adventurous, more timid people but never seem to influence the professional gunman). After listening to the marshal's threat, the outlaw rebuffs the lawman in no uncertain terms. At this point, the marshal has but one course of action left open: he now must back up his threat with action. The two characters now meet in the street to have their *showdown* with the eyes of all the citizens upon them. As events have pushed both protagonists into a situation nearly beyond their control, the marshal knows he must fight because to back down, or retreat, would be tantamount to giving up all control of the town forever. The marshal also realizes his ability to control is based on his power and strength. Conversely, to display weakness would lessen his ability to control some of the citizens of the town who, in the future, would see if they too could back down the authority. In most old movies, the marshal successfully defeats the outlaw, and the citizens go back to their daily lives confident that the control of their society rests in the hands of an invulnerable leader.

The teacher who relies on coercive strategies is, in many respects, like the marshal just described. A student may disrupt order in the class, just as the outlaw disrupted order in the town, and the teacher may issue a threat to frighten the student, just as the marshal attempted to frighten the gunfighter. Threats did not always work for the marshal, and they do not always work for teachers who sometimes receive rebuffs from their students. Just as the marshal had to back up threats with action, so do teachers. The teacher who uses coercive strategies to control the group is just as certain to have show-downs as was our fictitious marshal. Like our lawman, the teacher knows that retreating is a poor option because all eyes are focused on the event. If the teacher allows the deviant student to continue the misconduct without backing up the previous threat of punishment, other students in the group are likely to attempt a similar power play in the future. Unfortunately, this is where the analogy ends; real life is often very different from old movies. In real life, many marshals were either shot by gunmen or backed down from the danger. In the classroom, teachers, too, may retreat and lose confrontations. Although it is rare that such a loss results in physical danger, teachers can suffer from such defeats and can be hurt even more when they choose to retreat from the confrontation. The type of damage done to the teacher is that which is manifested in an inability to control future disruptions. Such a teacher has been outgunned.

The teacher who chooses to use coercive strategies must be prepared to maintain a strong power base from which to operate. If anything ever happens to erode the teacher's power, the ability to influence students through coercion will quickly wane. Teachers who abuse the use of coercive strategies (i.e., use them to excess) put themselves in leadership positions that are often-times difficult to maintain. This means that a teacher who enters the classroom with the intention to manage the setting with a *fast gun* and an *iron fist* must have the strength of character and leadership skill necessary to maintain the position of authority. The teacher who tries to coerce and cannot sustain a position of authority through strong action is likely to retreat and appear vulnerable to many of the students. Such a teacher usually finds it difficult or impossible to regain leadership by turning to remunerative and normative strategies. Leadership through coercion is not recommended. It is advisable for teachers to enter the classroom with the notion that control can best be maintained through normative and remunerative approaches.

An Example of Coercion: Use of Punishment

Although you should try to maintain control in other ways, a time may come when you will face a situation where one or more students are disturbing your class on a regular basis. Punitive measures (i.e., coercion) may be the only alternative. If this time does come (and it is hoped that it would come only infrequently), you must have a precise plan of action. Coercive strategies are best applied only after considerable forethought and after other strategies have failed.

When the teacher decides that punishment is in order, it is of the utmost importance that the punishment fit the individual(s) involved as well as the infraction committed. It must be remembered that punishing seven-year-olds is a very different matter than punishing seventeen-year-olds. Also, punishment, to a great extent, is actually a state of mind; that which seems severe to one individual may not even bother another. In a social setting such as a classroom, punishment must appear due and fair to both the students being punished as well as to the other students in the classroom. It is nearly impossible to use coercive measures with one student and not affect the attitudes and behaviors of other students in the classroom.

It is recommended that punishment never take the form of striking a student or withholding affection. There are simply too many risks involved to ever justify this course of action. The striking of another human being brings rise to certain ethical questions, and such questions must be solved in the minds of each individual involved. Corporal punishment of a child by a parent is a significantly different question than corporal punishment of a student by a teacher. The possibility that such teacher behavior could result in litigation is real, and its true effectiveness is doubtful. Punishment, then, will be discussed here as it refers to restricting students, taking away one or more of their privileges or belongings, or talking to students in a derisive way.

It must be recognized that, even by those who feel strongly against the use of coercive strategies, research evidence supports that the intensity and duration of punishment is positively related to the rapidity and the degree of suppression of unwanted behaviors (Walters & Grusec, 1977). In other words, if a teacher wants a student to stop exhibiting some behavior, that teacher can punish the student and the student will stop the behavior if the punishment is severe enough. The longer and harder the punishment, the more likely the behavior will be suppressed. It is not a question, therefore, of utility being considered in the use of punishment because punishment can stop undesired behavior. The question of concern is an ethical one. Should punishment be used? Does punishment have harmful effects on students' future behaviors and personalities? Walters and Grusec suggest that nonphysical punishments which avoid ridicule and other attacks on the student's self-esteem are not harmful and can actually aid in the socialization process. They also suggest that the student who receives punishment will not necessarily associate negative reactions with the teacher if the teacher is also seen as a reinforcing agent, not just a punishing agent.

It is clear that punishment can produce the desired results: suppression of unwanted behavior. However, not only does the use of coercive strategies require a strong power base in the social setting, the teacher also must be aware that punishment can have negative psychological effects if the student's self-esteem is attacked. Punishment must be administered only when the student involved has a clear understanding of why he or she is being punished. Although there is reason to believe that the misuse of punishment can do more harm than good, it is not necessary to conclude that this coercive strategy should never be used to influence the behavior of students. Punishment, when used in a proper, humane fashion, can be an invaluable socialization strategy in the classroom setting.

Personal attacks on students must be avoided and punishment should focus on the unwanted behavior, *never the students*. In order to function productively, students must feel that they are an important part of the classroom group. If the teacher makes a habit of scorning certain students or making jokes at their expense, these students are likely to lack any feeling of belonging. Personal attacks weaken students' self-concepts and any lowering of self-esteem can lead to poor academic performance and an augmentation of disruptive behavior. Personal attacks on students by a teacher are generally viewed as unfair and inexcusable by all students, not just the students being ridiculed. Any chance that the teacher has to develop normative control strategies will be seriously jeopardized after the use of personal attacks. Students in this predicament are not likely to be normatively influenced by a teacher who practices personal attacks against them.

At all cost, teachers must avoid embarrassing students in front of their peers. This type of behavior is destructive in that it will void future attempts at developing normative strategies and will increase the likelihood of subsequent student rebellion. Especially in the case of students in the upper elementary and secondary grades, students often feel they must rebel against a teacher who belittles them in front of their peer group. For example, an adolescent who is told by the teacher to "Take a seat or I will put you in one!" has no alternative left open. If this student takes the seat, his peer group may tease him because he allowed the teacher to put him down in such a rude fashion. The student, who may really prefer to take a seat and avoid the problem, will often feel compelled to rebuff his teacher. Now the teacher is truly in a difficult position. In situations such as this, it is easy for the teacher to be put in a position where retreating is imminent. What does the teacher do if the student feels pushed enough to tell the teacher to back up the threat?

Coercive strategies should not be used to influence students through fear of public embarrassment. If students are not treated with dignity, the teacher is not likely to be viewed as a professional worthy of respect. This type of abusive behavior on the part of a teacher will create an image that students can learn to detest. Students often rebel against such a teacher out of revenge. The avoidance of embarrassing personal or public attacks on a student is an absolute maxim of effective classroom management.

When the teacher finds it necessary to use punishment, it is important to explain clearly to the student why the punishment is being administered. Giving the student a rationale for the use of punitive measures not only helps the student relate his or her behavior to that of the teacher but also creates an image of fair play on the teacher's part. This image of fairness can be used as a foundation for the development of subsequent normative control strategies. The development of a rationale for punishment can also be very beneficial to teachers. If the teacher takes the opportunity to create such a rationale, it will become much easier for that teacher to deal with subsequent disruptions and to decide upon a punishment which is suitable for the circumstances involved. Teachers frequently misinterpret the disruptive behavior of students. After developing a rationale for the punishment of students, the teacher will come to a point where the students' behavior is seen in a more realistic light. When this happens, the behavior and the students can both be reacted to more justly.

Punishment should be administered in such a way as to allow students soon to redeem themselves with the teacher. In the meantime, the teacher must not hold grudges against students after the punishment has been administered. Since a major objective of any coercive strategy is for the student to associate the disruptive behavior with some negative consequence, it is important for the student to understand that punishment is not being administered due to a personal conflict with the teacher. All group members have a need to be cared for and to feel that they belong. When someone as significant as the teacher shows disapproval, students may feel so threatened that it becomes difficult for them to function in a meaningful way. Such students need to be given an opportunity to receive some type of positive display of approval from the teacher. Upon receiving approval from the teacher, students can then ascertain that it was the unwanted behavior, not a personal dislike, which caused the teacher to use punitive measures. Students who feel that the teacher still respects them are much more readily influenced by normative strategies than are students who feel that their teacher dislikes them and wishes they were not part of the group.

For the safety of both the student and the teacher, the teacher should avoid any overt display of anger or emotion when administering punishment. Because coercive strategies are to be used only after much forethought and wise judgment, the teacher should avoid any type of angry outburst that could result in a snap decision. The calm, confident teacher is much less likely to make a mistake in judgment and, therefore, is much more likely to develop an image necessary for the successful use of normative strategies. Anger and emotion on the part of the teacher may foster such behavior, in return, on the part of the students. By the teacher remaining even-tempered, a calming effect will develop among the students which will generally result in the diminishing of further difficulties. Finally, as the teacher works to develop a more productive relationship with parents, it is important to avoid any emotional displays in the classroom that might lead to the deterioration of such a relationship. It is difficult for parents as well as administrators to support teachers who continually lose their tempers with students.

While punishment can suppress unwanted behaviors, it often has a tendency to be temporary in its effectiveness. Punishment too frequently tends to focus on merely one isolated behavior and fails to deal with the actual cause of disruptive behaviors. Punishment should be seen only as a temporary means of deterring particular student behaviors that are creating an immediate classroom disturbance. The teacher may regain control of the classroom and continue instruction, but disturbances frequently recur because the underlying cause of the problem still exists. As a result, punishment must be used only as a small portion of a larger strategy designed to change disruptive behavior by alleviating its cause.

If a student repeatedly exhibits disruptive behavior, the teacher has two problems to address. First, the teacher must immediately regain control over the group in order that instruction may continue. Second, the teacher must help the student deal with the cause of the misbehavior because, even if the disturbance no longer exists within the classroom, there may be disturbances within the student which make it impossible for the student to function successfully. Punishment may very well help the teacher control the first problem, but coercive strategies will never help to alleviate and may even exacerbate the second. If the deviant behavior continues and is accompanied by repeated punishment, the student's self-concept may be damaged in such a way that even more defiant activity will characterize future behavior. It is easy to see that punishment can produce an effect opposite from that which the teacher desires. If a student is being disruptive because of anger or fear, punishment might even aggravate the situation causing further disruption.

The use of punishment is a very controversial topic, and many educators and psychologists alike feel that it should never be used to influence a student's behavior (Kohn, 2001). Hill (1981) suggests that this is probably so because reinforcement is more pleasant and produces a closer and friendlier relationship between teacher and student than does punishment. Teacher use of punishment is associated with negative behaviors. In this light, it is likely that educators and psychologists prefer positive reinforcement over punishment because of humane values, not because positive reinforcement is relatively more effective at changing behavior. While the misuse of punishment has several weaknesses, as does the misuse of positive reinforcement, most teachers use some type of punishment when students repeatedly display disruptive behaviors.

MAJOR THEORETICAL MODELS OF CLASSROOM MANAGEMENT

The relationship between the psychological and sociological views of the classroom is significant. Principles of psychology provide needed direction as teachers design strategies to shape the behavior of individual students who may be exhibiting undesirable classroom behaviors. These principles are valuable to teachers in helping to determine the individual learning, motivational, and developmental characteristics of a student in order that the student's behaviors can be better understood and a meaningful curriculum and instructional experience provided.

Sociological principles provide the teacher with an important group perspective of managing behavior. From these principles, the teacher learns that the behavior of an individual must be examined in terms of total group dynamics and that a student's behavior can often be explained in terms of interaction with peers. Also, an individual student's behavior is frequently influenced by social status in the group. The teacher should be aware, for example, of whether students are very popular with their peers, members of a small fringe group on the periphery of the total group, or social isolates having little significant interaction with other group members. Most importantly, teachers must be conscious of the fact that, when they correct the deviant behavior of one student in the group, this action will often affect the behavior of other students who witness the interaction. Kounin (1970) refers to this phenomenon as the *ripple effect.* Understanding the principles of learning theory, human development, and group dynamics will help in developing rational and consistent leadership behaviors needed to manage the classroom. Teachers who develop this level of understanding will exhibit their own unique set of leadership characteristics. The body of information known as *psychology* helps us as we endeavor to understand human behavior, and *sociology* helps us as we try to understand the impact of one person's behavior on an entire group of people. As we discuss the role of the teacher as a manager of student behavior, we should hold in mind that, although teachers frequently deal with individual student behavior, they typically deal with individual behavior within the context of a social group. The method that a teacher uses to manage an individual student within the classroom setting will impact other students within the classroom. Additionally, the way certain students conduct themselves within a classroom setting is likely to impact the behavior of other students in the classroom.

No discussion of classroom management would be complete without the inclusion of the major contributions made by those who have developed specific theories of group management. These theories are often referred to as *models* because they attempt to serve as examples for imitation or as descriptions of possible cause-and-effect relationships which help the teacher to better visualize procedures for managing students. Since there are several different models, there is, likewise, no complete agreement among theorists as to how best to manage group behavior. Some theorists examine the classroom from a psychological viewpoint, resulting in models different from those who tend to analyze it from a sociological perspective. Nevertheless, though they differ, much can be learned from their examination. Following this review, you will be able to form your own individual concept of classroom management that is suitable both to your personality and teaching style. This unique concept can be developed by selecting components from the different models presented and combining them to form a comprehensive, personal approach to management. Such synthesizing will help you to stay in a position where new ideas and techniques can be added readily to further refine your classroom management skills.

In the latest edition of *Building Classroom Discipline*, Charles (2008) describes how approaches to classroom management have changed since the mid-1980s when *Effective Teaching* was first published. Charles discusses a bridge going from the twentieth to the twenty-first century formed by theories such as those proposed in *Choice Theory in the Classroom* (Glasser & Dotson, 1998), *Discipline That Works: Promoting Self-Discipline in Children* (Gordon, 1989), and *Beyond Discipline: From Compliance to Community* (Kohn, 2006). A factor that all three of these approaches have in common is placing within the student a major part of the responsibility for classroom behavior. These theories see the student as proactive and responsible, not as someone who will be compliant to the control of outside forces. The teacher's leadership role is seen not as a leader who manipulates and restricts students while demanding compliance but one where more emphasis is placed on normative control strategies. The teacher creates a climate or environment in the classroom that allows and encourages students to take responsibility for their own and the group's functioning. For further study see Wiseman and Hunt (2008, p. 91) for a detailed overview of the models to be discussed.

Theorists	Focus of Management Models
1. Rudolf Dreikurs	The focus is on analyzing behavior problems to determine their source of origin and responding to them.
2. Hiam Ginott	The focus is on improving communication in order to avoid alienating students inhumanely.
3. B.F. Skinner	The focus is on shaping student behavior with positive reinforcement.
4. Jacob Kounin	The focus is on teachers learning behaviors that will allow them to become better leaders in the classroom.
5. William Glasser	The focus is on empowering students to become better group members.
6. Thomas Gordon	The focus is on teachers using counseling techniques to improve communication with their students.
7. Lee & Marlene Canter	The focus is on teachers asserting their right to teach and their students' right to learn.
8. Fred Jones	The focus is on keeping students engaged in academically appropriate activities.
9. David & Roger Johnson	The focus is on students resolving their own conflicts.
10. Alfie Kohn	The focus is on students becoming intrinsically motivated to value good behavior.

Figure 7-3. Management theorists and management models.

Rudolph Dreikurs

Rudolf Dreikurs' background in psychoanalytic theory permeated his theory of group management. Dreikurs (1968) and Dreikurs and Cassell (1972) state that children develop certain significant defense mechanisms designed to protect their self-esteem. Dreikurs felt that these protective mechanisms were needed by some students because of harmful, early relationships with members of their families (i.e., parents and siblings). Dreikurs suggested that all student behavior has a specific underlying purpose and that when behaving inappropriately the student is doing so in pursuit of a goal. The mildest form of misbehavior is done to *seek attention*. The next most severe form of misbehavior has *seeking of power* as the goal. A form of misconduct designed to get *revenge on another individual* is the next most severe. Finally, the gravest type of misconduct is designed to obtain *special treatment from the teacher through an overt display of inferiority.* Dreikurs noted that students exhibit these deviant behaviors because they do not have the ability to make the necessary personal adjustments needed to coexist in the interpersonal structure of a peer group. This inability is due to self-esteem problems rooted in the students' early family life.

The primary role of the teacher in Dreikurs' model is to analyze the misconduct of a given student and then, in a one-to-one conference, help the student to understand the goals behind his own behavior. To help the student understand the need to avoid the above-mentioned goals for deviant behaviors, the student must experience what Dreikurs referred to as the natural consequences, sometimes called logical consequences, of his own misconduct. In the concept logical consequences, when certain misbehaviors are exhibited by students, certain logical consequences follow in terms of responses to these unwanted behaviors. Students should be encouraged to help the teacher establish rules for acceptable behavior and the consequences that will come as a result of misconduct. Teachers should not deal with punishment per se. Group control is the concept that natural, unpleasant consequences will always be the result of misconduct.

As Charles (1981) explains, Dreikurs' model is based on four major ideas. First, students must learn that they are responsible for their own actions. Second, students must develop self-respect while, at the same time, developing a respect for others. Third, members of the group have the responsibility to influence their peers to conduct themselves properly. Finally, students are responsible for knowing the rules for appropriate behavior and the consequences of misconduct.

The psychoanalytic background of Dreikurs surfaces in his model for behavior management. In order to fully utilize this design, the teacher must be able to analyze the individual behavior of students and determine the goals motivating such behavior. The teacher also must have the interpersonal skills necessary to help students understand their goals in order to change their behavior when necessary. This type of complex analysis and communication requires skill that usually comes only after considerable practice and training.

Hiam Ginott

Hiam Ginott (1971, 1969, & 1965) was a very well known child psychologist who wrote books and syndicated newspaper columns while regularly appearing on the "Today Show" in the 1960s and 1970s. Ginott stressed the importance of the teacher sending sane messages that focus on the behavior of the student, not the student as a person. Sane messages do not attack students on a personal level, yet they provide students with a model for behavior that they should demonstrate when confronting social issues with classmates. A teacher, noted Ginott, should serve as a model of a self-disciplined person for the students.

Ginott encouraged teachers to create an environment where students could feel genuine satisfaction while building their self-esteem. Instead of bossing students through positions of power, teachers are encouraged to allow students to make decisions in an environment characterized by cooperative learning activities.

Ginott's theory stresses the importance of a teacher who is a humane model and who confirms high expectations without exercising power over students. His theory can be seen as a foundation for the theories of Glasser, Gordon, and Kohn who, as cited earlier, are referred to as the bridges to the twenty-first century by Charles (2008).

B. F. Skinner

The present model will not be referred to as *Skinner's Model* because B. F. Skinner did not actually develop an approach which he labeled a model for classroom management. However, many of the concepts discussed earlier in this chapter under the heading *remunerative strategies* have been drawn together by other psychologists to form a model referred to as *applied behavior analysis* which is clearly associated with Skinner's work. The model was originally called behavior modification, but, because the term took on what some felt to be a negative connotation, the model is now called applied behavior analysis (Woolfolk, 2008; Aberto & Troutman, 2006). The applied behavior analysis model distinguishes between punishment and negative reinforcement, and punishment is not used. Negative reinforcement refers to a situation where students are removed from an unpleasant situation as a reward for exhibiting desired behavior.

The key principle of applied behavior analysis is that students will repeat behaviors for which they receive reinforcement and will stop exhibiting behaviors for which they receive no reinforcement. The basis of this model is focused upon the positive, rewarding appropriate behavior, as opposed to concentrating on the negative, punishing inappropriate behavior (McCaslin & Good, 1992). As a student begins to change to exhibit more acceptable behavior, the teacher will need to reinforce the student each time proper behavior is exhibited. As the acceptable behavior pattern becomes more commonplace, it can then be maintained through occasional reinforcement on an unpredictable, less systematic schedule.

There are several systems of applied behavior analysis that vary from an informal approach, where the teacher simply waits for students to exhibit desired behavior, to more structured systems, where the teacher elicits desired behavior through the systematic use of tangible rewards. In order to modify a student's behavior, the teacher must closely observe the selected student to determine the degree to which that student exhibits the unacceptable behavior. The teacher can use this entering or baseline behavior to determine whether the student is making progress toward changing to more acceptable behavior patterns. Following the identification of this baseline, the teacher then may establish a schedule of reinforcement for rewarding the student for proper conduct. The schedule may be based on time (e.g., a reward for every five minutes of appropriate conduct) or may be based on frequency (e.g., a reward for every two examples of appropriate conduct).

Applied behavior analysis has been praised by many behavioral psychologists (Alberto & Troutman, 2006; Zirpoli & Melloy, 2004) while criticized by other psychologists and educators (Kohn, 2001; Travers, 1977) on the basis that this manipulation of reinforcements focuses on symptomatic behavior without considering the causes of the maladaptive conduct (see the discussion under *remunerative strategies* in this chapter). As with most highly systematic models for classroom management, the successful use of applied behavior analysis techniques will come only after professional training has been received.

Jacob Kounin

Eggen and Kauchak (2007) base much of their discussion of essential management skills on the work of Jacob Kounin. Kounin's model (Kounin, 1970), which focuses more on total group characteristics than on individual teacher and student personalities, has contributed greatly to the study of effective group management. Five key constructs characterize this approach. First, when teachers correct the misbehavior of one student, this correction can have an effect on the total group. Kounin refers to this phenomenon as the *ripple effect*. Second, teachers must have the characteristic of *withitness* which means that the teacher is able to be aware of what is taking place in all parts of the classroom at the same time. Third, teachers must be concerned about the flow of the lesson. Transitions between learning tasks and momentum within the tasks must be smooth. Teachers must avoid rushing into an activity with little preparation (Kounin calls this *thrust*) as well as avoid spending too much time on one topic or activity. Optimum pacing must be maintained which will keep the students on task. Busy students are, as was stated earlier, much less likely to cause management problems. This leads to the fourth key point, teachers should have as a goal the maintenance of *group focus*, which is achieved by keeping all students alert and accountable for learning the concepts being studied. It is important that every student feel that the teacher is aware of each person's individual level of progress. Before students will feel the need to be alert and accountable for learning, the teacher must develop a system for consistently monitoring student progress. Finally, teachers must make every effort to structure the curriculum with general as well as specific learning tasks to avoid student boredom. Kounin suggests that this can be done by adding variety and diversity to the kinds of activities the students undertake and by placing individuals within a scope and sequence of academic events which ensures all students the opportunity for success. Students who are bored or feel that progress is unlikely are prone to create management problems.

Kounin's model is valuable in that it focuses upon leadership qualities related to group dynamics. The primary emphasis, as with Glasser (1993), discussed next, is on the teacher's ability to prepare a good learning environment where all students receive adequate feedback and perceive themselves as making academic progress. This emphasis on group characteristics becomes evident through such concepts as the *ripple effect* and *withitness*. Kounin's model is based on a very realistic view of classroom life. Most teachers, regardless of their teaching styles, will benefit from an understanding of the components of this model.

William Glasser

William Glasser (1992, 1969, & 1965) and Glasser and Dotson (1998) provide a general model for classroom management that he has labeled *Reality Therapy*, today referred to as Choice Theory. Glasser has a wide following among teachers in this country, and there are data which indicate that the model can have positive effects when applied appropriately (Good & Brophy, 1986). There is one significant commonality between the models of Glasser and Dreikurs; in both, students are responsible for their own behavior and must accept any negative consequences that might result from misbehavior. Glasser, like Dreikurs, also stated the importance of students helping in the establishment of rules for proper conduct. In contrast, Glasser indicates that rules should be established through a collaborative process often referred to as the *class meeting*. Rules, however, also can be established in a more individualized fashion where teachers meet with students outside of the whole group.

During the class meeting the teacher is a democratic stimulator of discussion, not an authority figure. All decisions are arrived at through majority rule. Any time that classroom rules and regulations must be adjusted or unique situations evolve, the group meets and decisions are revised by vote or consensus. The class meeting, therefore, is a regularly recurring event during the school year. Class meetings must be used to prevent possible behavior problems, not just to react to an unwanted behavior occurrence. Through class meetings, teachers can guide students to reflect and share feelings that can help them work through possible conflicts. Sharing ideas concerning the need for certain rules, and the possible consequences for violating these rules, can help everyone in the group better understand the importance of certain expectations for behavior. The preventive aspect of any model is particularly important since good managers are characterized by their ability to avoid management problems.

There are other important characteristics of Glasser's model. An overriding principle of this approach is that a disruptive student must learn that, in order to remain in the classroom, agreed-upon rules for appropriate behavior must be followed. Removal from the group occurs only after repeated behavior violations and is accomplished through a sequential process. First, the student is simply isolated from the total group and asked to devise a plan to ensure that the rules for proper conduct are followed in the future. If positive results are not forthcoming, the next step is described as in-school suspension; the student now must deal with the principal, not only the teacher. A further plan must be devised to ensure that misconduct will no longer take place. If this does not achieve the desired result, the student's parents or guardians must come to the school and take the student home. This removal is temporary in the hope that the student can return to school shortly and begin anew. Finally, if the above steps all fail, the student is expelled from the school. In order to decrease the likelihood of having to go this far, Glasser and Dotson (1998) emphasize the importance of educators focusing on the development of quality in the lives of students and teachers in order that schools become better places with fewer behavior problems and more positive accomplishments.

This technique can be very profitable providing the teacher can accept a democratic leadership role. If the teacher feels it necessary to make totally unilateral decisions, he or she will have a difficult time following Glasser's suggestions. While the model is very systematic and relates well to most classroom situations, in order to fully function within the boundaries of Glasser's recommended approach, you will need specialized training and an opportunity to observe other professionals who use the techniques in a classroom environment.

Thomas Gordon

Thomas Gordon's model (Gordon, 1974) of classroom management is referred to as Teacher Effectiveness Training (TET). Gordon's philosophy of control is based on Gestalt psychology similar to that of Carl Rogers. Rogers is noted for his technique of nondirective counseling.

Central to TET is the position that teachers must give up their role as powerful authority figures and be able to discuss differences they may have with students in a free and caring way. Students should not be coerced in any manner to behave. Rather, the teacher must discuss the unacceptable behavior with the student in what Gordon calls a *no lose* situation. If teachers demonstrate a concern and caring attitude toward students, those students, in turn, will demonstrate the same type of respect for their teachers.

When problems occur in the classroom, teachers and students must first determine to whom the problem belongs: the teacher, the student, or both. Problems that belong to the student involve such inhibitors to learning as fear and anxiety. Teacher-owned problems, on the other hand, involve behaviors such as student misconduct, which tends to frustrate the teacher because it interrupts the instructional flow. When the problem is owned by students, the teacher must *actively listen* to the students in order to be able to help them arrive at their own solutions. Active listening involves encouraging students to talk about their frustrations while showing them that the teacher does, in fact, see the problem as being serious. The teacher should never take a student's problems lightly, even in an attempt to reassure the student that everything will eventually be worked out.

Active listening requires that the teacher gives full attention to the student while attending to both the emotional as well as the intellectual content of what the student is saying (Sokolove, Garrett, Sadker, & Sadker, 1990). Feedback to students must be offered in an attempt to help them solve their own problems. Conversely, as Good and Brophy (1986) explain, when the problem is the teacher's, the teacher must take the initiative and send messages to the disruptive students in order to change their behaviors. The person who *owns* the problem must be the one who talks about it.

Gordon believes that teachers are likely to have difficulty in changing students' behaviors when they approach their students by confronting them with criticism. Such confrontations are labeled *you messages* in this model. Gordon suggests that the best way to change student behavior is through what he refers to as *I messages*. An *I message* is developed in three distinct parts. The first segment delineates the deviant behavior, the second describes the effect that such behavior has on the teacher, and the final part tells how such behavior makes the teacher feel. An example of an *I message* would be as follows: (1) when someone comes into class late, (2) it disrupts the flow of the lesson and disturbs the learning activities, (3) and I (the teacher) become very frustrated. The *I message* is a central concept to teacher effectiveness training and gives the teacher an opportunity to change student behavior without having to become involved in a power struggle or the use of coercive strategies.

The use of *I messages*, which focus on behaviors, not the student as a person, is based upon the assumption that all students can understand communications which are sent in what some linguists consider to be elaborate codes (Stubbs, 1983). Through *I messages*, the teacher is attempting to persuade students to change their unwanted behavior by giving them a rational explanation of the effects of this behavior. It is suggested that some students, especially those from lower socioeconomic conditions, do not as easily understand nor positively respond to such elaborate communications. These students frequently come from backgrounds where control strategies tend to be based on the authoritarian power of the adult in charge. Such students have, in the past, often responded to brief commands without being given an explanation of the commands nor a chance to voice their opinions. When placed in the middle-class environment of the classroom and given elaborate communications designed to help students subjectively empathize with their teacher, they are likely to misinterpret the communication. They may not associate such elaborate messages with the teacher's desire for them to change their behavior. In simple terms, students from some cultural and socioeconomic backgrounds may not be accustomed to authority figures using such rational, democratic control methods. They tend to be more familiar with a direct, authoritarian method.

Lee and Marlene Canter

Lee and Marlene Canter (Canter & Canter, 1976) developed an approach to effective classroom management which relies on the teacher's ability and willingness to be assertive in the classroom. Referred to as the *Assertive Discipline* model, this model is founded on the tenet that teachers using the approach will not allow disruptive students to interfere with the teaching/learning process. Teachers using this model develop responses to classroom disruptions which do not reinforce and perpetuate misbehavior. For example, when confronted with a disruptive student, the teacher does not make a public issue of the behavior by verbal reprimands but instead gives a nonverbal warning by recording the student's name on the chalkboard or whiteboard, or on the teacher's notepad. By refusing to allow the student to disrupt the teaching/learning process, the teacher continues teaching with a minimal loss of instructional time. If the student continues to disrupt and is still unwilling to change behavior, the teacher will, at that point, assign the first of several possible negative consequences which have been developed, perhaps in cooperation with the entire class. This is typically done by adding a check mark after the student's name to indicate that the first of several negative consequences has been assigned. The first negative consequence is often a short detention either after school or during school. If the student still maintains the disruptive behavior, the teacher continues with additional check marks until the student reaches the end of the list of negative consequences or decides to modify the disruptive behavior. The final negative consequence is usually referral to the administration of the school which often results in a call to the student's parents. During the entire process, the teacher asserts the teacher's right to teach and the right of other students to learn by refusing to engage the disruptive student in verbal battles or allow the student to interfere in any way with the teaching/learning process. Instead, the teacher calmly and confidently assigns consequences until the student stops the disruption or is removed from the class.

Beyond the assertive aspect of the teacher's behavior, this model is based on full involvement of all parties concerned with the education of the student. Parents, peers, teachers, and school administrators are all involved in the initiation of the model in the classroom or school. As a customary practice, at the beginning of the school year, parents receive documentation to be signed which describes the model as it will be implemented. The signing of the document indicates a general acceptance of the procedures to be followed. Information is provided to the parents detailing such basic aspects of the model as the list of positive and negative consequences to be utilized in the teacher's classroom along with a brief list of classroom rules. Such documentation is typically sent home by individual teachers who indicate in an accompanying letter that signing the letter and returning it to school signifies a willingness to support the management program as outlined. The goal is to develop a partnership among teachers, parents, students, and administrators regarding the behavioral management program to be utilized, a characteristic all too rare among management systems used in many schools. The key to the overall effectiveness of the approach is the degree of parental support that is generated. Through the assertive discipline model, parents must be in communication with the school and learn of both positive and negative consequences of their child's behavior in time to react and support the system.

Canter states that assertive discipline is based on presenting students with choices, and, by making such choices, students learn responsibility. A teacher using the assertive discipline approach recognizes that, in order to choose how to behave, students must know the rules and the negative consequences of choosing not to follow them. Rather than focusing exclusively on negative consequences, teachers trained in assertive discipline use positive reinforcement consistently to focus student attention on desired behavior and to encourage students to continue that behavior because of the recognition they receive (Canter, 1988).

As with other approaches to classroom management, there is some controversy over the use of assertive discipline (Eggen & Kauchak, 2007). Some experts have claimed that the techniques are confrontational and align teachers against their students while stressing conformity over self-control (Kohn, 2001; McLaughlin, 1994; Curwin & Mendler, 1988). Yet, many educators feel assertive discipline is a positive approach to management. Even given this controversy, assertive discipline has been used in many schools across the nation.

Fred Jones

Fred Jones (2000) supports his theory of Positive Discipline which is based on the premise that most behavior problems occur when students are not engaged in meaningful academic activity. It is the task of the teacher, therefore, to give students activities that they can focus upon while using their time constructively. Jones believes that students exhibit unwanted behaviors because they are allowed to be idle and waste time, not because it is their natures to be aggressive, unruly, or defiant. Teachers are encouraged to minimize the amount of "down time" in the classroom in order to lessen the opportunity for students to exhibit unwanted behavior. Specifically, Jones suggests that the teacher's ability to plan appropriate, exciting lessons and develop a positive learning environment is the key to becoming an effective classroom manager (Manning & Bucher, 2007).

It is felt that students waste time because (1) their assignments are too difficult, (2) they do not understand what the teacher expects them to do, (3) their assignments are too easy resulting in some students finishing too quickly and having nothing to do, and (4) they find the assignments boring. Teachers can counteract these problems by (1) using teaching methods that are appropriate for keeping students focused, engaged, and excited about learning, (2) using clear nonverbal communication to students, (3) arranging the classroom to facilitate communication, and (4) rewarding students who stay on task.

David and Roger Johnson

Since conflicts among students have become a serious problem that has disrupted the teaching-learning environments in many schools, some educators currently advocate that students themselves should be formally trained to resolve their conflicts in a constructive manner at school (Johnson & Johnson, 1997; Stevahn, Johnson, Johnson, Green, & Laginski, 1997; Johnson & Johnson, 1995). Johnson and Johnson developed the conflict resolution model to address this need. Through conflict resolution training, students learn to negotiate with one another in order to find constructive resolutions to their disagreements. When students have a dispute, one of two types of negotiations can take place: integrative or distributive. The *integrative* approach is developed to use creative problem solving in such a way as to increase the probability that both disputants can get what they want through their negotiations. When using the *distributive approach*, each disputant tries to maximize personal gain at the expense of the other party. The integrative approach works much better in school settings (Johnson & Johnson, 1995).

Many claims have been made for conflict resolution as a model which helps decrease management problems in schools (Tolson, McDonald, & Moriarty, 1992). Although many schools have adopted conflict resolution programs (Johnson, Johnson, Dudley, Mitchell, & Frederickson, 1997), more objective research is needed, especially in middle and high schools, to support the model (Johnson & Johnson, 1995).

In order for conflict resolution to be successful, it needs to become a total school program requiring specialized training for both teachers and students. Due to the amount of training and the number of specialized initiatives related to academic programs that already exist in most schools today, some educators have been reluctant to embrace an extensive program such as this that is separate from academic content. Stevahn et al. (1997) suggest that, in order to make conflict resolution more functional, the training should be integrated into the overall ongoing curriculum.

Johnson and Johnson (2004) report that training students in conflict resolution and peer mediation leads to fewer management problems in the classroom and throughout the entire school. Further, they report that students continue to use their conflict resolution strategies when dealing with confrontations at home and in the community. Proper training, of course, is the significant variable.

Alfie Kohn

Kohn can be thought of as a leading opponent of behaviorism. Kohn feels that both rewards (he often refers to rewards as "bribes") and punishments function only to change specific behaviors; they do not change value systems or individual character. As a result, rewards and punishments can cause only temporary compliance. They do not tend to bring about long-term changes in student traits such as self-reliance, creative thinking, or self-confidence. Kohn's theory is based on the tenet that, for long-term positive change to take place, students must internalize pro-social values while becoming part of a caring community. *Pro-social behavior* is behavior that is directed toward promoting the well-being of someone else. This is the opposite of *antisocial behavior* which is used to bring about a negative consequence for someone else. Instead of being trained like animals through the use of rewards and punishments, students should be enculturated into a learning community based on humane values such as kindness, fairness, and personal responsibility (Powell, McLaughlin, Savage, & Zehm, 2001). In order to realize this humane system of management, teachers should integrate values instruction into classroom management, foster a caring community throughout the school, and use positive discipline practices (Kidron & Fleischman, 2007). Kohn (2001) believes that teachers must communicate with students in a way that models to students a caring, unity-building attitude toward all people.

SELECTING MANAGEMENT MODELS

The information provided in this section is intended to serve as an overview of several possible management models. Teachers must determine which model or collection of models would be best suited to their particular personality and teaching situation. It is strongly suggested that more study be undertaken prior to making such a decision as only introductory information has been presented here, and the decision to implement any management model will be based on many factors. According to Curwin and Mendler (1988), as a minimum, the following questions should be considered, and answered, prior to implementing any management program in a school.

1. What happens to students who break rules? Punishments or consequences?
2. Is it realistically possible to reinforce the program consistently?
3. What do students learn as a result of the use of the program?
4. Are the principles of behavior as visible and as important as the rules?
5. Do students have a say in what happens to them?
6. Do teachers have discretion in implementing consequences?
7. Is adequate time given for professional development of teachers and administrators? Is the training completed in only a day or two? Is there continuous follow-up and administrative support?
8. Does the plan account for the special relationship between teaching and discipline style, or does it focus exclusively on student behavior? Does it encourage teachers to examine their own potential contributions to discipline problems?
9. Is the dignity of the students preserved? Are students protected from embarrassment?
10. Is the program consistent with the stated goals of the school?

In addition to consideration of these concerns, teachers planning a management program also should carefully consider what they are currently doing, if anything, to create their own discipline problems. Perhaps lessons are being presented that (1) stimulate little motivation, (2) do not provide for student academic or behavioral success, (3) provide very little, if any, student choice, and (4) deny students the opportunity to express feelings and opinions (Curwin & Mendler, 1988). It also is noted that most models function best when adopted by the entire faculty of a school as opposed to a single teacher in isolation. Careful attention should be given to the earlier section in this chapter which deals with what may be done to prevent classroom management problems.

COPING WITH SPECIFIC CONTROL PROBLEMS

All specific control problems should be approached with the long-term goal of solving or removing the cause of the problem. Such an approach will take time and effort on the part of the teacher, but the benefits should make the effort worthwhile. Suggestions concerning the treatment of several common management problems follow. You are reminded that all such problems must be reacted to with consideration given to the make-up of the total group and the personalities of the students involved. It would be a mistake to suggest that all students exhibiting a common behavior problem exhibit the behavior for the same reason. For example, all inattentive students are not inattentive for the same reasons. Charles (1976), while discussing a study by Ritholz, reports that the seven most common examples of misbehavior are as follows: (1) *inattention,* (2) *disruptive talking,* (3) *unruliness,* (4) *aggression,* (5) *attention-seeking,* (6) *defiance,* and (7) *dishonesty.* Each one of these behavior syndromes will be examined individually.

Inattention

Inattention is usually manifested in such behaviors as staring into space (i.e., daydreaming), doing unrelated work during class, or doodling or playing with objects on the desk (e.g., pencils or rubber bands). This type of behavior is disturbing to teachers for several reasons. Primarily, if attentive students decide to copy such inattentive behavior, the teacher will find it virtually impossible to conduct instruction. In situations such as these, the teacher is always concerned when observing inattentive students because the desire is that all students profit from the instructional process. There frequently is another reason teachers become disturbed when observing inattentive behavior. Teachers often take personal offense when students are inattentive feeling that the students are communicating that they, as teachers, are not motivating and are ineffective. This personal criticism, whether realistic or not, generally places the teacher in a defensive position.

What are the underlying causes of inattentive behavior? Inattention can be caused by a number of influencing factors, including both poor teaching and curriculum construction. If the teacher's instruction is characterized by a repetition of long, dry episodes, where students are given little opportunity and encouragement for active participation, many will become bored and, as a result, inattentive. Lessons that last for long periods of time while focusing on the same activity also frustrate students to the point where they simply lose interest and are no longer attentive. Aside from these factors, certain personal characteristics of the teacher can contribute to student inattentiveness. The monotonic voice that drones on, for example, has become a symbol of the stereotypical bore, and a teacher with such voice quality should not expect students to become excited listeners. Teachers who fail to use gestures or other movements to supplement their verbal communication often lose the students' attention. To complement gestures, teachers must also be cognizant of the positive impact of occasional humor in the classroom. Effective teachers frequently insert a humorous anecdote or joke at the precise moment where students' minds are beginning to wander. Probably the most significant consideration in the analysis of student attentiveness is the level of student participation allowed. Classrooms where students are given the opportunity to actively participate in their lessons, as well as the planning of activities and selecting of materials, constitute environments that foster student attentiveness.

The source of an attention problem also could be found in the students as opposed to the teacher or the curriculum. Some students may become inattentive even when the teacher is doing an excellent job and the curriculum is dynamic due to problems outside of school which are so serious that the classroom instruction simply represents insignificant demands. Teachers must make a deliberate effort to know their students in order to better understand them and their problems. Some students, unfortunately, have been allowed to be inattentive so frequently that they have made a habit of letting their minds wander. Some may have short attention spans simply because they have never been encouraged, reinforced, or even required to be attentive. Regardless of the cause, inattentiveness is a behavior which seems deviant to many teachers and solutions must be found to aid the inattentive student in developing a longer attention span.

There are ways a teacher can help inattentive students. For example, developing an effective question-asking strategy, as discussed in Chapter 4, is frequently beneficial in addressing this problem. Teachers may need to ask questions more regularly of those students who have the habit of not paying attention to class discussions. Drawing students into the lesson and making it necessary for them to remain alert are the purposes of these questions. In this regard, it often is helpful to ask the question first and then call upon the student. If the student is called upon before the question is asked, other students in the classroom may not pay attention to the question or the answer. Another consideration for the teacher is whether or not reinforcements are being used effectively. Just as it is important to reward students for being attentive, it is also necessary to withhold reinforcements when students are being inattentive. For example, when directions are given and students do not pay attention, teachers are reinforcing inattentiveness when they continually repeat the directions. When teachers make it easy for students to be inattentive, they are not only reinforcing the inattentive students but they are also communicating to the entire group that it is not really necessary to listen carefully. Careful listening is a learned behavior. Students who are inattentive are not likely to become careful listeners in one or two days; their behavior must be molded over time. It is the teacher's responsibility to be careful always to reinforce such students when they are attentive. Teachers should review the importance of careful listening with the group and ensure that no one will be reinforced for being inattentive.

Disruptive Talking

Disruptive talk is viewed as unacceptable verbal communication on the part of the student. Because teachers set their own individual standards for acceptable talk at different levels, it is possible that no other standard for acceptable behavior varies as much among teachers as the one that serves to define acceptable talking. And, many teachers change their level of acceptable talk from one day to another. These changes may very well be due to the teachers' change of mood. As might be expected, students often find it confusing when their teachers fluctuate in the amount of talk allowed. In an effort to avoid such confusion, teachers must be consistent and aware of the danger of punishing a student today for a behavior which was acceptable previously.

Talking can often disturb the learning process for students who are attempting to attend to instruction. Even more than being disruptive, the student who is constantly involved in idle talk is not likely to be achieving the desired learning outcomes. Furthermore, as was the case with inattentive students, teachers frequently take personal offense when students talk when it is felt they should be listening. Teachers tend to interpret this behavior to mean that students think their instruction is unexciting or of little value.

Students become involved in disruptive talk for several reasons. Even though these reasons are both numerous and varied, the teacher can control the environment to the extent that much of what can be viewed as the causes for such talk is eliminated. Disruptive talk often takes place because students do not understand the instruction or directions of their teacher. When teachers are not clear in their communications, students are likely to become confused and ask one another for clarification. Teachers should observe this type of student behavior and determine the need for further elaboration. Unfortunately, teachers frequently punish students when they are asking one another for help because the teachers erroneously assumes the talk is not related to the instruction. Another cause for idle, disruptive talk is unmotivating lessons. Teachers will be able to diminish much unwanted talking by developing motivating, participatory instruction which holds the interest of the students. Many problems associated with disruptive talk and inattentiveness can be solved by teachers simply projecting enthusiasm about the content under study and by adding greater variety to the type of instruction taking place.

Teachers will often profit greatly from a reexamination of what they perceive as being *disruptive talk*. It is not uncommon for students to become so excited about their work that they share their ideas with each other. The teacher should be pleased to see such interest and should be aware that this type of verbal interaction is an invaluable aid to learning. Students also may become engaged in unwanted talk because they have become excited over some unexpected event or special occasion. Happenings such as ball games, assemblies, birthdays, and classroom visitors frequently create a stir of emotion resulting in what may be interpreted as disruptive talk. Finally, disruptive talk can be a problem resulting from certain student traits. The outgoing, verbal student, for example, who completes assignments early may develop a habit of using all spare time visiting with other students. Talking to one's friends can be a most enjoyable pastime and a difficult habit to overcome. Added to this, conversation is *contagious* in that, if some students begin to talk freely, others will see and hear them and begin to talk with their neighbors as well.

Prevention of disruptive talk must begin with the teacher. If students are to be quiet during a given time period, they must have assignments which are both stimulating enough to hold their interest and adequate enough to keep them occupied for the entire class. Students who have an ample amount of work to complete at the proper level of instruction (i.e., neither too simple nor too difficult) are not likely to become involved in idle conversation. It is important that teachers also remind students about the proper conduct to be exhibited when unexpected events take place such as visitors coming to the classroom or going to special assembly programs. These types of interruptions in the typical schedule have the potential to arouse the interest and excitement of students. If teachers would take a moment to talk with their students about these events and to answer questions concerning them, problems should be at a minimum. Effective teachers do not try to fight to suppress this normal curiosity and excitement. If the teacher knows about such events before they happen, prior adjustments can be made to prepare the students instead of waiting until the last minute when the level of excitement is at its highest.

When an event occurs that arouses unwanted chatter, the teacher might discuss the problem and its cause afterwards with the entire class. The technique of the class discussion, sometimes referred to as the class meeting (discussed earlier in this chapter), has received much acclaim as a method of approaching such problems. While it is difficult for students to objectively examine their own behavior when they are excited, most can look back upon their behavior at a later point and determine what they did which was inappropriate and how best to avoid future recurrences.

Students who chronically exhibit disruptive talk may need to be isolated from the source stimulating their disruptive behavior. All that might need be done is to create seating arrangements that separate those students who insist upon talking to each other. Another effective method of controlling disruptive talk is the placing of talkative students in an area of the room which will usually be in close proximity to the teacher. Regardless of their talkative traits, students are less likely to continue unwanted talking when seated close to the teacher.

A final word of warning is appropriate. You should never have a classroom atmosphere where all student-to-student talk is discouraged. The classroom is a social as well as an academic setting and students need to interact both with their peers and their teachers if optimal learning is to take place. Although teachers cannot allow students to chat with each other in such a way as to diminish their own learning as well as the learning of their classmates, it would be ill-advised to set such rigid rules that students are afraid to ask questions or make appropriate remarks during a lesson. Much has been said about excessive talking. However, it should be remembered that the student who never or seldom speaks may have a learning problem or personal issue creating difficulty in communicating ideas to others. It would be a serious shortcoming if teachers developed classroom environments which fostered a lack of open communication.

Unruliness

Unruliness is defined as a state of general misbehavior where students seem to lack any control over their own actions. Examples of such behavior are *pushing other students, laughing loudly, getting out of one's seat without permission,* and *playing practical jokes.* Unruly students are not necessarily aggressive or defiant but simply conduct themselves in a way that is not desirable. Some students may exhibit this type of behavior on a regular basis. Unruly behavior is a group and situation-related concept and that which may be acceptable in certain groups or in certain situations might not be acceptable in others. To the degree that a student's home and community adopts the same standards of behavior as that of the school, that student's behavior will be seen as being compatible with and in conformity to the role expectations for a public school student. But, a student who comes from a background which does not reflect the standards of the school is much more likely to exhibit behavior seen as being unruly than is the student who has been rewarded for such behavior in his home and community. This factor can place the teacher in a difficult situation. When correcting the behavior of an unruly student, the teacher must avoid making statements that attack other individuals who exhibit such behavior. For example, if a student curses and is told by the teacher that only bad people curse, that student may become alienated if those in his home and community use such language. It is important to separate, at all times, actions from people when reacting to unruliness. In reference to the previous example, the teacher could inform the student that such language is not to be used in the classroom without referring to an individual as being bad or evil because he or she used such words.

Because general misconduct can be manifested in a number of different forms, the causes of unruliness are varied. Learning tasks assigned to a student can be so difficult or nonchallenging that the student becomes either overextended, frustrated, or bored. Such a learning environment frequently puts so much stress on certain students that they become unruly and difficult to control. Teachers who fail to create an appropriately stimulating learning environment for students are setting the stage for this state of general misbehavior. Unfortunately, unruliness, as is the case with most types of misbehavior, is both *catching* and *habit forming.* Students who observe their peers involved in inappropriate conduct are prone to participate in unruly behaviors themselves. When left unchecked, this type of misconduct becomes commonplace, making it even more difficult for students to stop their improper behaviors. Teachers can naturally expect a certain amount of lack of self-control from all students under some circumstances. Elementary students can become very excited over special events like holiday parties and magic shows just as older students when it is time for an important ball game or prom night. Teachers should not expect young people to always exhibit self-control and restraint as adults certainly do not always exhibit such qualities under comparable social conditions.

When dealing with students who are consistently unruly, the teacher must assume that the learning environment is lacking something which would make their social adjustment easier. Too frequently, students who consistently display this sort of general misconduct are unhappy with school because they cannot achieve a desired level of satisfaction from their academic progress. Such students may have learning difficulties which are being manifested in an overt behavior triggered by an environment that provides little reinforcement and satisfaction. The teacher, upon identifying such a student, should first view the student as one who is in need of a better placement within a more stimulating setting, not as a student in need of discipline. Teachers often forget that unruly behavior can be the symptom of an inappropriate learning activity and to attack the unruliness is only to attack a symptom, not the real cause of the misconduct. Unruly students are often those who are easily overstimulated or have shorter attention spans. Such students frequently need more structure in their activities and movement, especially until they have fully learned what is expected of them. They typically are less successful working on their own than under the supervision of a teacher because they are easily distracted. Class work is often more productive when they are seated in a section of the room where their peers cannot interfere with their learning. Sometimes it only takes a casual comment from a peer to distract such students and get them off task and involved in undesirable behavior. Total isolation from the group may eventually be necessary if they become stimulated to the point where proper conduct is unlikely. Such isolation should be in a *nonstimulating* area, and students should see it as an opportunity to be calm and under control more than as punishment. This isolation should be viewed as a direct result of the students' unwanted behavior and never a form of reward. It is important that the student who has developed a habit of unruliness also receive reinforcement for exhibiting desirable behavior. As already noted, such a student may receive very little positive feedback in or out of school. Reinforcement for desirable behavior will help the teacher get closer to the student to discover the real cause of the student's misconduct.

Aggression

Aggression on the part of students can present the teacher with immediate and serious problems. When students talk out of turn or are inattentive, the teacher can take some time to analyze the behavior and try to determine how best to deal with it. However, when students are being aggressive, the teacher may have to react quickly and decisively as the teacher has the responsibility of protecting the safety of every student in the classroom. It is important to remember that aggression is marked by a lack of emotional control. Students who are involved in fights or temper tantrums are not in the proper state of mind to reason or discuss problems. When such students are approached by the teacher, they very likely may be so upset that they will verbally or even physically attack. They need to be calmed by the teacher as quickly as possible. Verbal retorts by the teacher will only increase the student's level of frustration and increase the likelihood of even more severe aggression. *Aggression* is a much more intense behavior problem than is *unruliness.* An unruly student is usually bothersome and often distracting to other students. The aggressive student, on the other hand, can be physically or emotionally harmful. Aggression cannot, under any circumstances, be permitted in the classroom.

The causes of aggression can be extremely complex and some students who chronically exhibit aggression probably will only learn to curb their emotions after they have received professional help. Some students may have problems that are so deep-seated that they are actually emotional *time bombs* for whom it is virtually impossible to function in a highly active social setting such as a classroom. Fortunately, the number of these highly unstable students who should be removed from the school is very small. Most aggressive behavior results from momentary outbursts as a consequence of intense frustration.

Students who come from homes and communities where aggression is a relatively common behavior may exhibit hostile behavior themselves because they have seen others consistently do so. Aggression can also result from the frustration that is caused by repeated academic failures. Some students have had such difficult and unsuccessful learning experiences that they actually rebel against the school and teacher by overt, aggressive behavior. Oddly enough, this type of aggression is often seen by some psychologists as a healthy release of inner frustrations that would be much more serious if it were held within. Teachers, however, cannot allow this type of behavior to exist in the social structure of the classroom. Student aggression, besides its potential for personal harm, is a true threat to the teacher's leadership position.

In dealing with aggressive students, teachers must first try to calm them down before attempting to address the actual cause of their aggression. This can rarely be done by talking because aggressive students are generally so emotional at the time that conversation usually evolves into an argument which only augments the tension. In analyzing alternative actions to take, the age and size of the student(s) involved in the aggressive act will help to determine the teacher's approach. For example, if six-year-old students are having a fight, it would be reasonable for most teachers to stop the fight by restraining the most aggressive student until both students have calmed to the point where their anger and frustration can be discussed. It might be very unwise for secondary level teachers to wade into a fight between two sixteen-year-olds, boys or girls. When students this age are fighting and the teacher attempts restraint, the teacher is taking the risk of being hit and seriously hurt. Too, the student who is not held may continue the attack as the teacher restrains the adversary. It is usually advisable for a secondary teacher to send for help and direct bystanders to stay clear of danger while verbally trying to get the combatants to desist. The teacher who is dealing with younger students and feels that it is necessary to stop the fight by holding one of them should remember that it is wise to allow the students to stop struggling and arguing completely before attempting to get their cooperation. Since aggressive students can only be dealt with constructively after composure has been regained, it generally is best to separate them from all sources of tension as soon as possible and that, during the course of the aggressive behavior, the teacher refrain from verbal chastisement and emotional outbursts which will only further arouse the aggression (Brophy & McCaslin, 1992).

Long-term solutions require that teachers make it clear to students that physical aggression (e.g., fighting or throwing objects) and verbal aggression (e.g., sassing the teacher or calling names and bullying classmates) are unacceptable behaviors in any social group, especially the classroom. Students who are chronic problems must be either isolated from the group or punished by having certain privileges taken away. Attempts should be made to discuss the source of the aggression with the students after they have regained their composure. Students often exhibit aggressive behavior because something is happening at school that is causing them great frustration. The teacher should listen patiently to the students and attempt to help them relieve their frustrations. If the source of frustration is not removed, the students are likely to become chronically aggressive or develop a dislike for or mistrust of the total school environment. Fundamentally, aggression should be thought of as a symptom of a more complex problem. It is the role of the teacher to help students deal with their frustrations or to locate others who are more qualified to do so.

Attention-Seeking

For years, teachers and parents alike have discussed the fact that some students seem to break behavior rules simply to get the attention either of their peers or the adults in charge. These students often seek attention by trying to *entertain* other people in the group and, as a result, are frequently labeled *show-offs* or *class clowns*. Some younger students receive the label *tattletale* because they try to get the teacher's attention by *telling* when others have broken rules or done something of which the teacher would not approve. Peer pressure typically abates tattling as students get older (i.e., middle and secondary levels). It must be remembered, however, that excessive attention-seeking, like most other types of misconduct, is a symptom of some other problem.

Students who are attention-seekers are usually trying to compensate for a real unmet need. They may not be getting the kind of attention in their home life, or at school, that they need for proper social adjustment. Many *show-offs* and *class clowns* are actually insecure individuals searching for feelings of love and belonging. All attention-seekers are not unloved children with tyrannical parents or from broken homes, but some are. Finding the exact source of such problems is often difficult, sometimes even impossible, yet teachers can make things easier for these students through proper interventions.

Since attention-seekers are characterized by insecurity, the teacher must avoid *putting them down* by telling them they are silly or that they should act their age. Avoiding this temptation is often difficult because the chronic attention-seeker can try the patience of the most even-tempered of teachers, particularly at the end of a tedious day. Ironically, it is usually the most trying students who need the greatest understanding. There are, however, some important things that teachers can do to help change these unwanted student behaviors. While teachers should give attention-seekers attention to the degree that it is possible, they should reinforce them for only appropriate behavior. It will often be necessary to delay or redirect attention-seekers instead of refusing them. With this in mind, it is important that teachers plan to give such students some daily, individual attention in order that they may learn that they can receive approval without displaying deviant behavior. Although the *class clown* can sometimes be entertaining and provide a pleasant break even for the teacher, the teacher must avoid reinforcing such behavior if at all possible. Ignoring the attention-seeker is probably a more profitable approach than trying to use a coercive strategy to change the unwanted behavior. Attention-seekers, however, should be reassured that they are important, respected members of the group. Nevertheless, this must be done without giving rewards for seeking attention in unacceptable ways.

Defiance

Students who refuse to do what the teacher asks or boldly talk back to the teacher in a threatening way are categorized as defiant. The behavior of such students must concern teachers very much. The defiant student, probably more than any other, creates situations where the teacher, as leader of the group, could possibly exhibit retreating behavior. If the teacher gives directions to a student and that student refuses to follow the teacher's directives, the deviant behavior must be corrected or the teacher may no longer be seen as an effective leader. Nothing short of true physical danger should be seen as a greater threat to a group leader. Defiant students are communicating to the teacher that they no longer *must* do what they are told to do.

The causes of defiance are quite often deep-seated. Students usually have a level of anger and frustration that has reached a point that can no longer be contained. For these students, this anger and frustration may have been building up over years of negative school experience. Additional sources of defiant behavior could be found in the home. Students who have problems relating to authority figures in the home may very well react defiantly toward teachers and administrators in the school. While this may be the case, it is likely that the teacher still can have some control over the development of a defiant attitude. Something in the classroom atmosphere or even the teacher's own behavior could possibly be a cause of the defiance. For example, the teacher, unknowingly, could be doing something which makes students feel unliked or unwanted (e.g., never calling on them), or the teacher could unintentionally be placing one or more students in a stressful situation (e.g., a poor reader being embarrassed because of oral reading assignments as a classroom activity).

Teachers should be cautious when dealing with any hostile student knowing that such a student is not likely to comply automatically to their verbal commands. Interaction with such a student is apt to increase hostility because the student is often aware of the fact that serious deviant behavior has already been exhibited. Rather than take offense at what has already been said and done, the teacher should stay calm and, if at all possible, direct the hostile student out of the classroom. Removing such a student from the classroom has the advantages of (1) giving the student time to get under control, (2) taking away the peer audience which could reinforce further defiance, and (3) removing the need for the deviant student to *keep face* in front of the entire class.

All defiance is not so hostile as to require the immediate removal of the student involved. However, any act of defiance is reason enough for the teacher to hold a private conference with the student. A defiant student may have corrected the unwanted behavior, but the source of the anger and frustration causing the defiance might be expected to exist long after the original incident has passed. A teacher-student conference may help the student view the teacher as being fair and concerned about his or her well-being. Through this building of rapport, the student may be able to see why the teacher could act negatively. Since the teacher interacts with these students on a one-to-one basis, the teacher can feel free to admit mistakes and talk to the student about what can be done to improve the classroom climate and avoid future displays of defiance. Defiant behavior should never be ignored through retreating since such student behavior must be viewed as a type of power struggle. To lose such a power struggle is to relinquish the role of group leader which would certainly be disastrous to the teacher.

Dishonesty

Dishonesty is a trait which has always been viewed as unacceptable in the school setting. Probably the most common type of dishonesty is cheating;

this type of behavior no doubt takes place at all levels of schooling. Students in the early elementary grades may not have important exams to worry about, but they might decide to copy each others' quiz papers or get someone else to do their homework assignments. The telling of untruths and even stealing takes place in many social settings, not only in the school. Certain amounts of dishonest behavior are, regrettably, expected from school-age youths. Although teachers certainly can not condone dishonest conduct on the part of their students, it must be remembered that children and adolescents are still in the formative stages of their moral development. That which may seem to be very deviant to an adult may not seem to be such serious misconduct to students. For example, students may steal a copy of an exam before the testing date simply to have an adventure, not to really cheat and steal in the sense that a teacher may view this type behavior. Additionally, many children in the early elementary grades do not have clear concepts of *ownership* and *truth*. Nonetheless, teachers have the responsibility to help students learn acceptable standards for honest behavior and dishonesty should always be cast in a very unfavorable light. Teachers must remember, however, that students are not born with middle-class, adult standards of behavior common to most teachers. Students must learn acceptable behavior in the home, community, and school. In certain instances, some students do not appear to be learning acceptable behavior in the home or community.

Just as there are a variety of dishonest behaviors, there are a variety of causes for such behaviors. It is a reality of the times that many students come from home and community environments which condone and may even model dishonest behavior. Some students are likely to copy these behaviors and bring them into the school. Such students can get in the habit of relying upon dishonesty in order to function in the school environment. Some students habitually copy homework from others and cheat on tests to the point where they do not know how to exist in an academic setting without using such tactics. Cheating of this nature can be a characteristic of students having poor self-concepts. Many such students have failed so frequently that they feel it impossible to get acceptable grades without cheating. Some educational psychologists refer to this as a condition of *learned helplessness*. It is also possible that during adolescence students become involved in some less-than-honest deeds simply to appear courageous, adventurous, or mature in the eyes of their peer group. The problem that teachers and administrators face with this type of *rite of passage* behavior is that, if one student is successful in gaining peer approval through dishonest acts, other students may try to get approval through the same behaviors.

Dishonest behavior often does not pressure the teacher into the kind of immediate action that aggression or defiance demand. As long as dishonest behavior does not physically hurt other group members, many students are unaware of its existence. When stealing or cheating on tests become known by the group, however, the teacher can no longer only analyze the behavior. At this point, the teacher must take action to correct the unwanted behavior. It is necessary that students know the teacher does not condone dishonesty. Cases of dishonest conduct may require such corrective strategies as deprivation of privileges. Academic dishonesty possibly can impact the student's grade. First and foremost, it is important for the teacher to determine if the student is being assigned work on an appropriate instructional level as a student who cheats may be in a curriculum that is simply too demanding. If this is found to be the case, the student should be placed in a learning environment where success is possible without having to rely upon dishonest tactics. Even in dealing with a student who has been dishonest (e.g., cheated, stolen, or lied), the teacher must be cautious to not label the student. It must be clear that it is the deed that is unacceptable, not the student. If a student is labeled as a *cheat* or a *thief,* the possible ill effects of this labeling on the student's self-concept and further development and behavior is a consequence that should be avoided. Telling students they are bad or dishonest may cause them to think of themselves negatively and begin to more consistently assume the role of dishonest persons.

Chapter 8

THE TEACHER AS AN EVALUATOR OF STUDENT PERFORMANCE

Teachers continue to struggle with various assessment-related issues as the profession moves further into the twenty-first century. Justified or not, there is strong public opinion that students today are not achieving at satisfactory levels, especially when compared to students in other countries. Because of this, there has been a definite move toward holding teachers more accountable for their students' achievement on standardized tests and expecting increasingly higher and higher levels of performance at the same time. There also are those, however, who desire to place greater accountability on students themselves by setting achievement standards which must be reached before they may be promoted from grade to grade, and, ultimately, to high school graduation. Many school districts and states have already initiated such programs. In some situations this has created levels of extreme stress. Although for some students these increased levels of expectation do serve to motivate and bring about more focused and achievement-oriented behavior, in far more instances they create climates of frustration and student behavioral issues.

Such concern over accountability and dissatisfaction with students' academic performance has resulted in ongoing discussions of raising standards, raising the bar as some say, and the creation of more rigorous tests. The rather highly charged atmosphere that this has brought about has led to proposals for the development of national achievement tests for the measurement and comparison of student performance (Jarolimek & Foster, 1997). Although concerns over states' rights, local control of schools, and the difficulty involved in developing tests fair to all students are likely to challenge if not prevent the adoption of such tests, at least in the near future, the public's demand for excellence and high standards is projected to continue and to focus educators' attention on the assessment of student knowledge levels, more than anything else, and the degree to which both teachers and students are accountable for student performance on adopted assessment instruments.

While educators and the public are focusing on students' performance scores on standardized measures of achievement, others are examining alternative formats for measuring student learning (Cheek, 1993). Some of these alternative formats are referred to as authentic assessments. Supporters of alternative assessment approaches seek ways to measure student performance through means other than traditional paper and pencil tests. Alternative measures, it is argued, are more relevant to the true learning of students because they emphasize performance on the actual tasks to be measured, as opposed to students taking a test about the tasks which is a much more vicarious evaluation experience. Such alternative approaches to student evaluations are often referred to as authentic assessments (due to the perception that they are more real-world oriented) or performance-based assessments (Hoy & Hoy, 2009; Hunt, Wiseman, & Bowden, 2003; Kenny & Perry, 1994; Kritt, 1993).

The typical public school classroom is an environment that is both intricate and fast-paced. The teacher who is effective, who learns the many cause-and-effect relationships between teacher behavior and student behavior, between planning and implementation, between motivation and management, between leadership and followership, will have gained these insights, in part, through developing proficiency in evaluation. As professionals, teachers must evaluate student behavior as well as social climate by comparing actual behavior with stated expectations for behavior. Teachers also must evaluate student achievement, taking into consideration specified standards and to what degree their students master desired student learning outcomes. Through self-evaluation and reflection, these same teachers must evaluate materials, instruction, and their own overall classroom performance for the purpose of continuous improvement. Gareis and Grant (2008) describe a model for student learning that includes curriculum, instruction, and assessment and note that, in addition to knowing what to teach and how to teach it, teachers must also be able to determine the degree to which students have learned at any given point in time. The elements of curriculum, instruction and assessment, need to become integrated to form a unified whole in the learning process.

This chapter places emphasis on the evaluation of student performance. Several techniques will be suggested and described which aid in this important process. Through careful study of this chapter, readers will learn more about the following topics:

1. three steps in the evaluation process,
2. guidelines for developing teacher-made test items,
3. methods of alternative assessment,

4. procedures for assigning and reporting student grades, and
5. current issues impacting the assessment of students.

THE NATURE OF EVALUATION

Evaluation may be looked upon as a three-step process which begins with (1) the collection of information, continues with (2) the analysis of the information collected, and concludes with (3) the making of decisions (Wiseman, Hunt, Zhukov, & Mardaehev, 2007). For instance, when determining whether or not a student has mastered an instructional objective, the teacher observes the student's performance related to the objective (collecting information), compares the student's performance to valued criteria (analysis), and then decides, based on this analysis, if the student has met the learning expectations expressed through the objective (decision making). The teacher may decide from this review that the student has mastered the objective and move on to new content, or, determine that the student has not mastered the objective and reteach pertinent information related to it.

Evaluation decisions are not simple to make. Rather than thinking through the situation in a linear, sequential fashion, the teacher often is faced with a much more complex situation. As suggested in Figure 8-1, the process should be thought of as one in which the original three steps are considered and continually reconsidered in light of the input of additional information and ongoing interaction with students. Besides being a logically oriented process, evaluation is the means by which people make judgments concerning persons, ideas, and things. With this in mind, teaching is seen as being comprised of a series of ongoing judgments in which the teacher is constantly (1) observing the classroom and the related environment for information, (2) processing the information observed, and (3) making significant decisions for the ultimate improvement of instruction and student performance.

TYPES OF ASSESSMENT

As complex as student assessment is, there basically are only two types of assessment: formative assessment and summative assessment. Teachers must be able to use both of these types of assessment, practically on a daily basis, in order to provide students with the most optimal learning environment possible (Lemlech, 1998).

Formative assessment is the process of gathering and analyzing data about student performance in order to make decisions that facilitate the teacher's

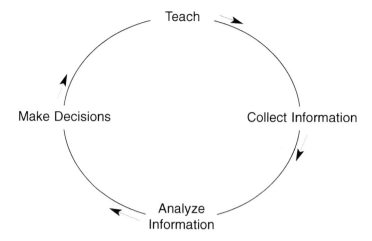

Figure 8-1. The Instruction/Assessment Cycle.

planning process (Wilen, Hutchison, & Ishler, 2008; Orlich, Harder, Callahan, Trevisan, & Brown, 2007). A teacher, for example, may give a pretest to determine entry knowledge or skill levels of students in order to provide needed information to plan units of instruction. The teacher who gives a test only to find that students have not mastered the material as expected may decide to reteach the material before moving to the next unit or area of study. This teacher is using the test to collect information, analyze the students' performance, and make a decision which facilitates planning for future instruction. Some teachers look upon formative assessment as *in route* assessment as it occurs in an ongoing manner during instruction and *in route* to the end of the instruction where summative assessment will be used.

Summative assessment, as opposed to formative assessment, is the process of gathering and analyzing data about student performance in order to determine what students have learned at the conclusion of a segment of instruction. Students typically are awarded grades based on such summative assessment. Summative assessment provides a summary of what the student has accomplished or achieved (Wilen et al., 2008; Orlich et al., 2007). It is this summary that helps the teacher in producing an evaluation report, i.e., grade, of the student's work or performance.

Whether formative or summative, student assessment should be related to the teacher's stated instructional objectives and based on what students are expected to learn, i.e., desired student learning outcomes, not on ancillary pieces of content that have been introduced during instruction. When teachers write their instructional objectives with identified learner outcomes, the criteria for assessment of student performance should be determined at that time. The instructional objectives, as well as the criteria for the assessment of student performance, should be well-known by and clear to the students. Learning activities should then be developed to guide students to mastery of the objectives. Assessment is conducted to determine if the instructional activities or strategies used by the teacher elicited the learning desired. As can be seen, the curriculum and instruction sequence begins with a statement of what students should learn (the objective), is followed by learning experiences that are designated and implemented to provide students the opportunity to master the objective (learning procedures or strategies), and ends with students being assessed on criteria based on the original objective. In some cases, the teacher may determine that appropriate learning has not taken place, and, as a result, remediation or reteaching takes place (formative assessment). In other cases, the teacher may determine that student learning is satisfactory and that the instruction is complete, record some grade illustrative of the students' performance in relationship to the objective, and begin instruction on a new segment of the unit (summative assessment).

Formal Testing

One common approach used for collecting assessment data is the use of traditional paper-and-pencil tests. Such tests are used for assessment in schools all over the world. Some researchers and educators suggest that a major use of tests should be the comparison of students' test scores on a classroom, school, district, state, national, or international basis (Atkin & Black, 1997). Others strongly disagree. It should be remembered, however, that while tests may contribute to the evaluation of a school, program, or classroom, they must not be allowed to define them (Chittenden, 1991).

For a number of years, measurement experts have warned educators of certain problems that may be inherent in the use of traditional paper-and-pencil tests (Lemlech, 1998). One such problem or limitation is test bias which should be a concern to anyone analyzing testing results (Eggen & Kauchak, 2007). A bias has occurred, for example, if a student's score is affected as a result of a lack of experiences due to such factors as race, gender, or geographical location. The use of stereotypical or unfamiliar language on a test also can bias the results as can the amount of prior experience students have had with tests. This is, a type of test wisdom can develop as a result of taking tests. Students who have had limited experience taking tests tend not to have this test wisdom and to not perform as well as students who are more accustomed to test taking (Lemlech, 1998). Further, some students suffer from what has been termed test anxiety, an uncomfortable and unpleasant reaction to a test that can lower performance (Eggen & Kauchak, 2007). Test anxiety also can be a problem with determining the accuracy of test results. Students with test anxiety tend to be less proficient test takers because they become nervous and lack self-confidence when confronted with testing situations. As a result of such factors as those mentioned here, a lower score than desired or anticipated on a given test could be the result of something other than the student's knowledge or understanding of the subject matter being tested. A score on any test is valid only to the degree that it reflects actual student ability, not such factors as test bias, anxiety, or experience with testing.

Categories of Tests

The two major categories of tests used in schools are standardized tests and teacher-made tests. The purpose of both types of tests is or should be to collect information about student abilities and knowledge in order to make instructional decisions. Standardized tests are developed in such a way as to ensure that students all over a state, the country, or even the world, undergo an identical experience when taking the same test (Popham, 2005). The directions, testing conditions, items, and format are standard for all test administrations. All tests are scored the same way, and results are reported in a standard fashion. Test items are developed through a standard process, and the items are field tested to ensure that they have reliability in measurement. Standardized tests typically come in two forms: norm referenced and criterion referenced. The same test could be either norm referenced or criterion referenced depending upon how the data are treated and reported (Pratt, 1994).

Norm-referenced tests are used to compare a student's score on the test with other students who took the same test; they compare a student's performance to that of a norm group (Borich, 2007). This is the most common type of standardized achievement test. Its format allows scores to be reported in percentile ranks based statistically on a normal curve distribution. Norm-referenced tests do not relate specifically to the goals and objectives of any particular school's curriculum, nor do they necessarily function as an effective measure of what has been taught in any given classroom (Ornstein & Hunkins, 1998). The Metropolitan Achievement Test, the Scholastic Aptitude Test (SAT), Advanced Placement Examinations, and The Praxis Series are examples of norm-referenced tests.

Criterion-referenced tests are another type of standardized test. Criterion-referenced tests compare a student's performance with an absolute standard, referred to as a criterion. The test reports a student's performance in relation to a set of specifically stated criteria. It does not compare one student's performance to that of another student. For example, a specific criterion might be the ability to multiply a three-digit number by a two-digit number. Since criterion-referenced tests can be designed to measure the skills or competencies of a given curriculum, these tests can reveal a student's ability to perform or display specific competencies that have been taught. State and local achievement tests are often in the criterion-referenced format.

The other major type of assessment instrument, the teacher-made test, is used regularly in virtually all classrooms. Most teachers rely on their abilities to develop test questions that allow them to determine the degree to which their students are mastering their instructional objectives. The development of good teacher-made tests, however, is a complex and sometimes underestimated process. Teacher-made tests are especially important as they give the teacher a greater local control of the assessment process and more immediate feedback related to student performance.

It might be thought that test construction begins with writing test questions; instead, several concerns must be addressed prior to writing the items themselves which will help make certain that the test is readable, appropriate, reliable, and valid. Reliability refers to the consistency of test results, e.g., if the same group of students could be retested several times and get about the same scores (Orlich et al., 2007). Reliability is reflected in the consistency or dependability of the results of an assessment (Gareis & Grant, 2008). Validity refers to the degree to which a test measures what it is intended to measure (Orlich et al., 2007). It is the extent to which inferences drawn from assessment results are appropriate (Gareis & Grant, 2008). As the teacher begins to prepare a test, clarity with respect to the test's purpose is the key to its successful development and eventual use. If a test is to be valid, it must be logically linked to the goals and objectives of the teacher's instruction.

When the basic purpose for giving a test is to determine if students have learned certain content which has been taught, the test should be designed specifically to reflect a summation of student learning in the given content area. Teachers frequently give this type of test and then record student scores for grading purposes. Such a summative test needs to be designed to measure only that information the teacher feels that students need to know or be able to do in order to demonstrate achievement of pre-stated objectives. Basic guidelines in developing teacher-made tests are included in Figure 8-2.

For the purpose of improving ongoing instruction, it is recommended that teachers diagnose their students prior to instruction in order to determine their entry strengths and weaknesses. Diagnostic evaluation or diagnosis is necessary to determine students' individual levels of competence, to identify those who may already know the material, and to help organize students for instruction (Burden & Byrd, 2007). The results of these diagnostic efforts are not used for grading purposes as was the case with summative tests discussed earlier. But, the results can be helpful in grouping students for instruction, making decisions concerning the need to reteach certain material, determining the readiness level of individual students as new content areas are

1. Be certain the test fully measures the objectives which were stated prior to instruction.
2. Always ask a sufficient number of questions to properly sample the content being tested.
3. Be conscious of the need to sample enough behavior over time and to provide students with adequate feedback concerning their performance.
4. Test early and often.
5. Compose test questions immediately after covering the material in the class.
6. Give detailed, written instructions.
7. Start the test with some warm-up questions.
8. Proofread the test form for errors.
9. Have another teacher evaluate the test for clarity and content.
10. Practice taking the test yourself so you have a good idea as to its difficulty and how long it will take to complete.

Figure 8-2. Basic guidelines for test construction.

approached, and identifying the causes of student failure, or success. Since diagnostic questions or tests are often thought of as a means to gather information for future structuring of learning experiences, they are referred to as being *formative*, as opposed to *summative*, in nature. After teachers have examined the results of their students' diagnostic performances, it becomes much easier to prescribe the best learning experiences for group as well as individual instruction.

Once the teacher has determined the purpose of a particular test, and understands how it relates to course goals and objectives, the overall plan of the test must be considered. Should the assessment be a type of written test or would an oral test be more suited to the material covered? There is a definite place for oral assessment where quick recall is the aim or where the teacher has taught certain oral communication skills and desires to see how well the students have learned them. In a similar vein, it is necessary for some subjects such as keyboarding, woodworking, or gymnastics to have a substantial performance testing component. Performance assessment is assessment that requires students to perform an activity or produce a product in order to demonstrate learning (Woolfolk, 2008). Regardless of the type of instrument, the kind of questions used should be determined by such conditions as the level of cognitive functioning desired, instructional objectives and desired learning outcomes, student maturity level, and student familiarity with the assessment format.

Even though the teacher may have a clear idea of the test's purpose and overall make-up, the development of a good instrument is still not assured. For instance, a general set of directions for taking the test is often omitted by many teachers because it is sometimes felt that formal directions are either superfluous or can be given orally by the teacher. Giving directions, though, can be very helpful to the student, especially on longer and more advanced tests. Directions need to be clear, concise, and on the students' reading level. Students who have had to struggle through difficult content only to be overwhelmed by the reading level of the test are in a situation that is unfair to them, and the test results are not apt to accurately represent what the student really knows or is able to do. Directions also should include all information and guidelines that students need in order to complete each question and to record each answer. Such directions are important so that students know what is expected with respect to the test overall, the point value awarded for each question, and what is to be done in response to each item. Although not part of the written directions, care also should be taken to develop optimal testing conditions, both physically and psychologically.

The actual arrangement of the test items may influence the performance of the students taking the test. For most testing purposes, test items can be arranged by a systematic consideration of the type of items used, the learning outcomes measured, the difficulty of the items, and the subject matter measured (Burden & Byrd, 2007). It is recommended that the least complex questions be placed at the beginning of the test and the more difficult ones toward the end. Figure 8-3 provides a test item hierarchy which can be a helpful guideline to follow in positioning questions on a teacher-made test and understanding the cognitive level of certain types of test items.

If a test has all five types of questions identified, i.e., true-false, completion, matching, multiple-choice, and essay, the true-false and completion questions should be at the beginning of the test with multiple-choice and essay questions located toward the end, assuming all other concerns are equal. Additionally, the content of the items should be considered. If several different parts of a subject are tested, common parts should be grouped together rather than located in different places throughout the test. The latter type of placement forces the student to consider a mental construct time and time again, rather than answering all questions about a certain topic at one time. For complex tests with many questions of many types, it is advised that teachers also group (1) question types in ascending order from the beginning, (2) similar content in question clusters, and (3) items of difficulty in ascending order within each content area.

Type of Test Items		Remembering 1.0	Understanding 2.0	Applying 3.0	Analyzing 4.0	Evaluating 5.0	Creating 6.0
Least Complex	1. True-False	B	X	–	–	–	–
	2. Completion	B	X	–	–	–	–
	3. Matching	B	B	X	X	–	–
	4. Multiple-Choice	X	B	B	X	X	–
Most Complex	5. Essay	X	X	B	B	B	B

Key:　X = Appropriate to the level indicated
　　　 B = Best level at which to use this item
　　　 – = Not ordinarily used to evaluate this level

Figure 8-3. Relationship of test items to Bloom's taxonomy of the cognitive domain as adapted from Anderson et al. (2001) and Merwin, Schneider, & Stephens (1974).

Types of Test Items

The five question types identified in Figure 8-3 can be grouped into two major categories, select and supply, by the type of response they require from students. Students may be asked to either select the correct answer from stated alternatives or to supply the proper answer in response to a question. *Selection items* include many of the most commonly used test questions (e.g., true-false, matching, and multiple-choice). Selection items have responses provided by the teacher from which students may choose. *Supply items* represent the remaining major types of written test questions (i.e., completion and essay). Supply items expect students to provide their own answers, not select from answers provided (Gareis & Grant, 2008).

Major benefits of selection items are that they (1) can provide great structure, forcing a single, predetermined, easy-to-evaluate response, (2) can be used to measure a variety of learning from simple to complex, and (3) are well suited to the coverage of a wide range of content on a single test. Requiring students to choose among different alternatives, or whether a statement is true or false, is the intellectual process necessary in answering these items. Selection items can be used at the remembering and understanding levels or, through the use of creatively written multiple-choice items, challenge the student at higher cognitive levels. When coupled with the ease of scoring that the selection item offers, it is little wonder that much classroom testing is of this type.

Evaluation that only requires the identification of correct answers and never the written development or demonstration of solutions to challenging problems, however, is an insufficient form of evaluation. Students, for example, should also be able to exhibit such behaviors as (1) supply the list of steps, in order, necessary to log on to a computer, (2) provide an explanation of how electricity is generated, or (3) describe the major characters and their relationships to each other in Hemingway's *A Farewell To Arms*. Responses to questions such as these require performances beyond the low cognitive level.

In order for higher intellectual skills to be fully assessed, the essay-type supply item is needed. Even though multiple-choice items can be written above the remembering level, their use beyond understanding is not extensive because of their difficulty in construction. Whereas the selection item often requires only recognition or recall, the supply item generally demands a more creative, at times open-ended, response on the part of the student. Some argue that, without at least some supply items, it is possible for test takers to have only the most minimal type of acquaintance with a subject. Because there is a decidedly low probability of students guessing or memorizing the correct answer for the supply-type of question, a more rigorous process of education typifies the class where supply items are used. While the grading of essay questions can be time consuming and mentally demanding, the phrasing of such questions and the test, as a whole, is fairly straightforward.

It is sometimes felt that extensive written work may penalize the less expressive of two students who knows the same amount of material as his or her more verbal counterpart. This is just one of several ambiguities that beset teachers when dealing with student assessment. Further complicating the grading of supply items is the problem of spelling and grammar. When and how much should spelling and grammar be counted on tests, especially when students are not native English speakers? Spelling and grammar in fact should influence the evaluation of supply items because written expression is an important aspect of a quality education. It will, of course, be up to each individual teacher to determine how much these factors influence a student's final grade.

Each question type has its own unique characteristics along with specific advantages and disadvantages. While selection questions may demand only an acquaintance with the subject and may seemingly require less in-depth understanding, sophisticated test construction can elicit rather high levels of thinking on these types of questions, especially when multiple-choice questions are used. If care is not taken, even supply-type questions, which are often known for requiring higher level responses, can elicit only low level cognitive performance. For example, if the response to an essay question is merely the remembered explanation of something taught in class, this is not considered to be a high cognitive performance.

The following discussion is presented to aid in the development of tests and test items that are challenging but which produce helpful information about students for evaluation purposes. Each of the five major types of test items previously mentioned is considered.

True-False Items

Perhaps because it is simple to construct, the true-false item is one of the most frequently used items in teacher-made tests. The true-false item, however, also has the least flexibility compared to other item types and can be difficult to use properly. For this very reason, it is advised by some educators that the use of true-false items be limited (Gage & Berliner, 1988; Travers, 1950). In spite of these cautions, teachers frequently use many true-false items. This is because, through their use, much subject matter can be tested in a short period of time, and the items are generally quite easy to score. But, true-false items typically measure only low cognitive learning, and this may not be the teacher's goal. As an example, although the true-false items that follow are acceptable, they measure only the lowest level of cognition.

    ___1. Dallas is the capital city of Texas.
    ___2. Alexander Bell invented the telephone.
    ___3. A spider is an insect.

Care should be given in the construction of true-false items to avoid misinterpretation and to make sure that what is expected of students is clear. For example, the following question is ambiguous because one does not know whether land area or population is the feature being referred to in the question.

    ___1. Alaska is the largest state.

This item can easily be improved with the addition of a short, clarifying phrase. For example:

    ___1. Alaska is the largest state in total land area.

True-false items also increase the probability of students guessing rather than actually knowing the correct answer. The guessing problem may be lessened somewhat by incorporating a greater number of items into a given test. However, it can be a difficult task to construct large numbers of meaningful true-false items. To use fewer questions, and to improve the item type, the modified true-false item is helpful. In the modified true-false item, the teacher underlines a specific part of the item and directs the students to give specific attention to this part of the item. To prepare the modified true-false item, the teacher states the directions as in the following example.

> **Directions:** If the item is correct, put the letter T for true in the blank provided, but, if it is incorrect, change the underlined word(s) to make it correct. (2 points each)

An additional option to modified true-false items is to omit the underlining and direct the student to underline the false portion, if encountered, and to write in the correction.

The following points are considered as advantages and disadvantages of using true-false items (Nilson, 2003).

Advantages	Disadvantages
1. Easy to interpret and grade.	1. There is a high guessing factor.
2. Can test a great deal of material in a short time.	2. Encourages the testing of trivial and low level cognition.
3. Useful as a diagnostic tool.	3. Items may be ambiguous.
4. Good for students who are poor readers.	4. Scores can be unduly influenced by guessing.

The guidelines in Figure 8-4 should be considered in the construction of effective true-false items.

---

1. Write short, direct statements in which a main idea is stated with only minimal additions.

2. Put only one idea, fact, or generalization in each statement.

3. Avoid words which are indefinite (i.e., be specific).

4. For clarity, state items positively rather than negatively.

5. Avoid clues such as *all*, *never*, *usually*, *every*, *always*, and *often*, which are typically indicative of false statements.

6. Avoid the tendency to create trivial items.

7. Include a minimum of 20 statements to lessen the influence of guessing.

8. Balance the number of true and false answers.

9. Write positive statements; negative and double negative statements are confusing to the student.

10. Allow at least thirty seconds per item to complete.

Figure 8-4. Guidelines for constructing true-false items.

Matching Items

The matching test item has great utility in test construction, even though it does have limitations. Commonly used at both the elementary and secondary levels, the item requires students to associate two groups of facts, concepts, or generalizations. It is this relating of two groups of words, phrases, or symbols that gives the item its versatility. For example, matching items may be constructed to associate such things as names with significant events in history, great paintings with techniques, or related scientific concepts with their applications. Consider the following example.

Directions: Place the letter of the event in the blank next to the matching name. (3 points each)

Name	Event
___1. G. Washington	a. Served the most years in the Presidency
___2. A. Lincoln	b. Known as the *Father of Our Country*
___3. F. Roosevelt	c. Was assassinated in Dallas, Texas
___4. R. Nixon	d. President during the Civil War
	e. Resigned from office due to scandal

Although it can be seen that the above example exhibits a tremendous economy of space, can be constructed without great difficulty, can be scored easily, and lowers the possibility of guessing, there still are pitfalls in using this type of item which need to be avoided. In constructing the matching item, two columns – a *premise* and a *response* – should be developed in which there is a definite similarity of terms. Notice in the following example that the premises are concerned with both plays and poetry. This mix-match of ideas should be avoided.

Premise	Response
___1. Hamlet	a. The hero searches for great deeds even when there are none
___2. Man of La Mancha	b A poem about the meaninglessness of our modern world
___3. The Hollow Men	c. The hero meets a tragic end
___4. Oedipus Rex	d. The protagonist kills his father
	e. The hero returns from the dead

When producing items to test one specific topic, keep all premise words homogeneous and refrain from including parts from another topic. Mixing classes of premises may create confusion for the student and allow clues to be given about those things to be matched. Another concern is the use of synonyms or words of the same or similar derivation in both the premise and response. For instance:

Premise	Response
___1. Great Lake	a. Lake Baikal
___2. Small barren sea	b. Lake Erie
___3. Largest lake in the world	c. Dead Sea
___4. A sea separating Africa and Europe	d. Mediterranean Sea
	e. Chesapeake Bay

Since it is obvious that the lakes and the seas match, there are really two separate question types with only two alternatives, each of which is much too simple.

Four is the minimum number of similarly paired terms to match and approximately ten the maximum. If more than ten items are desired for a matching exercise, it is recommended that the number of desired matching items be separated in groups of from four to ten.

The following points are considered as advantages and disadvantages in using matching items (Nilson, 2003).

Advantages	Disadvantages
1. Easy to grade.	1. There is a high guessing factor.
2. Relatively unambiguous.	2. Does not assess higher levels of cognition.
3. Assesses knowledge recall well.	3. Sometimes difficult to construct a common set of premises and responses.
4. Can test much material in a short time.	4. Can be difficult to avoid giving clues.

As an aid in preparing the matching type test item, consider the guidelines in Figure 8-5.

---

1. Use words or short phrases in both premise and response.

2. Eliminate clue words and mixing of topics.

3. Keep the number of response alternatives, if possible, between four and ten.

4. Lower the probability of guessing by adding extra responses.

5. Put all the premises and responses on the same page (to prevent possible student confusion in turning back and forth).

6. Arrange the response alternatives in a logical sequence (e.g., alphabetically). This is especially important if there is a long list of alternatives.

Continued on next page

7. Indicate the basis for the relationship between the two groups (e.g., if states are the premises and capitals the responses, be sure to label both columns appropriately).
8. Indicate whether some response items can be used more than once or not at all.
9. Keep premises and responses short and simple.
10. Allow at least thirty seconds per item to complete.

Figure 8-5. Guidelines for constructing matching test items.

Multiple-Choice Items

Acknowledged as one of the most versatile of all items (second only to the essay), the multiple-choice item can be laborious to construct. Whereas other selection items test remembering and understanding, multiple-choice items can be used to test at higher cognitive levels. No other item type, except essay, can be used so broadly. However, though the essay item may be easy to construct, it is also difficult to score. Multiple-choice items, conversely, are simple to score and challenging to construct.

In construction, multiple-choice items require a stem and from three to five alternatives offered as possible correct choices. Of these alternatives, it is recommended that one be obviously wrong, one correct, one similar to the correct answer, and the others somewhere between obviously incorrect and almost correct. The emphasis during item development is to make the student think and discern gross and slight differences between alternative answers called distracters. To be successful in responding to multiple-choice items, the student will be expected to analyze both the stem as well as each possible choice.

Even though multiple-choice items can be used to measure simple recall of facts and remembering other pieces of information, their usefulness is especially important when they are directed beyond this minimal level. It is advised that true-false and matching items be used to test lower cognitive performance since these items are relatively easy to construct, whereas multiple-choice items are not.

Examples of multiple-choice items are as follows:

Directions: Circle the letter that represents the correct answer in each item. (3 points each)

1. Which of the following is a primary color?

   a. Red
   b. Brown

c. Black

d. Orange

2. Where should you ride your bicycle when in traffic?

a. On the left side of the street

b. On the right side of the street

c. In the middle of the street near the dividing lines

d. It really does not matter if you are careful

3. Which of the following paintings most utilizes the idea of linear perspective?

a. Descent from the Cross

b. The School of Athens

c. Guernica

d. LeMoulin de la Galette

As previously noted, multiple-choice items can be constructed to test for intellectual performance beyond the low cognitive levels. The following multiple-choice items have been designed to test for student thought processing beyond remembering, understanding and applying (Santrock, 2008; Hunt & Metcalf, 1968).

4. America's entry into World War I was largely caused by the –

a. fear that the defeat of the Allies would lead to the overthrow of the republican government in France.

b. violation of Belgian neutrality.

c. fear of losses by the moneyed interests if the Allies were defeated.

d. declaration of war by Italy.

5. What was one of the immediate results of the War of 1812?

a. the introduction of a period of intense sectionalism.

b. the destruction of the United States Bank.

c. the defeat of the Jeffersonian Party.

d. the final collapse of the Federalist Party.

6. John Fitzgerald Kennedy is to Democrat as Ronald Reagan is to

_____.

a. Independent

b. Libertarian

c. Green

d. Republican

Note that item #4 is written as a completion-type item using the multiple-choice item format, item #5 is written as a conventional multiple-choice item where the student is expected to analyze the item choices and select the best answer to the question, and item #6 is written as an analogy-based item.

There are definite educationally valid reasons for using multiple-choice items when constructing a test. First, they can be graded quickly with immediate feedback provided. Second, they provide helpful practice in test taking for students since virtually all standardized tests use the multiple-choice item format. Finally, they can be constructed to measure higher levels of cognition. There are, however, cautions identified in the use of the multiple-choice item. For example, the construction of good multiple-choice items can be difficult, and it is easy to make them too difficult or ridiculously easy. Another concern grows out of the desire to have students communicate ideas. The multiple-choice item requires no writing on the part of students. If multiple-choice items are used exclusively, students would never be required to express their ideas in writing on a test. This, of course, is also true for other select item types.

The following points are considered as advantages and disadvantages in using multiple-choice items (Nilson, 2003).

Advantages	Disadvantages
1. Reduces some of the burden of testing in large classes.	1. Difficult and time-consuming to construct.
2. Easy and quick to grade by hand or scanner.	2. Encourages the testing of trivial and factual information.
3. Useful as a diagnostic tool.	3. Items may be ambiguous leading to student misinterpretations.
4. Can assess for both low and high levels of cognition.	4. Items are subject to giving clues where students can deduce the correct answer by elimination.

The guidelines in Figure 8-6 should be considered in constructing good multiple-choice items.

1. Avoid having an item with a multiple focus; there should be one central idea in each item.

2. Keep all wording concise and clear.

3. Make all alternatives, whether correct answer or distracter, of similar length.

4. Write all distracters, even those that are wrong, so that they are plausible.

5. Be sure that there are no clues in any of the distracters (e.g., all options must be grammatically consistent with the stem).

6. Include some items that require fine distinctions.

7. Minimize using the phrases *all of the above* and *none of the above.*

Continued on next page

8. Avoid items that merely ask a series of true-false questions.

9. Use three to five alternatives per item.

10. Estimate at least one minute for students to answer each question.

Figure 8-6. Guidelines for constructing multiple-choice items.

Completion Items

One of the most commonly used items, especially at the elementary level, is the completion (fill-in-the-blank) item. Although popular, the completion item is easy to use and easy to misuse. Since textbooks frequently still represent the primary learning aid for many teachers, it has become natural, because of the importance that teachers place on the text, for some teachers to take entire sentences from the text with key words omitted and turn them into completion items. Caution must be exercised when using such a procedure because the overuse of blanks may make even the simple task of recall difficult. For example, consider the following sample completion item:

Directions: Write in the space(s) provided the most appropriate answer(s) to complete the sentence. (4 points each)

1. Weather satellites are beneficial for weather _____ because they take _____ pictures.

The fact that *forecasting* (first blank) and *multiple* (second blank) make sense for correct responses does not simplify the task in the completion item above; for example, *watchers* (first blank) and *accurate* (second blank) also make sense, as well as other possibilities. Even if the sentence is quoted from a textbook, the item is not appropriate and would be better phrased as a short-answer question.

Completion items need to have a specific stem with a sufficient description of the missing word(s). For example:

1. Granite is a commercial rock which always contains _____ and _____.

Always contains is the specific description of *granite* that gives the student a valid indication of what is being requested in the response. When used in a direct manner, the completion item can be very useful. For example:

1. A noun names a_____ ,_____ or _____.
2. The name of the capital city of Montana is _____.
3. The molten material that flows from volcanoes is called _____.

A variation of the completion item, the short-answer item, requires only that students produce, i.e., supply, a sentence or perhaps a phrase to correctly complete the item statement. The teacher need only take a completion item and rephrase it in the form of a question to develop the short-answer item. For example:

1. What is a noun?_____
2. What is always found in granite?_____
3. What is one benefit of weather satellites?_____

A response to the short-answer item allows the student more freedom in supplying information beyond basic memorization. Such items represent a step, although a small step, toward approximating the complexities in answering essay items. For this reason, teachers should particularly refine their skills in constructing this type of item and in teaching students how to phrase their answers. Middle school and secondary teachers should not relegate this item only for use with the lower elementary or primary grades. This item type should be used regularly at all levels where students are capable of taking paper and pencil tests.

The following points are considered as advantages and disadvantages of using completion items (Nilson, 2003).

Advantages	**Disadvantages**
1. Easy to prepare and grade.	1. May include irrelevant clues.
2. Eliminates guessing.	2. Difficult to construct so that the response is clear.
3. Can test a large amount of material in a short time.	3. Does not assess higher levels of cognition.
4. Assesses knowledge/recall and vocabulary well.	4. May be difficult to grade if more than one answer may be correct.

The guidelines in Figure 8-7 should be considered in the construction of completion items:

---

1. Write the item so that only a single word or brief phrase is required and correct.

2. Use direct, clear sentences with the missing word(s) at or near the end of the sentence.

3. The missing word(s) should be the major point of the statement.

4. Determine the amount of clues that are appropriate for the grade level of the student. Use sentences directly from the text when you wish to prepare easier items for the early elementary grades, but create novel sentences for older students.

Continued on next page

5. Carefully use the length of the line. Shortly after introducing this question type in the early elementary grades, the length of the line should not vary as an aid in determining the answer; use the same length line for all items.

6. State during instruction that correct spelling is important.

7. Give any specifications that will ensure a unitary response such as in the following mathematics problem: A room that is 9 ft. by 3 ft. is _____ sq. ft. This specification ensures an answer in feet rather than inches or yards.

8. Avoid grammatical cues. For instance, use a/an and is/are to reduce cluing.

9. Use clear wording to elicit a unique response.

10. Allow at least thirty seconds to one minute per item to complete.

Figure 8-7. Guidelines for constructing completion items.

Essay Items

The usefulness of the essay item is in the flexibility that it allows the teacher and the freedom of response it allows the student. Essay items are especially helpful in measuring higher-order thinking including analysis, evaluating, and creating. Through the process of constructing a written, original response to a given problem or question, students can demonstrate their ability to understand a problem, organize the facts and concepts needed to answer it, and communicate effectively in writing. The essay item makes it possible for the teacher to observe students' thoughts in their essays as well as evaluate their written expression. Effective communication and the development of thinking skills are two of the most important outcomes of schooling. Because of this, the importance of the essay item cannot be overstated.

Essay items may ask the student to list, outline, explain, compare and contrast, defend, summarize, analyze, hypothesize, evaluate, and create. Such items are generally used to measure higher level thought processes. For example, consider the following sample essay items:

Directions: Place your responses on the pages provided. Each response should be no less than one and no more than two pages in length. Your responses should be in complete sentences and free of grammatical errors. (10 points each)

1. Describe how life might be in this country without any cars. Include at least two effects on mobility and the use of leisure time in your response.
2. Analyze the way your life might be if you lived in a communist country. Include reference to freedom of religion, education, and government participation in your response.

There primarily are three major reasons for using essay items: (1) they tend to measure higher levels of cognition, (2) they expect students to communicate their thoughts in writing, and (3) they tend to reward the use of ideas and creativity on the part of the student.

The disadvantage of using essay items comes in their scoring. Responses tend to be more subjective and individual, and it can be challenging to evaluate each student's response exactly the same way on the same set of criteria. Too, a student's vocabulary and writing skills may create a halo effect in that the teacher gives certain students good grades because their papers look good, not because their answers are necessarily complete and superior. The reverse is also a distinct possibility in reference to students with less language facility. As compared to supply items, the essay item will take longer for the teacher to score.

The following points are considered as advantages and disadvantages in using essay items (Nilson, 2003).

Advantages	**Disadvantages**
1. Can assess higher levels of cognition.	1. Time consuming to grade.
2. Develops writing skills.	2. Cannot test a lot of material on one exam.
3. Quick and relatively easy to construct.	3. Difficult to standardize grading.
4. Requires students to know the material in depth.	4. Penalizes students who work slowly or have weak writing skills.

The guidelines in Figure 8-8 should be considered in constructing essay items.

---

1. Carefully construct each question so that it gives sufficient direction to the student to complete the item as intended.

2. Outline a model answer to ensure greater objectivity and that the question is specifically phrased.

3. Include several shorter essay items rather than a few longer ones.

4. Write essay questions so that higher levels of student thought are required.

5. Use questions which the student will find new and challenging yet answerable; questions should expect the student to do more than produce a memorized answer.

6. Grade all essays without noting the name of the student.

7. While grading, write helpful, constructive comments on all students' papers.

8. Before they take the test, show the students examples of well constructed essay item responses.

Continued on next page

9. Give the point value for each question.

10. Estimate at least ten minutes per item to complete.

Figure 8-8. Guidelines for constructing essay items.

Alternative Assessment

Many educators believe that a student's performance on a traditional teacher-made test is not an accurate and complete measure of the student's true achievement. Critics of formal testing have argued that test results often can bear little resemblance to what students have actually learned (Jarolimek & Foster, 1997). The influence of Howard Gardner's research on multiple intelligences (Campbell, Campbell, & Dickinson, 1996: Armstrong, 1994; Gardner, 1993) has strongly influenced many educators to search for alternative methods of assessment that are more compatible with how students learn and that provide more real-world demonstrations of what has been learned. The authentic assessment movement was born in response to these criticisms with the goal being to develop assessments that are alternatives to traditional testing, that truly assess what students know and are able to do, and that assess real-life outcomes (Hoy & Hoy, 2009).

Informal Observation, Teacher Conferences, and Structured Behavioral Inventories

Informal observation is an important method for the teacher to use in collecting assessment data. This is particularly the case at the primary school level but is also relevant throughout the PK–12 grade continuum. This informal monitoring function, which must be carefully developed, demands that teachers know what student behaviors to look for and then fit this information into a meaningful set of cause and effect relationships. At the very least, variables that potentially fit this kind of relationship need to be studied in greater depth. For example, if a teacher desires for students, at the completion of a lesson, to know what to do in sequence and to exhibit comprehension of certain material, it is important that the teacher monitor students' reactions from the beginning of the lesson until the students have completed their tasks. Important cause and effect relationships concerning student behavior and the effectiveness of instruction will be identified in this process. All teachers should be skilled in posing probing questions to help answer the basic question, "What has been accomplished?"

Informal observation can take place in many ways as a teacher moves through the classroom monitoring students as they work. It is recommended that teachers make extensive observations as students work on their assignments taking careful note of such information as who is having problems and who is not being challenged. Such observations also should include the use of probing questions to determine progress. There is a degree of subjectivity to informal observation evaluation, and some teachers do not allow this type of feedback gathering to affect student grades. However, if the teacher feels that such evaluations add to the knowledge of a student's overall performance and growth, it may be appropriate to adjust a grade based on informal observation.

A common misconception of informal observation is that it is unstructured or unorganized evaluation. Although teachers often randomly observe students and note strengths and weaknesses to be addressed, the best type of teacher observation takes place when teachers have previously listed certain behaviors that students should manifest. The observation, then, should be designed to detect specific student behaviors that allow the teacher to evaluate the instructional objectives being addressed. It is not haphazard. The art teacher, for example, may have as a performance statement that students will draw a particular type of person. The criterion statement in the objective should list the criteria (e.g., clarity, size, and types of lines used) upon which the drawing will be evaluated. The teacher may then, by moving through the classroom, observe each student's work in light of these specific criteria. It is recommended that teachers list these criteria specifically in their lesson plans and make certain that their students are aware of them.

Teacher conferences can be used to discuss a student's work or behavior on a more personal (i.e., one-to-one) level. For such conferences to be productive, the teacher first should develop a list of specific broad and narrow questions to be asked. The kindergarten teacher, as an example, might ask a student to draw a picture of the student's family and then discuss the picture with the child. There must be an instructional purpose for this assignment, and the questioning should be structured to ascertain whether or not each student has understood and addressed that purpose. As a process, it will be helpful for the novice teacher to list the important questions on paper before the conference takes place.

Structured behavior inventories are checklists used by a teacher to guide observation and allow for the recording of findings. A common inventory is the Informal Reading Inventory used by most teachers of reading. This inventory allows the teacher to listen to a student read orally while marking mistakes on a printed copy of the paragraphs being read. This approach structures the observation of the student's reading and provides a lasting record of the performance that can be dated and filed for later reference. Such inventories can be developed by the teacher or found in any of several textbooks on teaching methods.

Evaluation, whether formal or informal, should be designed to determine if students are meeting stated instructional objectives. It is not adequate simply to say that an objective will be evaluated by teacher observation. The teacher needs to be able to state specifically (1) what student behaviors are being observed as a part of the evaluation process and (2) on what criteria the student's evaluation (perhaps grade) will be based (see Chapter 2 for further explanation).

Student Products: Exhibitions and Portfolios

Exhibitions and portfolios are two approaches to assessment that require a student product and a type of performance in context (Hoy & Hoy, 2009). Student products have become a popular source of assessment data in classrooms across the country. An exhibition is a type of performance assessment that has two special features. It is public, requiring students preparing exhibitions to take the audience into account. Second, the exhibition often requires many hours of preparation because it can be the culminating experience of an entire program of study. McDonald, Smith, Turner, Finney, and Barton (1993), in *Graduation by Exhibition: Assessing Genuine Achievement*, present a unique strategy for school reform identified as planning backwards from exhibition. The strategy received prominence in the late 1980s and early 1990s through a network of reform-minded schools called the Coalition of Essential Schools. The Coalition grew out of A Study of High Schools conducted under the chairmanship of Theodore Sizer. Instituting the exhibition as a graduation requirement involves fundamentally changing the roles, rules, and relationships in a school (1993, p. 24). Through exhibitions, students develop a better understanding of the qualities of good work and recognize these qualities in their own productions. They also benefit when they make decisions about the examples of their work to exhibit and communicate their reasons for the selections (Guskey & Bailey, 2001).

Though there are many ways to collect and organize examples of student products, the portfolio (efolio if the products are collected and stored in electronic form) has become the choice of many. The purpose of the portfolio is to tell a type of story of the student's growth, long-term achievement, and significant accomplishments in a particular academic area. It is a planned collection of student achievement that documents what a student has accomplished (Borich, 2007). It has long been a common practice for teachers to collect examples of student work, yet, with the advent of the portfolio concept, the responsibility of collection and organization of these examples goes to the student (Orlich et al., 2007; Jarolimek & Foster, 1997; Engel, 1994). In preparing a portfolio, students collect samples of their work over time to build a record of their growth toward the mastery of specific learning objectives. The best samples of a student's writing, for example, might be collected over a number of weeks to tell the story of that student's growth as a writer. This record of growth could be representative of a relatively short time (e.g., a grading period) or of a period encompassing a full semester or academic year. The portfolio approach to assessment is often referred to as an example of authentic assessment as it is intended to focus on more real-world and ongoing displays of student growth.

Goerss (1993) outlined several important guidelines that should help define the portfolio process as presented in Figure 8-9.

1. Students should have clear direction as to what to include in the portfolio.

2. Students must be taught a specified process for collecting, organizing, and classifying materials for inclusion.

3. Although the portfolio belongs to the individual student, it should be kept in the classroom.

4. Periodically, the portfolio should go home (especially at the end of grading periods) for parental review.

Figure 8-9. Guidelines for defining the portfolio process.

More recently, Wilen, Hutchison, and Ishler (2008) identified the following steps to serve as a guide for using portfolios as part of the assessment process (see Figure 8-10).

1. Identify your purpose for the portfolio and share that purpose with your students.

2. Identify the specific knowledge, skills, and dispositions that students are to demonstrate through the pieces they place in their portfolios. Share this information with your students and address them in the assessment rubrics.

3. Decide on which products to put into the portfolio and the number of samples to be included. The products should represent the knowledge, skills and dispositions being emphasized in the activity.

4. Build the portfolio rubric, preferably with your students. Decide on what will be considered excellent, satisfactory, poor in each category. For the knowledge objectives, use the key outcomes expected. Do the same for the skills and dispositions.

Figure 8-10. Steps for using portfolios in the assessment process.

While the teacher should discuss with the students the guidelines for what material is to be included, the teacher should not become too focused on specifically delineating what goes into the portfolio (Herbert, 1998). A primary purpose of the portfolio is to provide students with an opportunity to self-monitor and/or evaluate themselves. This can best be done by allowing the students to select what they want in the portfolio, through consultation and guidance from the teacher, not from a predetermined list of curriculum samples. The contents of the portfolio should represent a shared decision involving both student and teacher; this will increase the probability that important teacher-to-student interaction will take place. Portfolio development is an evolving process. As students become more familiar with the portfolio approach, less teacher direction concerning specific content decisions will be needed.

Herbert (1998) and Goerss (1993) note the importance of parental involvement in the process. Parents need to understand the importance of portfolios to the assessment process and the overall curriculum. This type of communication among parents and teachers is important regardless of the assessment process being used. When innovative procedures are adopted and parents are less familiar with their format and expectations, clear communication is a necessity to ensure the acceptance of the new procedures and ideas.

In order for the portfolio process to be meaningful for all concerned, evidence of student reflection must be apparent. The portfolio does not merely contain a sampling of student work, but also needs to include student reflections on why certain items are included and how these items illustrate that learning has taken place. Without students including their reflections, the portfolio takes on a scrapbook quality that is of much less value and that is difficult to assess in a meaningful way. Finally, the portfolio should not be a grouping of isolated events. Student reflections will serve to tie the portfolio items together and act as an avenue, i.e., means, to improve communication between the student and the teacher.

When using portfolios, the question arises as to how the teacher can best determine if student learning has truly taken place. There is always a concern that portfolios may be assessed on their attractiveness as opposed to their substance. In order to avoid such concerns, teachers, with input from students, need to develop specific assessment criteria and make students aware of these criteria prior to evaluating the portfolios. The specific criteria for evaluating portfolios often are referred to as scoring rubrics. Gareis and Grant (2008, pp. 146–148) describe a scoring rubric as a description of the nature of an acceptable response. Rubrics are very applicable in the assessment process when a student is providing any type of original response, such as on a completion or essay supply-type item on a teacher-made test or an exhibition or portfolio where individual performance or work is to be displayed. Three types of scoring rubrics are identified:

1. **Checklist:** A checklist is a list of behaviors or look-fors in a student response. Checklists are used for a quick grading of a response.
2. **Holistic Rubric:** A holistic rubric provides a defined level of expected performance that is applied to a student's overall performance or response but is not indicative of specific components of the performance or response. Holistic rubrics typically involve levels of performance, e.g., ranging from a 2 to a 6. Levels of performance reflect such performance categories as exemplary, proficient, developing/ needs improvement, and unsatisfactory.
3. **Analytical Rubric:** Analytical rubrics are reserved for more complex tasks. The analytical rubric is a scoring key that provides information regarding performance in each of the parts of the task, making it useful for diagnosing strengths and weaknesses. Students gain more information regarding their performance and teachers gain more information regarding a student's level of performance through this type of rubric. Developing and applying an analytical rubric can be time consuming for teachers, but the information the rubric provides can be very valuable.

Pate, Homestead, and McGinnis (1993) suggest that teachers should follow prescribed steps when developing scoring rubrics such as:

- analyze the learning task and list all important characteristics including process, content, mechanics, quality of presentation, sources, and neatness;
- develop a scale associated with these expectations which begins with the highest level (i.e., excellence) and clearly describes all criteria for as many levels as are necessary; and
- analyze each characteristic or criterion to determine their relative importance in order that an appropriate weight can be assigned to each.

Airasian (2005) recommends that the teacher consider the following guidelines when selecting observational criteria for products or performances.

1. Select the performance or product to be assessed and either perform it yourself or imagine yourself performing it.
2. List the important aspects of the performance or product.
3. Try to limit the number of performance criteria that can reasonably be observed and assessed.
4. If possible, have other teachers think through the criteria as a group.

5. Express the criteria in terms of observable student behaviors or product characteristics.
6. Avoid vague and ambiguous words, such as correctly, appropriately, and good.
7. Arrange the performance criteria in the order in which they are likely to be observed.
8. Check for existing performance criteria before constructing your own.

Figure 8-11 illustrates the process involved in developing a scoring rubric of the analytical type. In the final analysis of the material, a weight would be assigned to each criterion in order for the student products to be adequately and fairly assessed. Using the rubric developed in Figure 8-11, Figure 8-12 illustrates the weighing of criteria and how this can impact the assessment of a single product.

Task Description: Research and prepare a report and class presentation on an aspect of Hispanic culture introduced in class. The assignment is to be completed by researching a variety of print and electronic sources.

Procedures: Discuss your proposed topic with your teacher who will approve your final topic; begin your research; have a conference with your teacher when you have identified at least five sources; and have a conference with your teacher when you have written an outline/draft of your paper. After your draft has been discussed with your teacher, prepare the final report and plan your class presentation.

Evaluation: The final project will be evaluated using the enclosed rubric (see Figure 8-11).

Research Report and Oral Presentation Rubric

Critical Element	1 Incomplete	2 Improving	3 Satisfactory	4 Good	5 Excellent
Research Sources	The student gathered information that lacked relevance or identified no appropriate sources in any format.	The student gathered information from a limited range of appropriate sources but made little attempt to balance format types.	The student gathered mostly appropriate sources in a variety of formats (books, journals, electronic sources).	The student gathered information from a variety of quality, highly appropriate sources in a variety of formats (books, journals, electronic sources).	The student gathered information from a variety of quality electronic and print sources. Sources are relevant, balanced and include critical readings relating to the topic.

Continued on next page

Research Report and Oral Presentation Rubric *(continued)*

Content	The report provides numerous inaccurate statements with few details and/or weak support. The paper is less than 4 pages in length.	The report provides some inaccurate information, with limited details/support. The paper is a minimum of 4 pages in length.	The report provides basic information, with some details/support. The paper is a minimum of 4 pages in length.	The report provides accurate, in-depth information, with some specific details/support. The paper is a minimum of 5 pages in length.	The report provides accurate, in-depth, relevant information, with specific, sufficient details/support. The paper is a minimum of 6 pages in length.
Expression of ideas	The paper lacks clear and logical development of ideas with weak transitions between paragraphs. Conclusions are not supported by evidence.	The paper is somewhat clear with logical development of ideas and some transitions between paragraphs. Stronger evidence needed to support conclusions.	The paper is clear with logical development of ideas and adequate transitions between paragraphs. Conclusions are supported with adequate evidence.	The paper is clear with logical development of ideas and good transitions between paragraphs. Conclusions are supported with substantial evidence.	The paper is exceptionally clear and convincing with thorough development of ideas and excellent transition between paragraphs. All conclusions are supported with convincing evidence.
Conventions	The written report contains numerous spelling, punctuation and grammar errors that are distracting and confusing to the reader.	The written report contains numerous spelling, punctuation and grammar errors that are distracting to the reader.	The written report contains a few spelling, punctuation, or grammar errors that do not distract the reader.	The written report contains no errors that detract from the meaning.	The written report contains virtually no errors.
Citations/ Documentation	The student provided citations that were incomplete or inaccurate, and provided no way to check the validity of the information gathered.	The student cited some sources and provided little or no supporting documentation to check accuracy.	The student cited most sources in proper format and documented sources to enable accuracy in checking.	The student cited all sources of information accurately to demonstrate the credibility and authority of the information presented.	The student cited all sources of information accurately to demonstrate the credibility and authority of the information presented.

Continued on next page

Research Report and Oral Presentation Rubric *(continued)*

Oral Presentation/ Organization	The audience cannot understand the presentation because the information is not sequenced.	The student jumps around creating confusion and difficulty for audience to follow.	Student presents information in a logical sequence that audience can follow.	Student presents information in a logical sequence that audience can easily follow.	Student presents information in a logical, interesting sequence that audience can easily follow.
Oral Presentation/ Delivery	The audience has great difficulty hearing. Presenter reads notes and seldom or never makes eye contact.	The presenter makes only occasional eye contact and needs many reminders from audience to speak up. Mostly reads from notes.	The presenter may need reminders from audience to speak up. Generally consistent with maintaining eye contact. May need reminders from audience to speak up. Some reliance on notes.	The presenter has strong presence. Can be heard by all in the audience without assistance. Consistently maintains eye contact. May need a single reminder from audience to speak up. Minimal reliance on notes.	The presenter has strong presence. Can be heard by all in the audience without assistance. Consistently maintains eye contact. No reliance on notes.
Oral Presentation/ Visuals	The audience is unable to read the visuals. Graphics detract from the presentation and are messy and inappropriate.	Visuals are not accessible to all of the audience. Graphics may be messy and/or inappropriate. They do not add to the presentation.	Visuals are readable from all parts of the room. Graphics are neat and add to the presentation.	Visuals are attractive and readable from all parts of the room. Graphics are clear and enhance the presentation.	Visuals are attractive and readable from all parts of the room. Graphics are clear and professional looking and enhance the presentation.

Figure 8-11. A sample scoring rubric to be used to assess a secondary research report and oral presentation.

The written and presentation assignment illustrated in Figure 8-12 has a total potential value of 175 points, the 175 points would be achieved if a student scored an excellent rating on each of the critical elements: *research sources* (5 x 6 = 30), *content* (5 x 6 = 30), *expression of ideas* (5 x 6 = 30), *conventions* (5 x 4 = 20), *citations/documentation* (5 x 3 = 15), *oral presentation/organization* (5 x 3 = 15), *oral presentation/delivery* (5 x 4 = 20), and excellent on *oral presentation/visuals* (5 x 3 = 15). As can be seen from an examination of Figure 8-12, the student in this case earned 136 of the total 175 points possible. The

	Incomplete 1	Improving 2	Satisfactory 3	Good 4	Excellent 5	Score x Weight	Total
Research Sources (weight = 6)			X			3 x 6	18
Content (weight = 6)			X			3 x 6	18
Expression of ideas (weight = 6)					X	5 x 6	30
Conventions (weight = 4)					X	5 x 4	20
Citations/Documentation (weight = 3)		X				2 x 3	6
Oral Presentation/ Organization (weight = 3)				X		4 x 3	12
Oral Presentation/ Delivery (weight = 4)					X	5 x 4	20
Oral Presentation/ Visuals (weight = 3)				X		4 x 3	12

Figure 8-12. A teacher-developed rating scale using weighted scores adapted from Hunt, Wiseman, & Bowden (2003).

teacher who has given this assignment will determine the student's grade on the assignment using the predetermined system for points earned as related to the points-to-grade standard.

The above example is one that would likely be found in a secondary setting; it could easily be modified for a middle school level assignment. However, major modifications would need to be made if an expository writing assignment were to be assessed in an early childhood setting. The following example, as seen in Figure 8-13, is more typical of a kindergarten rubric; notice that icons are used in place of words to designate proficiency levels.

Kindergarten Writing Rubric

	😊	😐	🙁
Picture	I drew a picture with lots of details.	I drew a picture with some details.	I drew a picture with no details.
Sentence and Punctuation	I wrote a sentence with a capital letter and a period.	I wrote a sentence but forgot the capital letter or I forgot the period.	I did not write a sentence. I forgot to use a capital letter and a period.
Spacing	I put spaces between all my words.	I put spaces between some of my words.	I did not put spaces between my words.

Figure 8-13. Kindergarten expository writing rubric.

Using scoring rubrics allows teachers to clearly communicate expectations to students and provides a forum for the teacher and the student as they discuss the student's progress. This process helps ensure that students are being assessed on substantive, clear criteria and that a product will not be deemed good simply because it is attractive. The emphasis must be placed on the quality of the material, not the attractiveness of the container or the eye appeal of the presentation.

Unhappiness with traditional paper and pencil tests has led many individual teachers and instructional teams to develop alternative assessment procedures in classrooms across the country. Figure 8-14 provides a list of guidelines teachers should consider when deciding to use alternative methods of assessment.

---

1. Begin with a diagnosis of the students giving attention to such factors as individual academic preparation, social backgrounds, developmental levels of preparedness, and other considerations concerning student homogeneity and diversity.

2. List desired outcomes for the unit of study. Attention should be given to national, state and local standards as well as the personal goals for the individual students involved. This must focus on the personal aspects of assessment and instruction if all students are to have success in a challenging, dynamic curriculum.

3. Develop the assessment tasks. The following guidelines should be of assistance in developing the actual tasks.

   • *Standards should reflect multiple tasks that can be used for measurement.* If the system is to improve upon traditional assessment systems, students must make choices from options. This is the only avenue to true authenticity.

   • *The tasks should be personalized to the students being assessed.* Students must have input and ownership if assessment is to be successful. Assessment cannot be seen as something teachers do to students.

   • *The tasks should resemble real-life experiences that students can relate to their own lives.* If learning is to be continuous and meaningful, authenticity is necessary in instruction and assessment.

   • *The assessment tasks must mesh with the instructional tasks.* Teachers cannot teach at one level of understanding and measure students' growth at another level. At times it should be difficult to observe the classroom and determine if instruction or assessment is in progress. Assessment should be thought of as a learning experience.

4. Develop procedures for student self-evaluation. Assessment is too critical to the student's overall learning to allow it to take place without careful planning and organization.

Continued on next page

5. Review and revise the tasks that have been developed. Careful attention should be given to gaining feedback from teacher colleagues as well as students.

6. Consider the scoring rubrics to be used. Rubrics must define the tasks completely. Teachers must also give attention to possible student responses and how they will be scored during both teacher evaluation and self-assessment.

7. Revise the tasks after they have been used. This formative assessment is based on teacher and student review of the processes.

Figure 8-14. Guidelines for developing alternative assessment procedures adapted from Hunt, Wiseman, and Bowden (2003).

GRADING AND RECORD MANAGEMENT

Grading is a process used to classify students, often using letter or number designation, on the basis of their performance on summative assessments. While grading can be a somewhat controversial topic, grading, in some format, is applied and expected in schools across the nation. The grading issue may not seem controversial until the effects of actual grades received are assessed. Many educators and parents decry the deleterious effects of constant failure on the self-concept of children and adolescents. Because of this, teachers must be cautious of the manner in which grades are determined and how this information and other evaluative data are communicated to students and their parents. Grades, along with other forms of feedback, are part of the information used to keep students abreast of their progress. The more frequently this is done, the less frequently misunderstandings will occur.

Because of variations in student ability, experience, and achievement, teachers also are faced with challenges in establishing effective approaches to record management. Students complete assignments at different speeds and with different levels of understanding and quality. Properly grouping or working with students on an individual basis will meet many student needs. Without an orderly management system to coordinate assignments, however, any teacher can become confused as to which assignments are due at a particular time and what those students who have completed assignments early should do next.

Grading Procedures

Teachers traditionally have varied in the procedures they use to determine or calculate student grades. Although some procedures are more systematic and effective than others, all teachers, eventually, must choose a system that coincides with their personal philosophy of student evaluation, which relates clearly to their goals and objectives for instruction, and which conforms to the system that has been adopted in their school and district. Regardless of the system, it is important that every teacher make grading procedures clear to students before summative evaluation takes place. The following approaches to grading are commonly used by teachers across the country: (1) *grading on the curve*, (2) *scaling grades*, (3) *inspection method*, (4) *standard grading scale*, and (5) *criterion-referenced*.

Grading on the Curve

Some teachers employ what is popularly referred to as grading on the curve. In using this approach, teachers assume that student abilities are dispersed around a central point in a consistent way. The middle half of the grades are labeled as being Cs. Approximately 20 percent of the grades immediately above C are awarded Bs, and approximately 20 percent of the grades immediately below C are awarded Ds. There remain two small groups: one, approximately 5 percent extremely above average receiving As and another, approximately 5 percent, extremely below average receiving Fs. Such a system is not advisable in the typical classroom situation because it falsely assumes that grades on teacher-made tests are, or even should be, normally distributed in a fashion expected of standardized tests.

Scaling Grades

Many teachers prefer a procedure called scaling grades. In this procedure, the teacher takes the highest score achieved by any student and treats it as if it is 100 percent correct and scales all other grades based upon it. For example, if the highest raw score obtained on a test was 92 percent, eight points would be added to that score to make it total 100 percent, and eight points would then be added to each of the other test scores (e.g., a raw score of 75 percent would then become 83 percent). At this point, teachers assign grades to scores using the new scale. This system should never be used to hide the fact that some students are not doing as well as is expected or desired or the fact that the test items being used inadequately sample the students' learning.

Inspection Method

The inspection method of grading is another procedure that some teachers use. Using this method, the teacher records all test scores on a continuum from high to low, and then assigns the same grade to each student in the same cluster. The best way to display such scores is in a frequency continuum as shown in Figure 8-15. Considering the scores presented, it can be seen how they "group themselves" in clusters for a class of twenty-five students.

Scores	Frequency Of Score	Grade Achieved
98	2	A
95	3	A
88	2	B
86	3	B
85	1	B
84	4	B
78	2	C
77	1	C
76	2	C
71	1	D
70	1	D
65	1	F
61	2	F

Figure 8-15. Worksheet to employ the inspection method of grade assignment.

This unscientific procedure has its basic weakness in that most distributions can be broken down in several different ways. Consequently, the system is considered unreliable by many, and individual grades are hard to justify.

Standardized Grading Scale

Another, and probably more common, procedure is the use of the standardized grading scale. This procedure is recommended over the rather subjective inspection approach. Many teachers are required, or simply prefer, to use the grading scale established for the school in which they teach. It is not uncommon, however, for teachers to formulate their own scales. A traditional scale could be as follows: A = 90–100%, B = 80–89%, C = 70–79%, D = 60–69%, and F = below 60%. In this system student performances are compared to the standards of the scale, not to each other.

Criterion-Referenced Grading

A final type of grading, called criterion-referenced grading, is currently used by many teachers for some, or all, of their grading procedures. Criterion-referenced grading is used to denote mastery of material. In this approach, student performance is compared to announced, fixed standards. There are no student-to-student or student-to-class comparisons. This procedure seeks to determine whether or not students possess competence in the stated objectives of instruction. The only comparison is to the learning of the material, e.g., *met* or *not met*. Did the student learn the material at an acceptable level or not? The teacher's major task in interpreting performance is to initially set the standards for successful completion. Minimal competency might be set at 70 percent mastery of the material. This is typically done in a pass-fail manner. In criterion-referenced grading, the grade report form can vary significantly. Parents usually receive a report card on which all the objectives (criteria) are checked as met or not met. Criterion-referenced grading and reporting has been growing in use, particularly with primary grade children. Communicating achievement in this fashion is seen to be less threatening to students while still adequately expressing progress to parents. Some parents, however, perhaps because they were products of more traditional grade reporting systems, or because they desire to compare the performance of their children to that of other students, prefer to receive reports that reflect performance in letter grades.

Whatever the approach taken, it is critical that grades be an honest and accurate representation of student performance. Further, grades should reflect the priorities in the curriculum. If a student receives a passing grade, that student should have mastered the objectives of the program of study that has been taught. Because grading can impact a student's life, the process must be based on professional decisions relating student performance to actual curriculum objectives (Pratt, 1994). Unfortunately, this is not always the case. For example, some teachers assign grades that are influenced by conduct as opposed to only reflecting academic performance (Farkas, Sheehan, & Grobe, 1990) when conduct was never stated as a grading criterion.

Reporting Student Performance

Once grades have been determined for a grading period, teachers typically send home some type of report to parents using the school or district-adopted reporting form. Acting *in loco parentis*, teachers have a responsibility to keep parents informed about the progress of their children. Since all students do not put into their parents' hands the schoolwork that the teacher sends home, teachers must not surprise parents at the end of the grading period with a less-than-expected report. To avoid such surprises, and the difficulties that arise from them, teachers should communicate with parents regularly through one of the following techniques: (1) telephone or send home a written message to parents concerning student progress, especially for those students who are performing at a level less than desired, (2) send home a weekly or biweekly progress report or packet of student work to be signed by the parents, or (3) request a conference with parents. Teachers who make the effort to communicate student achievement in these ways will be rewarded by having more parents who take greater interest in their children's schoolwork, require and support their children to do better work (e.g., spend more time on homework or study for regular tests), and do not become dissatisfied and call or come to the school wanting to know why poor performance is taking place.

Careful record keeping procedures also must be utilized in order for teachers to be able to report accurate student achievement information to parents. It is recommended that teachers keep complete, updated records of their students' scores along with individual folders, electronic or hard copy, containing examples of each student's work. A complete record system and examples of student work will allow teachers to make a more accurate assessment of performance over time and prove helpful when communicating progress to the students as well as their parents during a conference or at other times.

Many schools are attempting to move to a reporting system based more on student performance instead of using a single number or letter to represent the quality of a student's learning. These performance-based report systems or report cards give parents information reflecting three different learning criteria: *Product* (quality of work done on tests or alternative procedures), *Process* (quality of effort and thought students exhibit), and *Progress* (the personal improvement the student has realized). Such progress reports often give a much fairer and more complete statement of the student's actual performance (Guskey, 1994; Wiggins, 1994).

ASSESSMENT ISSUES

Several important issues currently are being discussed in the profession that pertain to student assessment, and many continue to debate the proper role of assessment in the movement toward higher academic standards. Since the late 1980s and the first Bush Administration's America 2000, which later became Goals 2000 in the Clinton Administration, and through the No Child Left Behind Act (NCLB) under the second Bush Administration, establishing and maintaining high academic standards for students throughout the

PK–12 grade continuum has been a stated expectation. One goal, leading the world in science and mathematics achievement, has been a driving force in both the political and educational arenas since the work of the National Education Goals Panel (1991) and continues to be an important goal today as we assess national progress in science, technology, engineering, and mathematics (STEM).

Many educators and, significantly, many taxpayers believe that tougher standards and greater accountability will fix the nation's ailing schools. However, there also are many who fear that a misguided emphasis on high academic achievement and increased rigor in standards will cause teachers to make curriculum and instructional decisions designed to raise student test scores that will be detrimental to many students (Gough, 1995).

Types of Standards

Several categories of standards are considered by lawmakers and educators alike (Lewis, 1995). *Content standards* are those which establish what should be learned in a given content or subject area. *Performance standards* are those which set acceptable levels of achievement necessary to reach proficiency. *Opportunity-to-learn standards* describe the working conditions and the resources necessary to provide all students an equal opportunity to meet the performance standards. *World-class standards*, often referred to simply as *world standards*, are expectations held for American students based upon the content presented to and level of achievement expected of students from other countries. All of these standards are being put in place with the expectation that students be assessed in order to verify that challenging content is being mastered while requiring that students apply what they have learned.

Concerns about Standards Assessment

Certainly few would argue against the position that schools should have high expectations for students or that the curriculum should have substance and a sound degree of rigor. Nevertheless, many educators are concerned that the standards movement will lead to a type of education where teachers merely teach-to-the-test and quality will be judged only on student production of test scores (Sizer, 1995). Others fear that it is a serious mistake to set standards that are overly specific and prescriptive because such attempts at specificity and precision were already shown to be counterproductive in the behavioral objective movement of the 1960s. Eisner (1995) questions the wisdom of creating standards that require the same things from all students in each content area. Students, he notes, are diverse, not uniform, and attempts to ignore their innate and individual differences could be counterproductive, misleading, and harmful. A particular standard could be rigorous and difficult for one student while a peer might find the same standard easy and not challenging (Reigeluth, 1997). If, for example, it is decided that all students must complete three units of mathematics beginning with Algebra I in order to graduate from high school, questions of assessment are likely to be raised. Specifically, how rigorous will the assessment in Algebra I, Plane Geometry, and Algebra II be if a student must pass all three courses before receiving a diploma? Some point out that high standards in all courses must be maintained in order to ensure that every student is being well prepared. At the same time, others note that such a system of high standards creates a situation where many students will become disenfranchised and drop out of the system.

Much concern has been voiced in the popular media and in professional literature about American students' performance on World-Class Standards (Gandal, 1997). Assessment results of the Third International Mathematics and Science Survey (TIMSS), for example, were released to the public in the late 1990s. At that time, there was much frustration that the results, as reported, indicated that American students did not do as well or know as much as students in some other countries such as Korea, Singapore, and Japan (Atkin & Black, 1997). American students finished slightly below average on the TIMSS mathematics test and only slightly above average on the science test (Bracey, 1997). Although much remains to be said about the impact of World Class Standards on future educational policy and reform decisions, many educators warn that concerns about world comparisons should not overshadow what may be more important educational issues such as school funding and the impact of poverty on learning (Biddle, 1997). Other educators, e.g., Bracey (1998), question the validity of making comparisons among American students and students from other nations who are sometimes much older than their American counterparts, have had differing amounts of content preparation, are products of drastically different educational systems, and may be from quite different cultures.

Having high standards and standardized standards-based tests are very much a part of the fabric of today's education system. In spite of criticisms, such testing is widespread. As a result of the federal No Child Left Behind (NCLB) legislation, the following are evident (Eggen & Kauchak, 2007):

- every state has adopted standards in reading, math, and science;
- all states have testing programs designed to measure the extent to which students meet the standards;
- all states are required to issue overall ratings of their schools based on their students' performance on the tests; and
- states must close or overhaul schools that are identified as failing.

The use of standardized tests and high-stakes testing have significantly changed the ways that schools do business. Some policymakers identify that high-stakes state standards-based testing will have a number of positive effects (Santrock, 2008) such as:

- improved student performance,
- more time teaching the subjects tested,
- high expectations for all students,
- identification of poorly performing schools, teachers, and administrators, and
- improved confidence in schools as test scores increase.

On the other hand, critics of the current use of standardized tests and high-stakes testing identify important areas for concern:

- dumbing down of the curriculum with greater emphasis on rote memorization than on problem-solving and critical thinking skills,
- teaching to the test, and
- discrimination against low-socioeconomic-status (SES) and ethnic minority students.

The evaluation and assessment of student learning are among the most serious, complex, and delicate tasks that educators perform. While teachers need to explore new routes to excellence through assessment, the tools they have used have often provided limited insights into the capabilities of their students. Assessment instruments frequently have little predictive validity and basing decisions solely on feedback from their use is short sighted and will often prove unsuccessful. Figure 8-1, introduced earlier in this chapter, illustrates that the instructional/assessment process is a four-part cycle. Teachers must spend significant time collecting and analyzing large amounts of data before making decisions. Assessment instruments, both standardized and teacher-made, are but two components of the total evaluative process. Without the necessary reflection and insight into the entire educational experience, teachers run the risk of making uninformed, unproductive decisions from which their students and society will suffer.

REFERENCES

Airasian, P. (2005). *Classroom assessment: Concepts and applications* (5th ed.). Upper Saddle River, NJ: Pearson Education, Inc.

Alberto, P. A., & Troutman, A. C. (2006). *Applied behavior analysis for teachers* (7th ed.). Upper Saddle River, NJ: Merrill/Prentice-Hall.

Alderman, M. (2004). *Motivation for achievement: Possibilities for teaching and learning* (2nd ed.). Mahawah, NJ: Lawrence Erlbaum.

Anderson, J. (2005). *Cognitive psychology and its implications* (6th ed.). New York: Worth.

Anderson, L., Krathwohl, D., Airasian, P., Cruikshank, K., Mayer, R., Pintrich, P., Raths, J., & Wittrock, M. (Eds.). (2001). *A taxonomy for learning, teaching, and assessing: A revision of Bloom's taxonomy of educational objectives.* New York: Longman.

Anderson, P. (1999). *Nonverbal communication: Forms and functions.* Mountain View, CA: Mayfield.

Anderson, R. (1984). Role of the reader's schema in comprehension, learning, and memory. In R. Anderson, J. Osborn, & R. Tierney (Eds.), *Learning to read in American schools: Basal readers and content texts.* Hillsdale, NJ: Erlbaum.

Anderson, R. (1978). Schema-directed processes in language comprehension. In A. Lesgold, J. Pellegrino, S. Fokkema, & R. Glasser (Eds.), *Cognitive psychology and instruction.* New York: Plenum.

Anderson, R. (1977). The notion of schemata and the educational enterprise: General discussion of the conference. In R. Anderson, R. Spiro, & W. Montague (Eds.), *School and the acquisition of knowledge.* Hillsdale, NJ: Erlbaum.

Argyle, M., & Dean, J. (1965). Eye contact, distance and affiliation. *Sociometry, 28,* 289–304.

Armbruster, B. (1996). Schema theory and the design of content-area textbooks. *Educational Psychologist, 21,* 253–276.

Armento, B. (1997). Teacher behaviors related to student achievement on a social science concept test. *Journal of Teacher Education, 28*(3) 46–52.

Armstrong, T. (1994). *Multiple intelligences in the classroom.* Alexandria, VA: Association for Supervision and Curriculum Development.

Armstrong, D., Henson, K., & Savage, T. (1997). *Teaching today: An introduction to education* (5th ed.). New York: Macmillan.

Ashton, P., & Webb, R. (1986). *Making a difference: Teachers' sense of efficacy and student achievement.* White Plains, NY: Longman.

Atkin, J. M., & Black, P. (1997). Policy perils of international comparisons: The TIMSS case. *Phi Delta Kappan, 79*(1), 23–28.

Ausubel, D. (1968). *Educational psychology: A cognitive view.* New York: Holt, Rinehart, and Winston.

Ausubel, D. (1978). In defense of advance organizers: A reply to the critics. *Review of Educational Research, 48,* 251–259.

Ausubel, D., & Robinson, D. (1969). *School learning: An introduction to educational psychology.* New York: Holt, Rinehart, and Winston.

Barbe, W. B., & Milone, M. (1981). What we know about modality strengths. *Educational Leadership, 38*(5), 378–380.

Bartlett, F. (1932). *Remembering: An experimental and social study.* Cambridge, UK: Cambridge University Press.

Bartlett, F. (1958). *Thinking.* New York: Basic Books.

Beane, J. A. (1993). Problems and possibilities for an integrative curriculum. *Middle School Journal, 25*(1), 18–23.

Beane, J. A. (2001). Reform and reinvention. In T. Dickinson (Ed.), *Reinventing the middle school.* New York: Rutledge Falmer.

Beck, C. R. (1998). A taxonomy for identifying, classifying, and interrelating teaching strategies. *The Journal of General Education, 47*(1), 37–62.

Bedrova, E., & Leong, D. J. (1996). *Tools of the mind: The Vygotskian approach to early childhood education.* Upper Saddle River, NJ: Merrill.

Berliner, D. C. (2002). Educational research: The hardest science of all. *Educational Researcher, 31*(8), 18–20.

Berliner, D. C., & Casanova, U. (1996). *Putting research to work in your school.* Arlington Heights, IL: IRI/Skylight Training and Publishing, Inc.

Berlinger, W. W., & Yates, C. M. (1993). Formal operational thought in the gifted: A post-Piagetian perspective. *Roeper Review, 15*(4), 220–224.

Biddle, B. J. (1997). Foolishness, dangerous nonsense, and real correlates of state differences in achievement. *Phi Delta Kappan, 79*(1), 9–13.

Biehler, R., & Snowman, J. (2006). *Psychology applied to teaching* (11th ed.). Boston: Houghton-Mifflin.

Birdwhistell, R. (1970). *Kinesics and content.* Philadelphia: University of Pennsylvania Press.

Blair, T. (1988). *Emerging patterns of teaching.* Columbus, OH: Merrill.

Bloom, B. (1976). *Human characteristics and school learning.* New York: McGraw-Hill.

Bloom, B. (1980). The new direction in educational research: Alterable variables. *Phi Delta Kappan, 61*(5), 382–385.

Bloom, B., Englehart, M., Furst, E., Hill. W., & Krathwohl, D. (1956). *Taxonomy of educational objectives. Handbook I: Cognitive Domain.* New York: David McKay.

Blumenfeld, P., Soloway, E., Marx, R., Krajcik, J., Guzdial, M., & Palincsar, A. (1996). Motivating project-based learning: Sustaining the doing, supporting the learning. In D. Berliner & U. Casanova (Eds.), *Putting research to work in your school* (pp. 153–157). Arlington Heights, IL: IRI/Skylight Training and Publishing, Inc.

Borich, G. (2007). *Effective teaching methods: Research-based practice* (6th ed.). Upper Saddle River, NJ: Pearson Education, Inc.

Borko, H., & Niles, J. (1982). Factors contributing to teachers' judgments about students and decisions about grouping students for reading instruction. *Journal of Reading Behavior, 14,* 127–140.

Borko, H., & Niles, J. (1987). Descriptions of teacher planning: Ideas for teachers and researchers. In V. Richardson-Koehler (Ed.), *Educators' handbook: A research perspective.* New York: Longman.

Bracey, G. W. (1997). The new lost generation? *Phi Delta Kappan, 78*(7), 578–579.

Bracey, G. W. (1998). TIMSS, rhymes with "dims," as in "witted." *Phi Delta Kappan, 79*(9), 686–687.

Brandt, R. (1992). On making sense: A conversation with Magdalene Lampert. *Educational Leadership, 51*(5) 26–30.

Bredekamp, S., & Copple, C. (Eds.). (1997). *Developmentally appropriate practice in early childhood programs* (Rev. ed.). Washington, DC: NAEYC.

Brenner, M., Mayer, R., Moseley, B., Brar, T., Duran, R., Reed, B., & Webb, D. (1997). Learning by understanding: The role of multiple representations in learning algebra. *American Education Research Journal, 34*(4), 663–689.

Brophy, J. (1981). Teacher praise: A functional analysis. *Review of Educational Research, 51*(1), 5–32.

Brophy, J. E. (1987). *Educating teachers about managing classrooms and students.* Occasional Paper No. 115. East Lansing: Institute for Research on Teaching, Michigan State University.

Brophy, J. E., & Good, T. L. (1986). Teacher behavior and student achievement. In M.C. Wittrock (Ed.), *Handbook of Research on Teaching* (3rd ed.). New York: Macmillan.

Brophy, J., & McCaslin, M. (1992). Teachers report of how they perceive and cope with problem students. *Elementary School Journal, 93*(1), 3–68.

Bruner, J. (2004). *Toward a theory of instruction.* Cambridge, MA: Belknap Press.

Bruner, J., Goodnow, J., & Austin, G. (1956). *A study of thinking.* New York: Wiley.

Bruning, R., Schraw, G., & Ronning, R. (1995). *Cognitive psychology and instruction* (2nd ed.). Upper Saddle River, NJ: Prentice-Hall.

Bruning, R., Schraw, G., Norby, M., & Ronning, R. (2004). *Cognitive psychology and instruction* (4th ed.). Upper Saddle River, NJ: Merrill/Prentice-Hall.

Burden, P., & Byrd, D. (2007). *Methods for effective teaching: Promoting K–12 student understanding* (4th ed.). New York: Pearson Education, Inc.

Campbell, L., Campbell, B., & Dickinson, D. (1996). *Teaching and learning through multiple intelligences* (2nd ed.). Boston: Allyn & Bacon.

Canter, L. (1988). Let the educator beware: A response to Curwin and Mendler. *Educational Leadership, 46*(2), 71–73.

Canter, L., & Canter, M. (1976). *Assertive discipline.* Santa Monica, CA: Canter and Associates.

Carnegie Council on Adolescent Development. (1995). *Great transitions: Preparing adolescents for a new century.* New York: Carnegie Corporation of New York.

Carroll, J. (1970). The formation of concepts. In B. Beyer & A. Penna (Eds.), *Concepts in the social studies – Bulletin 45.* Washington, DC: National Council for the Social Studies.

Charles, C. M. (1976). *Educational psychology: The instructional endeavor* (2nd ed.). Saint Louis, MO: C. V. Mosby.

Charles, C. M. (1981). *Building classroom discipline.* New York: Longman.

Charles, C. M. (2008). *Building classroom discipline* (9th ed.). New York: Allyn & Bacon.

Cheek, D. W. (1993). Plain talk about alternative assessment. *Middle School Journal, 25* (2), 6–10.

Chittenden, E. (1991). Authentic assessment, evaluation, and documentation of student performance. In V. Perrone (Ed.), *Expanding student assessment.* Reston, VA: Association for Supervision and Curriculum Development.

Chomsky, N. (1957). *Synthetic structure.* The Hague: Mouton.

Chuska, K. (2003). *Improving classroom questions* (2nd ed.). Bloomington, IN: Phi Delta Kappa.

Clark, C. M., & Yinger, R. J. (1979). *Three studies of teacher planning.* Research Series No. 55. East Lansing: Institute for Research on Teaching, Michigan State University.

Colton, A. B., & Sparks-Langer, G. M. (1992). Restructuring student teaching experiences. In C.D. Glickman (Ed.), *Supervision in transition.* Alexandria, VA: Association for Supervision and Curriculum Development.

Cooper, H. M., Lindsay, J. J., Nye, B. A., & Greathouse, S. (1998). Relationships among attitudes about homework assigned and completed and student achievement. *Journal of Educational Psychology, 90,* 70–83.

Cooper, H. M., & Valentine, J. (2001). Using research to answer practical questions about homework. *Educational Psychologist, 36*(3), 143–153.

Cooper, J. (Ed.). (1986). *Classroom teaching skills* (3rd ed.). Lexington, MA: D.C. Heath.

Cooper, J. (2006). *Literacy: Helping children construct meaning* (6th ed.). New York: Houghton-Mifflin.

Crable, R. (1979). What can you believe about rhetoric? In J. McKay (Ed.), *Exploration in speech communication.* Columbus, OH: Charles E. Merrill.

Cruickshank, D. (1985). Applying research on teacher clarity. *Journal of Teacher Education, 35*(2), 44–48.

Cruickshank, D. (1987). *Reflective teaching: The preparation of students for teaching.* Reston, VA: Association of Teacher Educators.

Cruickshank, D. (1990). *Research that informs teachers and teacher educators.* Bloomington, IN: Phi Delta Kappa Educational Foundation.

Curwin, R., & Mendler, A. (1988). Packaged discipline programs: Let the buyer beware. *Educational Leadership, 46*(2), 68–71.

de Ramirez, L. L. (2009). *Take action! Lesson plans for the multicultural classroom.* Upper Saddle River, NJ: Pearson Education, Inc.

Delgado-Gaiton, C. (1992). School matters in the Mexican American home: Socializing children to education. *American Educational Research Journal, 29*(3), 495–516.

Dempster, F. (1991). Synthesis of research on reviews and tests. *Educational Leadership, 48*(7), 71–76.

Dewey, J. (1933). *How we think.* Lexington, MA: D.C. Heath.

Doyle, W. (1986). Classroom organization and management. In M. Wittrock (Ed.), *Handbook of research on teaching* (3rd ed.). New York: Macmillan.

Dreikurs, R. (1968). *Psychology in the classroom* (2nd ed.). New York: Harper and Row.

Dreikurs, R., & Cassell, P. (1972). *Discipline without tears.* New York: Hawthorn Books.

Driscoll, M. (1994). *Psychology of learning for instruction.* Boston: Allyn & Bacon.

Dunn, R., Dunn, K., & Price, G. (1981). Learning style: Research vs. opinion. *Phi Delta Kappan, 62*(9), 645–646.

Dunn, R., Dunn, K., & Price, G. (1989). *Learning style inventory.* Lawrence, KS: Price Systems, Inc.

Eggen, P., & Kauchak, D. (2007). *Educational psychology: Windows on classrooms* (7th ed.). Upper Saddle River, NJ: Pearson Education, Inc.

Eggen, P., & Kauchak, D. (2006). *Strategies and models for teachers: Teaching content and thinking skills* (5th ed.). Boston: Allyn & Bacon.

Eisner, E. W. (1995). Standards for American schools: Help or hindrance? *Phi Delta Kappan, 76*(10), 758–764.

Elawar, M., & Corno, L. (1985). A factorial experiment in teachers' written feedback on student homework. *Journal of Educational Psychology, 77*(2), 162–173.

Ellett, C. (1990). *A new generation of classroom-based assessments of teaching and learning: Concepts, issues and controversies from pilots of the Louisiana STAR.* Baton Rouge, LA: College of Education, Louisiana State University.

Ellis, S., Dowdy, B., Graham, P., & Jones, R. (1992, April). *Parental support of planning skills in the context of homework and family demands.* Paper presented at the Annual Meeting of the American Educational Research Association, San Francisco.

Ellwein, M. C., Graue, M. E., & Comfort, R. E. (1990). Talking about instruction: Student teachers' reflections on success and failure in the classroom. *Journal of Teacher Education, 41*(4) 3–14.

Emmer, E., Evertson, J., Clements, B., & Worsham, M. (1996). *Classroom management for secondary teachers* (4th ed.). Englewood Cliffs, NJ: Prentice-Hall.

Emmer, E. T., Sanford, J. P., Clements, B. S., & Martin, J. (1982). *Improving classroom management and organization in junior high schools: An experiential investigation.* R & D Report No. 6153. Austin: The University of Texas at Austin, Research and Development Center for Teacher Education.

Engel, B. S. (1994). Portfolio assessment and the new paradigm: New instruments and new places. *Educational Forum, 59* (Fall), 22–27.

Epstein, J. (1990). School and family connections: Theory, research, and implications for integrating sociologies of education and family. In D. Unger, & M. Sussman (Eds.), *Families in community settings: Interdisciplinary perspectives.* New York: Haworth Press.

Evertson, C. M., Anderson, C. H., Anderson, L. M., & Brophy, J. E. (1980). Relationships between classroom behaviors and student outcomes in junior high mathematics and English classes. *American Educational Research Journal, 17*(1) 43–60.

Evertson, C., Emmer, B., Clements, B., Sanford, J., & Worsham, M. (1994). *Classroom management for classroom teachers* (3rd ed.). Upper Saddle River, NJ: Prentice-Hall.

Falk, J., & Balling, J. (1996). The field trip milieu. In D. Berliner, & U. Casanova (Eds.). *Putting research to work in your school* (pp. 88–92). Arlington Heights, IL: IRI/Skylight Training and Publishing, Inc.

Farkas, G., Sheehan, D., & Grobe, R. P. (1990). Coursework mastery and school success: Gender, ethnicity, and poverty groups within an urban school district. *American Educational Research Journal, 27,* 807–827.

Fischer, B., & Fischer, L. (1979). Styles in teaching and learning. *Educational Leadership, 36*(5), 245–254.

Freiberg, H., & Driscoll, A. (2005). *Universal teaching strategies* (4th ed.). Boston: Allyn & Bacon.

Gage, N., & Berliner, D. (1988). *Educational psychology* (4th ed.). Chicago: Rand McNally.

Gagne, E., Yekovich, C., & Yekovich, F. (1993). *The cognitive psychology of learning* (2nd ed.). New York: Harper-Collins.

Gagne, R. (1985). *The conditions of learning* (4th ed.). New York: Holt, Rinehart, and Winston.

Gallagher, J., & Aschner, M. (1963). A preliminary report of the analysis of classroom interaction. *Merrill-Palmer Quarterly, 9,* 183–194.

Galloway, C. (1982, April). *Please listen to what I'm not saying.* Presentation to Reflections: An Invitation to Successful Teaching, Coastal Carolina College of the University of South Carolina, Myrtle Beach, South Carolina.

Gandal, M. (1997). *What students abroad are expected to know about mathematics: Defining world class standards,* Vol. 4. Washington, DC: American Federation of Teachers.

Gardner, H. (1983). *Frames of mind.* New York: Basic Books.

Gardner, H. (1993). *Multiple intelligences: The theory in practice.* New York: Basic Books.

Gardner, H., & Boix-Mansilla, V. (1994). Teaching for understanding – Within and across the disciplines. *Educational Leadership, 51*(5) 14–18.

Gareis, C., & Grant, L. (2008). *Teacher-made assessments: How to connect curriculum, instruction, and student learning.* Larchmont, NY: Eye on Education.

Gilzow, D. F. (2001). Japanese immersion: A successful program in Portland, Oregon. *ERIC News Bulletin, 24* (1 & 2), 1–3.

Ginott, H. (1965). *Between parent and child.* New York: Avon.

Ginott, H. (1969). *Between parent and teenager.* New York: Macmillan.

Ginott, H. (1971). *Teacher and child.* New York: Macmillan.

Glasser, W. (1965). *Reality therapy: A new approach to psychiatry.* New York: Harper and Row.

Glasser, W. (1969). *Schools without failure.* New York: Harper and Row.

Glasser, W. (1992). *The quality school: Managing students without coercion* (2nd ed.). New York: Harper-Perennial.

Glasser, W. (1993). *The quality school teacher.* New York: Harper-Perennial.

Glasser, W., & Dotson, K. (1998). *Choice theory in the classroom.* New York: Harper-Collins.

Glickman, C., Gordon, S., & Ross-Gordon, J. (2007). *Supervision and instructional leadership: A developmental approach* (7th ed.). Boston: Allyn & Bacon.

Goerss, K. V. (1993). Portfolio assessment: A work in process. *Middle School Journal, 25*(2), 20–24.

Goldman-Eisler, F. (1961). A comparative study of two hesitation phenomena. *Language and Speech, 4,* 18–26.

Good, T., & Brophy, J. (1986). *Educational psychology: A realistic approach* (3rd ed.). New York: Holt, Rinehart, and Winston.

Good, T., & Brophy, J. (2003). *Looking in classrooms* (9th ed.). Boston: Allyn & Bacon.

Good, T., & Brophy, J. (1997). *Looking in classrooms* (7th ed.). New York: Longman.

Goodwin, S. S., Sharp, G. W., Cloutier, E. F., & Diamond, N. A. (1983). *Effective classroom questioning.* Paper Identified by the Task Force on Establishing a National Clearinghouse of Materials Developed for Teaching Assistant Training. ERIC Document Reproduction Service No. ED 285–497.

Gordon, T. (1989). *Discipline that works: Promoting self-discipline in children.* New York: Random House.

Gordon, T. (1974). *T.E.T. teacher effectiveness training.* New York: Wyden.

Goss, C., & O'Hair, D. (1988). *Communicating in interpersonal relationships.* New York: Macmillan.

Gough, P. B. (1995). Finding good teachers for city schools. *Phi Delta Kappan, 76*(10), 739.

Grabe, M., & Grabe, C. (2007). *Integrating technology for meaningful learning* (5th ed.). Boston: Houghton-Mifflin.

Griffin, G. (1986). Clinical teacher education. In J. Hoffman, & S. Edwards (Eds.), *Reality and reform in clinical teacher education.* New York: Random House.

Gueguen, N., & DeGail, M. (2003). The effect of smiling on helping behavior: Smiling and good Samaritan behavior. *Communication Reports, 16,* 133–140.

Guilford, J. (1959). Three faces of intellect. *American Psychologist, 14,* 469–479.

Gumperz, J. J. (1996). On teaching language in its sociocultural context. In D. I. Slobin, J. Gerhardt, A. Kyratzis, & J. Guo (Eds.), *Social interaction, social context, and language: Essays in honor of Susan Ervin-Tripp* (pp. 469–480). Mahawah, NJ: Erlbaum.

Gunns, R., Johnston, L., & Hudson, S. (2002). Victim selection and kinematics: A point-light investigation of vulnerability to attack. *Journal of Nonverbal Behavior, 26,* 120–159.

Guskey, T. R. (1994). Making the grade: What benefits the student? *Educational Leadership, 52*(2), 14–20.

Guskey, T., & Bailey, J. (2001). *Developing grading and reporting systems for student learning.* Thousand Oaks, CA: Corwin Press.

Harrow, A. (1972). *A taxonomy of the psychomotor domain: A guide for developing behavioral objectives.* New York: David McKay.

Harry, B. (1992). An ethnographic study of cross cultural communication with Puerto Rican American families in the special education system. *American Educational Research Journal, 29*(3), 471–488.

Heck, S., & Williams, C. (1984). *The complex roles of the teacher.* New York: Teachers College Press.

Heckman, P. E. (1994). Planting seeds: Understanding through investigation. *Educational Leadership, 51*(5) 36–39.

Henson, K. T. (1996). *Methods and strategies for teaching in secondary and middle schools* (3rd ed.). White Plains, NY: Longman.

Herbert, E. A. (1998). Lessons learned about student portfolios. *Phi Delta Kappan, 79*(8), 583–585.

Herrell, A. L. (2000). *Fifty strategies for teaching English language learners.* Upper Saddle River, NJ: Merrill.

Hill, W. (1981). *Principles of learning: A handbook of applications.* Sherman Oaks, CA: Alfred.

Hoetker, J., & Ahlbrand, U. (1969). The persistence of recitation. *American Educational Research Journal, 6,* 145–167.

Hoover-Dempsey, K., Bassler, O., & Burow, R. (1995). Parents' reported involvement in students' homework: Strategies and practices. *Elementary School Journal, 95*(5), 435–449.

Hoy, A., & Hoy, W. (2009). *Instructional leadership: A research-based guide to learning in schools* (3rd ed.). New York: Pearson Education, Inc.

Hunt, G., & Bedwell, L. (1982). An axiom for classroom management. *The High School Journal, 66*(1), 10–13.

Hunt, G., Wiseman, D., & Bowden, S. (2003). *The modern middle school: Addressing standards and student needs* (2nd ed.). Springfield, IL: Charles C Thomas.

Hunt, J. (1961). *Intelligence and experience.* New York: Ronald.

Hunt, J. (1964). The implications of changing ideas on how children develop intellectually. *Children, 11*(3), 83–91.

Hunt, M., & Metcalf, L. (1968). *Teaching high school social studies.* New York: Harper and Row.

Hunter, M. (1984). Knowing, teaching and supervising. In P. Hosford (Ed.), *Using what we know about teaching.* Alexandria, VA: Association for Supervision and Curriculum Development.

Huzinga, J. (1970). *Homo Ludens: A study of the play element in culture.* New York: Harper & Row.

International Society for Technology in Education. (2007). *National educational technology standards for students.* Retrieved June 8, 2008, from www.iste.org.

International Society for Technology in Education. (2008). *Educational Technology Standards for Teachers.* Retrieved August 4, 2008, from www.iste.org.

Ishii, S. (1987). *Nonverbal communication in Japan.* Tokyo: The Japan Foundation.

Jackson, P. (1990). *Life in classrooms.* New York: Columbia University Press.

Jacobs, H. H. (Ed.). (2004). *Getting results with curriculum mapping.* Alexandria, VA: Association for Supervision and Curriculum Development.

Jacobsen, D. A., Eggen, P., & Kauchak, D. (1999). *Methods for teaching: Promoting student learning.* Upper Saddle River, NJ: Merrill/Prentice-Hall.

Jarolimek, J., & Foster, C. D., Sr. (1997). *Teaching and learning in the elementary school* (6th ed.). Upper Saddle River, NJ: Merrill/Prentice-Hall.

Jhally, S., & Katz, J. (2001, Winter). Big trouble, little pond. *Umass,* pp. 26–31.

Johnson, D. W., & Johnson, R. T. (1992). Encouraging thinking through constructive controversy. In N. Davidson, & T. Worsham (Eds.), *Enhancing thinking through cooperative learning.* New York: Teachers College Press.

Johnson, D. W., & Johnson, F. (1997). *Joining together: Group theory and group skills* (6th ed.). Boston: Allyn & Bacon.

Johnson, D. W., & Johnson, R. T. (1989). *Leading the cooperative school.* Edina, MN: Interaction.

Johnson, D. W., & Johnson, R. T. (1999). *Learning together and alone: Cooperative, competitive, and individualistic learning* (5th ed.). Boston: Allyn & Bacon.

Johnson, D. W., & Johnson, R. T. (1995). *Teaching students to be peacemakers* (3rd ed.). Edina, MN: Interaction.

Johnson, D. W., & Johnson, R. T. (2004). The three Cs of promoting social and emotional learning. In J. Zins, R. Weissberg, M. Wang, & H. Walberg (Eds.), *Building academic success on social and emotional learning* (pp. 40–58). New York: Teachers College Press.

Johnson, D. W., Johnson, R. T., Dudley, B., Mitchell, J., & Frederickson, J. (1997). The impact of conflict resolution training on middle school students. *The Journal of Social Psychology, 137*(1), 11–21.

Jones, F. (2000). *Positive classroom discipline* (3rd ed.). New York: McGraw-Hill.

Joyce, B., Weil, J., & Calhoun, E. (2004). *Models of teaching* (7th ed.). Boston: Allyn & Bacon.

Kagan, D. (1992). Implications of research on teacher belief. *Educational Psychologist, 27,* 65–90.

Karweit, N. (1989). Time and learning: A review. In R. E. Slavin (Ed.), *School and classroom organization.* Hillsdale, NJ: Erlbaum.

Kauchak, D., & Eggen, P. (1998). *Learning and teaching: Research-based methods* (3rd ed.). Needham Heights, MA: Allyn & Bacon.

Kenny, E., & Perry, S. (1994). Talking with parents about performance-based report cards. *Educational Leadership, 52*(2), 24–27.

Kidron, Y., & Fleischman, S. (2007). Research matters: Promoting adolescents' prosocial behavior. *Educational Leadership,* Retrieved May 31, 2007, from www.ascd.org/portal/site/ascd/template.

Klausmeier, H. J. (1988). The future of educational psychology and the content of the graduate programs in educational psychology. *Educational Psychologist, 23,* 203–220.

Klausmeier, H. J., & Sipple, T. S. (1982). Factor structure of the Piagetian stage of concrete operations. *Contemporary Educational Psychology, 7,* 161–180.

Knapp, M. (1972). The field of nonverbal communication. In C. Stewart (Ed.), *On speech communication.* New York: Holt, Rinehart, and Winston.

Knapp, M. L., & Hall, J. A. (1992). *Nonverbal communication in human interaction.* Fort Worth, TX: Holt, Rinehart, & Winston.

Kohn, A. (2006). *Beyond discipline: From compliance to community.* Alexandria, VA: Association for Supervision and Curriculum Development.

Kohn, A. (2001). *Punished by rewards: The trouble with gold stars, incentive plans, As, praise, and other bribes.* New York: Houghton-Mifflin.

Kounin, J. (1970). *Discipline and group management in classrooms.* New York: Holt, Rinehart, and Winston.

Kovalik, S. (1994). *ITI: The model – integrated thematic instruction* (3rd ed.). Kent, WA: Books for Educators.

Kozloff, M., LaNunziata, L., Cowardin, J., & Bessellieu, F. (2001). Direct instruction: Its contributions to high school achievement. *The High School Journal, 84*(2), 36–54.

Krathwohl, D., Bloom, B., & Masia, B. (1964). *Taxonomy of educational objectives. The classification of educational goals. Handbook II: Affective domain.* New York: David McKay.

Kritt, D. (1993). Authenticity, reflection, and self-evaluation in alternative assessment. *Middle School Journal, 25*(2), 43–45.

Kyllonen, P., Lohman, D., & Snow, R. (1981). *Effects of task facets and strategy training on spacial task performance* (Technical Report No. 14) Stanford, CA: Stanford University Aptitude Research Project.

Lemlech, J. K. (1998). *Curriculum and instructional methods for the elementary and middle school* (4th ed.). Upper Saddle River, NJ: Merrill/Prentice-Hall.

Lessons at the Museum. (2008). Retrieved June 10, 2008, from http://www.edweek. org/ew/articles/2008/06/11/41museum.h27.html?tmp=1256746218.

Lewis, A. C. (1995). An overview of the standards movement. *Phi Delta Kappan, 76*(10), 744–750.

Lewis, D., & Greene, J. (1982). *Thinking better.* New York: Rawson, Wade.

Linn, M., & Barbules, N. (1993). Construction of knowledge and group learning. In K. Tobin (Ed.), *The practice of construction in science education.* Washington, DC: American Association for the Advancement of Science.

Mackenzie, A., & White, R. (1996). Field work in geography and long-term memory structures. In D. Berliner, & U. Casanova (Eds.), *Putting research to work in your school* (pp. 88–92). Arlington Heights, IL: IRI/Skylight Training and Publishing, Inc.

Maclay, H., & Osgood, C. (1959). Hesitation phenomena in spontaneous English speech. *Word, 15,* 19.

Mager, R. (1962). *Preparing instructional objectives.* Palo Alto, CA: Fearson.

Manning, L., & Bucher, K. (2007). *Classroom management: Models, applications, and cases* (2nd ed.). Upper Saddle River, NJ: Pearson Education, Inc.

Martorella, P. (1986). Teaching concepts. In J. Cooper (Ed.), *Classroom teaching skills* (3rd ed.) Lexington, MA: D.C. Heath.

Marzano, R. (2007). *The art and science of teaching: A comprehensive framework for effective instruction.* Alexandria, VA: Association for Supervision and Curriculum Development.

Marzano, R. (2003). *What works in schools: Translating research into action.* Alexandria, VA: Association for Supervision and Curriculum Development.

Maslow, A. H. (1968). *Toward a psychology of being* (2nd ed.). New York: Van Nostrand.

Maslow, A. H. (1970). *Motivation and personality* (2nd ed.). New York: Harper and Row.

McCarthy, B. (1990). Using the 4Mat system to bring learning styles to schools. *Educational Leadership, 48*(2), 31–36.

McCaslin, M., & Good, T. (1992). Compliant cognition: The misalliance of management and instructional goals in current school reform. *Educational Researcher, 21*(3), 4–17.

McCroskey, J. (1972). *Introduction to rhetorical communication* (2nd ed.). Englewood Cliffs. NJ: Prentice-Hall.

McDonald, J., Smith, S., Turner, D., Finney, M., & Barton, E. (1993). *Graduation by exhibition: Assessing genuine achievement.* Alexandria, VA: Association for Supervision and Curriculum Development.

McKenzie, G. (1979). Effects of questions and test-like events on achievement and on-task behaviors in a classroom concept learning presentation. *Journal of Educational Research, 72*(6), 348–351.

McKenzie, G. (1980). Improving instruction through instructional design. *Educational Leadership, 37*(9), 664–667.

McLaughlin, J. J. (1994). From negative to negotiation: Moving away from the management metaphor. *Action in Teacher Education, 16*(1), 75–84.

Mehrabian, S. (1969). Significance of posture and position in the communication of attitude and status relationships. *Psychology Bulletin, 71,* 359–72.

Mehrabian, A. (1981). *Silent messages: Implicit communication of emotions and attitudes* (2nd ed.). Belmont, CA: Wadsworth.

Merrill, D., & Tennyson, R. (1977). *Teaching concepts: An instructional design guide.* Englewood Cliffs, NJ: Educational Technology Publications.

Merwin, W., Schneider, D., & Stephens, L. (1974). *Developing competency in teaching secondary social studies.* Columbus, OH: Charles E. Merrill.

Miller, D. (2002). *Reading with meaning.* Portland, ME: Stenhouse.

Minami, M., & Ovando, C. J. (2004). Language issues in multicultural context. In J. A. Banks & C. A. M. Banks (Eds.), *Handbook of research on multicultural education* (pp. 567–588). San Francisco, CA: Jossey-Bass.

Morine-Dershimer, G. (2006). Instructional planning. In J. Cooper (Ed.), *Classroom teaching skills* (7th ed., pp. 20–54). Boston: Houghton-Mifflin.

Murphy, J., Weil, M., & McGreal, T. (1986). The basic practice model of instruction. *Elementary School Journal, 87,* 83–95.

National Board for Professional Teaching Standards. (1991). *Toward high and more rigorous standards for the teaching profession* (3rd ed.). Detroit, MI: Author.

National Council for Accreditation of Teacher education. (2008). *Professional standards for the accreditation of teacher preparation institutions.* Washington, DC: Author.

National Education Goals Panel. (1991). *Measuring progress toward the national education goals: Potential indicators and measurement strategies discussion document* (U.S. Government Printing Office No. 292–323/40246). Washington, DC: U.S. Government Printing Office.

Nichols, S. L., & Berliner, D. C. (2007). *Collateral damage: High-stakes testing corrupts America's schools.* Cambridge, MA: Harvard Education Press.

Nilson, L. B. (2003). *Teaching at its best: A research-based resource for college instructors* (2nd ed.). Boston: Anker.

Nucci, L. (1987). Synthesis of research on moral development. *American Educational Research Journal, 28*(1), 117–153.

O'Donnell, A., & O'Kelly, J. (1994). Learning from peers: Beyond the rhetoric of positive results. *Educational Psychology Review, 6,* 321–349.

O'Flahavan, J., Hartman, D., & Pearson, D. (1988). Teacher questioning and feedback practices: A twenty-year retrospective. In J. Readence, R. Baldwin, J. Konopak, & P. O'Keefe (Eds.), *Dialogues in literacy research* (pp. 183–208). Chicago: National Reading Conference.

O'Hair, D., Friedrich, G. W., Wiemann, J. M., & Wiemann, M. O. (1997). *Competent communication* (2nd ed.). New York: St. Martin's Press.

Olson, D. R. (2004). The triumph of hope over experience in the search for "what works": A response to Slavin. *Educational Researcher, 33*(1), 24–26.

Orlich, D., Harder, R., Callahan, R., Kauchak, D., Pendergrass, R., Keogh, A., & Gibson, H. (1990). *Teaching strategies: A guide to better instruction* (3rd ed.). Lexington, MA: D. C. Heath.

Orlich, D., Harder, R., Callahan, R., Trevisan, M., & Brown, A. (2007). *Teaching strategies: A guide to effective instruction* (8th ed.). New York: Houghton-Mifflin.

Ornstein, A. C., & Hunkins, F. P. (1998). *Curriculum: Foundations, principles, and issues* (3rd ed.). Boston: Allyn and Bacon.

Ornstein, A., & Lasley, T. (2000). *Strategies for effective teaching* (3rd ed.). Boston: McGraw-Hill.

Palincsar, A., & Brown, A. (1984). Reciprocal teaching of comprehension – fostering and comprehension monitoring activities. *Cognition and Instruction, 2,* 117–175.

Passe, J. (1999). *Elementary school curriculum.* Boston: McGraw-Hill.

Pate, P. E., Homestead, E., & McGinnis, K. (1993). Designing rubrics for authentic assessment. *Middle School Journal, 25*(2), 36–41.

Perrone, V. (1994). How to engage students in learning. *Educational Leadership, 51*(5) 11–13.

Perry, B., & Conroy, J. (1994). *Early childhood and primary mathematics.* Sydney: Harcourt Brace.

Piaget, J. (1970). *Science of education and psychology of the child.* New York: Orion Press.

Pierce, W., & Lorber, M. (1977). *Objectives and methods for secondary teaching.* Englewood Cliffs, NJ: Prentice-Hall.

Poole, M., Okeafor, K., & Sloan, E. (1989, April). *Teachers' interactions, personal efficacy, and change implementation.* Paper presented at the Annual Meeting of the American Educational Research Association, San Francisco.

Popham, W. (2005). *Classroom assessment: What teachers need to know* (4th ed.). Boston: Allyn & Bacon.

Porter, A. C., & Brophy, J. E. (1987). *Good teaching: Insights from the Work of the Institute for Research on Teaching.* Occasional Paper No. 114. East Lansing, MI: The Institute for Research on Teaching, Michigan State University.

Powell, J. H., Casanova, U., & Berliner, D. C. (1991). *Parental involvement: Readings in educational research, a program for professional development, a National Education Association Project.* Washington, DC: National Education Association.

Powell, R., McLaughlin, H., Savage, T., & Zehm, S. (2001). *Classroom management: Perspectives on social curriculum.* Upper Saddle River, NJ: Merrill/Prentice-Hall.

Pratt, D. (1994). *Curriculum planning: A handbook for professionals.* Fort Worth, TX: Harcourt Brace.

President's Educational Technology Initiative. (1999). Retrieved June 9, 2008, from http://clinton2.nara.gov/WH/EOP/OP/edtech.

Price, E., & Driscoll, M. (1997). An inquiry into the spontaneous transfer of problem-solving skill. *Contemporary Educational Psychology, 22,* 472–494.

Purkey, W. (1976). *Self-concept and school achievement.* Englewood Cliffs, NJ: Prentice-Hall.

Quinn, Z., Johnson, D., & Johnson, R. (1995). Cooperative versus competitive efforts and problem solving. *Review of Educational Research, 65*(2), 129–143.

Reigeluth, C. M. (1997). Educational standards: To standardize or to customize learning? *Phi Delta Kappan, 79*(3), 202–206.

Reisman, F., & Payne, B. (1987). *Elementary education: A basic text.* Columbus, OH: Merrill.

Reynolds, A. (1992). What is competent beginning teaching: A review of the literature. *Review of Educational Research, 62*(1), 1–35.

Richert, A. E. (1990). Teaching teachers to reflect: A consideration of programme structure. *Journal of Curriculum Studies, 22,* 509–527.

Rinne, C. H. (1998). Motivating students is a percentage game. *Phi Delta Kappan, 79*(8), 620–628.

Rosenshine, B. (1970). Enthusiastic teaching: A research review. *The School Review, 78,* 499–515.

Rosenshine, B. (1987). Explicit teaching. In D. C. Berliner, & B. V. Rosenshine (Eds.), *Talks to teachers* (pp. 75–92). New York: Random House.

Rosenshine, B., & Furst, N. (1971). Research in teacher performance criteria. In B. O. Smith (Ed.), *Research in teacher education.* Englewood Cliffs, NJ: Prentice-Hall.

Rosenshine, B., & Stevens, R. (1986). Teaching functions. In M. Wittrock (Ed.), *Handbook of research on teaching* (3rd ed., pp. 376–391). New York: Macmillan.

Ross, D. D., Bondy, E., & Kyle, D. W. (1993). *Reflective teaching for student improvement.* New York: Macmillan.

Ross, J. A., & Regan, E. M. (1993). Sharing professional experience: Its impact on professional development. *Teaching and Teacher Education, 9*(1), 91–106.

Rowe, M. (1969). Science, silence, and sanctions. *Science and Children, 6,* 6.

Rowe, M. (1972, April). *Wait-time and rewards as instructional variables: Their influence on language, logic, and fate control.* Paper presented at the National Association for Research in Science Teaching, Chicago.

Rowe, M. (1986). Wait-time: Slowing down may be a way of speeding up. *Journal of Teacher Education. 37*(1), 43–50.

Santrock, J. (2008). *Educational psychology* (3rd ed.). Boston: McGraw-Hill.

Sarasin, L. (1998). *Learning style perspectives: Impact in the classroom.* Reston, VA: Association for Supervision and Curriculum Development.

Schlechty, P. (1976). *Teaching and social behavior: Toward an organizational theory of instruction.* Boston: Allyn & Bacon.

Schramm, W. (Ed.). (1945). *How communication works in the process and effects of mass communication.* Urbana, IL: University of Illinois Press.

Schunk, D. (2004). *Learning theories: An educational perspective* (4th ed.). Upper Saddle River, NJ: Merrill/Prentice-Hall.

Sereno, K., & Bodaken, E. (1975). *Trans-per: Understanding human communication.* Boston: Houghton-Mifflin.

Shepherd, G., & Ragan, W. (1982). *Modern elementary curriculum.* New York: Holt, Rinehart, and Winston.

Siegel, I. E. (1990). What teachers need to know about human development. In D. D. Hill (Ed.), *What teachers need to know: The knowledge, skills, and values essential to good teaching.* San Francisco: Jossey-Bass.

Silver, H., Strong, R., & Perini, M. (2007). *The strategic teacher: Selecting the right research-based strategy for every lesson.* Alexandria, VA: Association for Supervision and Curriculum Development.

Sizer, T. (1995, April 2). Making the grade. *Washington Post Education Review,* p. 12.

Slavin, R. E. (1990). *Cooperative learning: Theory, research, and practice.* Boston: Allyn & Bacon.

Slavin, R. E (1994). *A practical guide to cooperative learning.* Needham Heights, MA: Allyn & Bacon.

Slavin, R. (1995). *Cooperative learning: Theory, research, and practice* (2nd ed.). Boston: Allyn & Bacon.

Slavin, R. (1996). Cooperative learning in middle and secondary education. *Clearing House, 69*(4), 200–203.

Smith, H. A. (1995). Nonverbal teacher behavior. In L. W. Anderson (Ed.), *International encyclopedia of teaching and teacher education* (2nd ed.). Cambridge, UK: Cambridge University Press.

Smith, L. R. (1985). A low-inference indicator of lesson organization. *Journal of Classroom Instruction, 21*(1), 25–30.

Smith, L. R., & Sanders, K. (1981). The effects of student achievement and student perception of varying structures in social studies content. *Journal of Educational Research, 74*(5), 333–336.

Snow, R. (1988). Aptitude complexes. In R. Snow, & M. Farr (Eds.), *Aptitude, learning, and instruction: Vol. 3., Cognitive and affective process analyses.* Hillsdale, NJ: Erlbaum.

Snowman, J., McCown, R., & Biehler, R. (2009). *Psychology applied to teaching* (12th ed.). Boston: Houghton-Mifflin.

Snyder, S., Bushur, L., Hocksema, P., Olson, M., Clark, S., & Snyder, J. (1991, April). *The effect of instructional clarity and concept structure on students' achievement and perception.* Paper presented at the annual meeting of the American Educational Research Association, Chicago.

Sokolove, S., Garrett, S., Sadker, M., & Sadker, D. (1990). Interpersonal communication skills. In J. Cooper (Ed.), *Classroom teaching skills.* Lexington, MA: Heath.

Steffy, B., Wolfe, M., Pasch, S., & Enz, B. (Eds.). (2000). *Life cycle of the career teacher.* Thousand Oaks, CA: Corwin Press.

Sternberg, R., & Williams, W. (2002). *Educational psychology.* Boston: Allyn & Bacon.

Stevahn, L., Johnson, D. W., Johnson, R. T., Green, K., & Laginski, M. (1997). Effects on high school students of conflict resolution training integrated into English literature. *The Journal of Social Psychology, 137*(3), 302–313.

Stowell, L. P., Rios, A. R., McDaniel, J. E., & Christopher, P. A. (1996). *Working with middle school students.* Westminster, CA: Teacher Created Materials, Inc.

Stubbs, M. (1983). *Language, schools, and classrooms* (2nd ed.). London: Methuen.

Sugrue, M., & Sweeney, J. (1969). Check your inquiry-teaching technique. *Today's Education, 50*(5), 44.

Tabachnick, B. R., & Zeichner, K. (1991) Reflections on reflective teaching. In B. Tabachnick, & K. Zeichner, *Issues and practices in inquiry-oriented teacher education.* Philadelphia: Falmer Press.

Tiletson, D. (2000). *10 best teaching practices: How brain research, learning styles, and standards define teaching competencies.* Thousand Oaks, CA: Corwin Press.

Tolson, E., McDonald, S., & Moriarty, A. (1992). Peer mediation among high school students: A test of effectiveness. *Social Work in Education, 14,* 86–93.

Travers, R. (1950). *How to make achievement tests.* New York: Odyssey Press.

Travers, R. (1977). *Essentials of learning.* New York: Macmillan.

Tusing, K., & Dillard, J. (2000). The sounds of dominance: Vocal precursors of perceived dominance during interpersonal influence. *Human Communication Research, 26,* 148–171.

U.S. Department of Education. (1987). *What works: Research about teaching and learning.* Washington, DC: U.S. Government Printing Office.

Van Houten, R. (1980). *Learning through feedback: A systematic approach for improving academic performances.* New York: Human Sciences Press.

Van Paten, J., Chao, C., & Reigeluth, C. (1986). A review of strategies for sequencing and synthesizing instruction. *Review of Educational Research, 56*(4), 437–471.

Vygotsky, L. S. (1962). *Thought and language* (E. Hanfmann, & G. Vokar, Trans.). Cambridge, MA: MIT Press. (Original work published in 1934).

Walker, M., & Trimboli, A. (1989). Communicating affect: The role of verbal and nonverbal content. *Journal of Language and Social Psychology, 8,* 229–248.

Waller, W. (1932). *The sociology of teaching.* New York: John Wiley and Sons.

Walters, G., & Grusec, J. (1977). *Punishment.* San Francisco: W. H. Freeman.

Weinert, F., & Helmke, A. (1995). Interclassroom differences in instructional quality and individual differences in cognitive development. *Educational Psychologist, 30,* 15–20.

Weinstein, C., & Mignano, A. (1993). *Elementary classroom management.* New York: McGraw-Hill.

Weinstein, C., & Mignano, A. (2003). *Elementary classroom management: Lessons from research and practice* (3rd ed.). New York: McGraw-Hill.

Weiss, I., & Pasley, J. (2004). What is high quality instruction? *Educational Leadership, 61*(5), 24–28.

White, R., & Lippitt, R. (1960). *Autocracy and democracy: An experimental inquiry.* New York: Harper and Row.

Wiggins, G. (1994). Toward better report cards. *Educational Leadership, 52*(2) 28–37.

Wiles, J. (2004). *Curriculum essentials: A resource for educators* (2nd ed.). Boston: Allyn & Bacon.

Wiles, J., & Bondi, J. (1989). *Curriculum development: A guide to practice.* Columbus, OH: Merrill.

Wilen, W., Hutchison, J., & Ishler, M. (2008). *Dynamics of effective secondary teaching* (6th ed.). New York: Pearson Education, Inc.

Wiseman, D. (1975). The logical aspects of classroom instruction. In H. Walding (Ed.), *The general teaching model,* Conway. SC: School of Teacher Education, Coastal Carolina College.

Wiseman, D. (1983). Using instructional contracts in the middle school classroom. *Middle School Journal, 14*(2), 13–15.

Wiseman, D., & Hunt, G. (2008). *Best practice in student motivation and management in the classroom* (2nd ed.). Springfield, IL: Charles C Thomas.

Wiseman, D., & Hunt, G. (2007). The teacher as an evaluator of student performance. In D. Wiseman, G. Hunt, V. Zhukov, & L. Mardahaev (Eds.), *Teaching at the university level: Cross-cultural perspectives from the United States and Russia* (pp. 143–161). Springfield, IL: Charles C Thomas.

Wiske, M. S. (1994). How teaching for understanding changes the rules in the classroom. *Educational Leadership, 51*(5), 19–21.

Wood, J. (2008). *Communication mosaics: An introduction to the field of communication* (5th ed.). Belmont, CA: Thomson Wadsworth.

Wood, D., Bruner, J. C., & Ross, G. (1976). The role of tutoring in problem solving. *Journal of Child Psychology and Psychiatry, 17,* 89–100.

Woolfolk, A. (2008). *Educational Psychology* (10th ed.). New York: Pearson Education, Inc.

Yinger, R., & Clark, C. (1983). *Self-reports of teacher judgment.* (Research Series No. 134). East Lansing, MI: Michigan State University Institute for Research on Teaching.

York-Barr, J., Sommers, W., Ghere, G., & Montie, J. (2005). *Reflective practice to improve schools: An action guide for educators* (2nd ed.). Thousand Oaks, CA: Corwin Press.

Zabel, R. H., & Zabel, M. K. (1996). *Classroom management in context: Orchestrating positive learning environments.* Boston: Houghton-Mifflin.

Zirpoli, T. J., & Melloy, K. J. (2004). *Behavior management: Applications for teachers and parents* (4th ed.). Upper Saddle River, NJ: Merrill/Prentice-Hall.

INDEX